How Resourceful Employees
Build and Preserve Wealth
at Work

IN

OUR

REACH

TONY VERHEYEN

Certified Employee Benefits Specialist®

and Award-Winning Instructor

Printed in Elm Grove, Wisconsin, in the United States of America.

ISBN: 978-1-7354156-9-7 (Hardcover)
ISBN: 978-1-7354156-8-0 (Paperback)
ISBN: 978-1-7354156-7-3 (eBook)

Library of Congress Control Number: 2020922684

Disclaimers. This publication is sold with the understanding that the publisher and author is not engaged in rendering legal, accounting, investment, insurance, or tax advice, or any other professional service to the reader. If expert advice or assistance is required, the services of a competent professional person should be sought. Although most portions of this book are non-fiction, some are fiction. Fictitious names, characters, and places are products of the author's imagination, and any resemblances to actual events or places or persons, living or dead, is entirely coincidental.

Book cover design and stepladder image provided by Brenna Verheyen, front cover photography by Enrico Bettella via Unsplash (username "Henry_Be"), and back cover photography by Jodi Lukach. Technical support for hardcover edition provided by The Book Cover Whisperer: ProfessionalBookCoverDesign.com.

First printing edition 2021.

The Richfield Companies, LLC
P.O. Box 222
Elm Grove, WI 53122-0222

www.inourreach.com

To Michelle, my best friend and soulmate. She encouraged me to start this project, walked with me step-for-step, and gave me the strength to finish.

And to Bob Love, a selfless hero and unwavering ally. He embodied the spirit of leaders that go the distance to help employees at all levels succeed.

CONTENTS

Section V: A Protecting Mindset

Section VI: An Unrelenting Devotion

Conclusion: You Are The Biggest Difference

WE DON'T NEED TO WALK ALONE

We're all instinctive dreamers leading full lives. We can't reliably predict the future, but possess the ability to imagine and shape it. In our efforts to build and preserve wealth, we are compelled to make assumptions, take risks, and do our best with the resources that are in our reach. Although our journeys are separate and unique, we do not need to walk alone.

According to the U.S. Department of Labor, nearly 159 million Americans derived part or all of their economic vitality in February 2020 by working as employees.[1] In exchange for full-time or part-time employment, their employers paid them and frequently provided valuable perks. Coupled with other helpful resources in the public domain, the vast majority of these people should have been in solid financial shape.

Unfortunately, that wasn't true. In an era characterized by low unemployment, 4-in-10 were "usually" or "always" living paycheck-to-paycheck.[2] In a period of abundance, roughly the same numbers confessed that they would have needed to borrow money or sell something to pay an unexpected $400

---

[1] Bureau of Labor Statistics News Release, "The Employment Situation – February 2020," News Release (Washington, DC, U.S. Department of Labor, 2020, Summary Table A).

[2] CareerBuilder Press Release, "Living Paycheck to Paycheck is a Way of Life for Majority of U.S. Workers, According to New CareerBuilder Survey" (Chicago and Atlanta, CareerBuilder, 2017).

bill.[3] And in the information age, most were baffled by basic financial planning concepts.[4] The Great Recession officially ended years earlier, but many continued to exhibit the telltale signs of financial dysfunction: drained savings, unpaid bills, soaring debt, stolen identities, strained relationships, and stress-related illnesses.

If they couldn't keep their heads above water in a vibrant economy, how did they expect to thrive during any type of significant financial crisis? Well, in March 2020, the Coronavirus pandemic struck and tens of millions of people found out.

I wasn't born into wealth, and I'm not a YouTube star, real estate mogul, or bitcoin billionaire. I'm a proud worker bee who's spent most of the past 25 years earning my living by helping organizations manage their benefit plans and by delivering award-winning workplace financial education services.[5]

Given the vital nature of these programs to both employers and employees, I've been compelled to develop a broad based and multidisciplinary understanding of financial planning. Throughout my career, I have: held various insurance licenses and securities registrations; scrutinized countless vendors, products and services; studied many aspects of personal finance that are relevant to the diverse population that I serve; developed a robust curriculum of financial planning workshops; advised hundreds of employers; and earned the respected Certified Employee Benefits Specialist (CEBS) designation from

---

[3] Board of Governors of the Federal Reserve System, "Report on the Economic Well-Being of U.S. Households in 2019" (Washington, DC, Federal Reserve Board, 2020, pgs. 2,3).

[4] Madeline Farber, "Nearly Two-Thirds of Americans Can't Pass a Basic Test of Financial Literacy" (July 12, 2016, Fortune, Web, www.forbes.com, December 29, 2020).

[5] Tony Verheyen, "Richfield's financial readiness services help client earn 'Best of Show' from Profit Sharing/401(k) Council of America" (Elm Grove, WI, The Richfield Companies, October 4, 2007).

the International Foundation of Employee Benefit Plans and the Wharton School of the University of Pennsylvania.

And since 2006, I have personally shown tens of thousands of employees how to make the most of the resources in their reach. Over 98% of those that attended my seminars and submitted feedback surveys rated my content and delivery as "excellent" or "good." Many offered written comments like "I wish this had been presented 25 years ago," "This has been a huge help and much appreciated," and "I loved the unbiased comments," and some hugged me. But a small number mocked me, yelled at me for delivering hidden pay cuts, and accused me of contributing to the Great Recession. No worries: that's the nature of this topic.

Along the way, I've presented my thoughts to students in university classrooms, organizational leaders in boardrooms, plan managers at industry conferences, regulators from federal agencies, and movers-and-shakers on Capitol Hill and in the White House. Most recently, as the Executive Director for the Plan Sponsor Council of America and a representative of the Save Our Savings Coalition, I helped staff members from the U.S. House Ways & Means Committee and the U.S. Senate realize the impact of tax policy on participants in workplace retirement plans.[6]

I generally champion the free enterprise approach to improving financial wellbeing, but the gradual transfer of liabilities from employers to employees is endangering some of the people that I help. As growing numbers of organizations shed 20th Century human capital constraints such as permanent full-time workforces, retirement pension plans, retiree medical benefits, and affordable health care, it's becoming clear that the onus to prepare for an uncertain future is shifting to individuals and families that won't be ready.

---

[6] Plan Sponsor Council of America, "Employee Benefits & Workplace Retirement Programs" (presentation, Save Our Savings Coalition, Washington, DC, May, 2017).

Many policymakers, academics, and industry leaders think that the lack of financial preparedness exhibited by people that are struggling is driven by financial illiteracy. They conclude that such individuals, many of whom are or will be in the workforce, can't or won't take the right steps, and must be nudged or shoved into prescribed behaviors. Their proposed solutions often include mandatory coursework in primary and secondary schools, involuntary enrollment in one-size-fits-all programs, and penalties for non-compliance.

I have a different take. Although I agree that many people struggle to understand financial concepts, jargon, and legalese, I don't perceive those that I meet during my workplace interactions to be "illiterate;" a pejorative label that isn't much different than calling them "ignorant" or "uneducated."

Based on my personal experience helping employees at all levels, most adults that want to build and preserve wealth are capable of doing it. Unfortunately, many of them haven't awakened to the precarious nature of life in the 21st Century. They're preoccupied with their busy lives, impeded by rosy time's-on-my-side assumptions, and derailed by zombie-like tendencies. And, ironically, they're walking the same worn path, albeit unconscious and alone.

It doesn't need to be this way, at least for people that work for organizations that provide competitive pay, training, benefits, and other perks. I am confident that they can succeed if they adopt conscious approaches to financial wellbeing, strengthen four core financial mindsets, and maintain unrelenting devotions to achieving doable financial goals.

In my opinion, most just need a simple framework for sustainable results; the equivalent of a financial stepladder.

In Our Reach gives you insights into what some of your resourceful peers are doing, and it puts those same strategies in your reach. It offers practical steps that can lead to quick and noticeable improvements, and it teaches you enduring concepts that'll prepare you for circumstances that are too big or too complex for easy-button solutions.

The book consists of two general sections that serve as bookends to four topical sections.

➤ *Section I: A Conscious Approach.* The vast majority of employees that I encounter don't work with financial advisors. By choice or by default, they manage most or all aspects of their personal finances on their own. This might be necessary and practical, but it exposes them to avoidable missteps, missed opportunities, and frustration. To get you rolling, I identify three attributes that drive financial outcomes that I observe among those that I help, and I share a simple framework to make your efforts easier.

➤ *Section II: A Saving Mindset.* Few achievements in personal finance create as much satisfaction and peace-of-mind as securing solid income and adequate savings. Strengths in these areas can overcome weaknesses elsewhere. In this section, I call you to take steps to increase your workplace earnings, improve your spending habits, and save for your liquidity needs.

➤ *Section III: A Borrowing Mindset.* No aspect of personal finance draws more interest or debate among employees than borrowing. The money gurus notoriously warn of its perils, but properly leveraging credit and debt can lead to wealth building opportunities that might otherwise be unattainable. Here, I offer ideas and techniques to improve your utilization of these tools.

➤ *Section IV: An Investing Mindset.* Ready or not, the necessity to invest for critical long-term goals is shifting to employees. In this section, I explain concepts and strategies related to common investing objectives: funding future post-secondary education; paying for future health-related expenses; and having adequate future retirement income.

➤ *Section V: A Protecting Mindset.* Employees and their loved ones are vulnerable to all types of threats, but finding the right protection isn't easy. In this part of the book, I'll share insights and strategies that'll help you improve your ability to use insurance to manage risks associated with typical aspects of life.

➤ *Section VI: An Unrelenting Devotion.* Whether employees go-it-alone or engage financial advisors, results matter and maintaining an unrelenting devotion to moving forward is crucial. To close, I urge you to occasionally verify that you're heading in the right direction, and to formally search for the right professionals if you're not.

To get the most from *In Our Reach*, I suggest that you read Section I and complete the recommended activities. Then, return to the table of contents and prioritize your reading based on the mindsets that you want to improve. And read Section VI once you're moving forward.

Also, I want you to generate and maintain as much momentum as possible, and encourage you to keep a journal or smart device nearby so that you can immediately convert ideas to actions. However, I implore you to avoid writing or inserting sensitive information in the book because I don't want your efforts to backfire if your copy lands in the wrong hands.

Finally, I'm eager to continue the dialogue with you, and will strive to provide you with more insights, materials, and updates at www.inourreach.com.

SECTION I

A CONSCIOUS APPROACH

CHAPTER 1

SUCCESS BEGINS WITH A MINDSET

I magine that you've arrived at your favorite meeting place for an introductory visit with a financial advisor. You've never met the person, but were encouraged to connect by a mutual friend who felt that it might be good for you. You don't know a lot about them and they presumably don't know much about you.

Wait! Scratch that...

During my 25-year career teaching and counselling employees, I've noticed that most don't work with financial advisors. By choice or default, they manage their household budgets, save for future consumption, sign complex lending agreements, and make investment and insurance decisions without professional help. They are, in part or whole, *DIY financial planners*.

Since that might be you, it'll help to flip the script.

Let's instead picture you as the financial advisor meeting with a potential client for the first time. Other than hearsay volunteered by your friend, you're starting from scratch. Before you can help the individual, you need them to reveal who they are, what's important to them, where they are in life, and where they hope to go.

As they open up, you acquire basic information, such as their age, family situation, employment status, income, and debts. You also gain deeper insights. Perhaps you discover that they're the epitome of financial fitness, or you spot unhealthy tendencies that completely undermine their efforts. Or you learn that they're somewhere in between. Regardless, you have a better understanding of the path that they're on, and the future that they envision for themselves and those they cherish.

Ok, now step back.

So, who's the client here? *You are.* And who's the financial advisor? *You are.* Since you're acting in both roles, it's vital for you to recognize three key *DIY financial planner* attributes as you move forward.

Your Mindsets

Dabo Swinney, the Head Football Coach for Clemson University, was interviewed on the field a few minutes after his team won the 2018 NCAA Division I National Championship. In response to a reporter's questions about his team's victory, he talked about the year of preparation that led to it and referred to the key ingredient in any long-term endeavor: a mindset.

Mindsets aren't just the rah-rah platitudes of coaches, leaders, and motivational speakers; they're real. Based on my work with *DIY financial planners*, they account for peoples' financial behaviors and habits, and are the bedrock upon which they build and preserve wealth. And, in a way, they're similar to jigsaw puzzles.

The inside puzzle pieces are collections of statements and opinions that people regard as true or false, and they're shaped by lessons learned throughout life. In personal finance, I find that the relevant ones stem from: education, like parents that teach their kids that "money can't buy happiness;" observations, such as individuals that reject long-term planning because they watched loved ones fail after doing all of the right things; and experiences, like victims of identity theft that go to extremes to protect their personal information.

The border pieces are ways of thinking and acting that reflect outlooks for the future, and they ultimately cause mindsets to be strong, weak, or conflicted. Here, some of the people that I encounter possess can-do attitudes. They use phrases like "I'll do whatever it takes" or "Let's do this now" when they like what they hear. Others are constrained by self-defeating can't-do attitudes and are predisposed to sabotaging themselves. As the following example illustrates, the former are often more likely to do what's necessary...

> During a legacy-planning workshop, a dozen employees agreed that dying without their Last Will & Testament would most likely hurt the people that they loved. But when I asked how many had previously created one, only a few admitted that they had.
>
> I replied, "Well, I have good news! For those of you that don't have them, your employer has hired a reputable law firm to provide each of you with a Will. It's free, confidential, and 100% yours."
>
> The attendees that had already completed it on their own openly griped. Those that hadn't were visibly pleased. I spent a few minutes explaining the benefit and showing them how to begin, and then offered to help them take the first step. One jumped at the chance (and had a Will within a week), but the rest never acted.
>
> Months later, the Benefits Manager and I wondered what kept the others from taking advantage of the new benefit, and decided to ask each of them individually. The responses were variations of "It's not worth it," "It won't matter anyway," or "I don't have time to think about it."

For better or worse, mindsets aren't permanent and must be cultivated. Sometimes weak ones can be improved with simple exercises. Other times, strong ones can be dislodged by traumatic events like divorces, illnesses, and unemployment, and restoring them requires considerable effort. In the case of the latter, I know firsthand how fast they can change...

> In August 2005, I started a business to help employers manage their workplace benefit plans and provide their employees with unbiased financial education. It took a year to create the services, and I was excited to go "live" with them in September 2006. But three days into the product rollout, two work-companions and I witnessed a mur-

der in Aurora, Colorado. Other than the victim, nobody else was phys-
ically hurt.

I thought I was unaffected, but something inside me snapped a
few weeks later; it was as if a muscle tore somewhere in my body. In
an instant, I abandoned lifelong beliefs about restraint and thrift, and
adopted a new mantra: "life's too short to have regret and too long
to have regret, so live it the way you want to now." It felt like a posi-
tive response to a despicable tragedy, but it wasn't. I stopped caring
about my financial future, and it took me a year to get back on track.

Given the interconnected relationship between peoples' evolving beliefs
and attitudes, and the fractured nature of personal finance, I don't see that a
single guiding mindset (e.g., "millionaire mindset", "abundance mindset",
"profit mindset") is practical for those that I help. But like the rails of a stepladder, there are four distinct ones that I regularly observe among those that
I serve: saving, borrowing, investing, and protecting.

Your Approach

In addition to mindsets, peoples' approaches to the countless financial
scenarios that they encounter throughout their lives are important. Two aspects of this attribute are very relevant.

Life Stages

Like innings of a ballgame, chapters of a book, or acts of a play, *life stages*
are distinct and common phases that people experience during their journeys
from the cradle to the grave. Some commence with celebrated milestones
and others follow shocking setbacks, but most can be characterized by typical
needs and circumstances that correspond with progressions in age.

Many of the people that I help view their lives in several sequential stages that begin with their first real jobs, military service, or other non-career experiences. Next, they marry, buy homes, and try for kids, and those events often occur in their 20s and 30s. Assuming that all goes well, they advance in their occupations and prepare their children for adulthood. That ushers them into their 40s or 50s. From there, their focus shifts to reimagining their futures and preparing for whatever comes after they stop working for a living. By the time they reach their 60s or 70s, they're ready to retire and take steps to prolong their quality of life, maintain their health, and create their legacies.

Alternatively, some people prefer uncomplicated successions. The most common example are those that distinguish between pre-retirement stages whereby they accumulate wealth and post-retirement stages where they spend it; two halves divided by one transition. And others choose less traditional models whereby they remain single, get divorced (and maybe remarry), raise kids in single-parent or blended families, exit and reenter the job market for countless reasons, or never officially retire.

The concept of life stages is useful in personal finance. First, it provides perspective about the here and now. Second, it offers a sense of what might be on the horizon. And third, it sheds light on what others are doing. Ultimately, it helps *DIY financial planners* assess, plan, act, and adjust.

Situation Management

I find that most employees understand life stages, but few are aware of the impact of situation management on their efforts to get ahead. Here's an exchange that often occurs during my conversations with them:

> Employee: *It was a bad decision. Can you help me?*
> Me: *I think so. But can you tell me why you did it?*
> Employee: *Honestly, I don't know what I was thinking...*

Situation management seldom receives the attention that it deserves in personal finance. It's often swept aside, but it's essential to people's efforts to build and preserve wealth because it's the bridge that connects intentions and outcomes.

Following are some of the most common financial predispositions that I observe among the employees that I meet.

➢ *Bound or Unbound.* Some bind their financial goals and expectations to popular yardsticks and perceptions of what's required. A typical example are people that adhere to strict household budgets until they accumulate desired amounts in their emergency savings accounts. Others refuse to tie themselves to any metrics or guideposts.

➢ *Conformist or Contrarian.* Some follow the herd. They act on what they see or hear others do, such as selecting the same investments or hiring the same financial advisors as their friends. Contrarians are inclined to do the opposite of what they see others doing.

➢ *Emotional or Logical.* Some admit to acting on emotion. While it can feel good and satisfy deeper psychological needs, it can also create problems. Typical examples that I observe are married couples that embark on big spending sprees as they attempt to rekindle their faltering relationships, and employees that convert their long-term retirement investments to cash based on unverified information and irrational fears. Other people are logical to extremes.

➢ *Reflective or Impulsive.* Some think that it's foolish to act without engaging in thorough reflection. Normally, that isn't bad, but it often kills their momentum and leads to procrastination. I witness this several times a year when employees take too long to choose their benefits during their workplace open enrollments and miss the chance to sign up. Conversely, others engage in knee-jerk reactions that can be equally harmful.

These tendencies aren't to be judged because there are times and places for each, and none necessarily guarantee success or failure. But they affect outcomes, and it's clear to me that many people aren't conscious of them when they confront financial opportunities and challenges.

Your Resources

In terms of the scope, quantity, and quality of resources, there's never been a better time for employees to be *DIY financial planners*. They're surrounded by institutions and professionals (or *financial partners*) that have the potential to give them most or all of what they need.

At work, employers with more than a handful of employees often provide assortments of wealth building and preserving resources. They have considerable leeway in the design and administration of their programs, and usually hire vendors to support their efforts. And though they're driven by degrees of self-interest, they increase the options available to eligible employees.

Beyond work, other organizations offer valuable resources. Government agencies act as watchdogs, regulators, enforcers, and educators, and are renowned for the backstop safety nets that they manage and fund, like Social Security, Medicare, and Unemployment Insurance. Non-profit groups supply free and low-cost information, education, counselling, and assistance. And, personal service providers sell products and solutions that can fill most of the remaining gaps.

However, the abundance of resources gives some people headaches, and they struggle to leverage them. To add insult to injury, the products, services, and rules: frequently change; periodically overlap or conflict with each other; and aren't always in consumers' best interests. This inevitably leads to workplace interactions like this...

While teaching a group of employees about a caregiving tool that their employer introduced a few years earlier, an attendee interrupts me. She's very agitated and says "Wait. Are you serious? This could've helped me with my mom!"

Her statement is followed by a brief pause as her coworkers and I process her comment. Then another attendee chimes in "Yeah, I had no idea we had this either. But to be honest, I'm still not sure that I know what it does."

The second admission creates a buzz and a handful of people let the two know that they've been missing out. One individual responds "Guys, HR rolled this out to us 3 or 4 years ago, and I'm pretty sure they talk about it every year during annual enrollment." Another says,

"I don't want you to feel bad, but I used this for my 82-year-old mom last year and it was a life saver."

The exchange is followed by an awkward silence. At least one person feels very disappointed, and everyone in the room realizes that they don't talk to each other enough.

Some of the people that I help are understandably overwhelmed, but the resourceful ones revel in their good fortunes. By instinct or training, I find that they do two things that their peers typically don't (or don't do often enough):

✓ *They take control.* This requires dedication. It includes identifying available resources, assessing their relative value, confirming the ability to use them, and learning how to properly activate them.
✓ *They demand more.* This takes backbone. It includes engaging financial partners, pushing them to do more, scrutinizing their recommendations, and holding them accountable for desired results.

Resourceful employees concentrate on getting as much value as possible from whatever's in their reach and on filling gaps where they exist. That's because they know that they're serving the interests of the most important clients in the world: themselves and those that they cherish.

NOW IT'S YOUR TURN
Address mental health issues that cause weak or conflicted mindsets

If depression, addiction, or exposure to trauma are undermining your efforts to build and preserve wealth, take 15 minutes now to identify and engage mental health care professionals. This is critical to the rest of your journey, and you might find that they're in your reach via current financial partners for little or no cost.

CHAPTER 2

A BETTER PATH

Before shuffling to their assigned seats, passengers boarding commercial jets often have opportunities to glance into the cockpits and witness remarkable scenes. Surrounded by toggle switches, computer screens, blinking lights and sounding alarms, their pilots and co-pilots focus intensely on pre-flight checklists and seem oblivious to the slow-motion cattle drives that are occurring behind them.

Like pilots, *DIY financial planners* vigorously focus on their to-do lists and timelines. With limited vision, they try to juggle their needs with those of their bosses, families, and anyone else that matters. Work deadlines, doctor's visits, and trips to grocery stores aren't as glamorous as flying airliners at 35,000 feet, but they're nonetheless important.

Similarly, many of the resources that are necessary to complete their respective missions are, or could be, provided by others. Just as grounds crews prepare the planes and air traffic controllers guide the flights, financial partners equip people with arrays of potentially useful products and services. The biggest challenge for those that I help is taking and maintaining command.

A Better Path

Although pilots are endowed with attributes that are necessary to fly, they need to be sufficiently trained before they can do it competently. And at some point during their careers, somebody must teach them time-tested procedures that are flexible enough to confront real-world complexities yet durable enough to be reliable in unforeseeable situations.

It's for this reason that I offer *DIY financial planners* a set of easy-to-follow steps to strengthen their four core mindsets.

Step One: Take Inventory

Many of the employees that I help blame their apathy for personal finance on the scattered nature of their resources and the endless barrage of communications that they receive from current and wannabe financial partners. The notifications, solicitations, and calls-to-action span from clear to incomprehensible, and the mess ultimately causes them to grow numb, tune out, and fall behind.

Taking inventory is a critical first step because it answers the question "What do I have?" For basic organization, it exposes non-essential items that can be discarded. For emergency preparation, it centralizes information that might be indispensable in crisis scenarios. And, for wealth planning, it rounds up and catalogs valuable resources, and facilitates constructive conversations with financial partners.

Generally, this step isn't technical, but it is administrative. As such, it requires time and effort to locate, organize, and safeguard information, and to confirm the purpose and application of available resources. Although valuable guidance found at work and in the public domain can assist in this process, many of the employees that I help start with the *At-A-Glance Worksheet* (**Appendix A**), *Document Checklist* (**Appendix B**), *Workplace Perks Checklist* (**Appendix C**), and *Personal Paycheck Audit* (**Appendix D**) in this book.

People that prefer to keep important information in paper-form should store their documents in secure and dry (and fireproof if possible) locations. Those that opt for electronic versions should place them on encrypted digital devices or secure cloud-based platforms. Regardless, they need to give trusted family, friends, or attorneys instructions to locate and access the items.

They should also properly dispose of obsolete documents that contain sensitive information. One solution is to use personal crosscutting shredders that typically retail for $75 to $200. Another is to collect materials in containers that can be taken to reputable businesses that'll charge fees to destroy them, or to free community document shredding events hosted by local organizations like churches, charities, or clubs. People that are interested in the latter option can learn more by contacting their area Chamber of Commerce.

There's one extra task associated with this step, and it's for those that are in marriages or long-term partnerships where household finances are combined. While it makes sense for them to divide responsibilities, many fail to exchange their information. This becomes dicey if a member of the duo isn't able to perform, so these people need to make ongoing efforts to share the "Who?", "What?", "When?", "Where?", and "Why?" of their assigned duties.

NOW IT'S YOUR TURN
Organize and safeguard your financial information and documents

Spend 15 minutes asking your financial partners about any resources that they offer that'll help you organize and safeguard your financial information and documents. Then schedule a time to complete this task.

Step Two: Assess the Situation

This is a natural continuation of the first step. As *DIY financial planners* take inventory, they instinctively begin to spot some of their shortcomings. But before advancing to goal setting, they should pause to answer questions like "Where will these resources get me?", "What do I need to update or cancel?", "What's working for me?" and "What's not working for me?"

Sometimes self-assessment is uncomplicated because the answers are obvious. Other times it's not. Luckily, an abundance of financial yardsticks exist to help people assess their situations and preparedness relative to their peers, aspirations, and life stage needs.

In addition to tools found in the public domain, many employees have powerful ones at work. For example, most retirement plan administrators offer in-person and online resources to help participants assess their readiness to retire, as well as their emergency savings, credit scores, college savings, and health savings. And a growing number of employers provide free or low-cost counselling and coaching services that can tell people where they stand.

But there are reasons to be cautious. First, some self-assessment tools employ dubious data and methods, and are built to initiate sales conversations with unsuspecting consumers. Second, anecdotal success stories touted by acquaintances are seldom reliable because they might exaggerate results, conceal failures, or exclude relevant details.

NOW IT'S YOUR TURN
Solicit life stage insights and support from your financial partners

Take 15 minutes now to initiate conversations with your financial partners. Ask about free and low-cost resources that'll help you anticipate and
plan for current and future life stages, and make it easier to manage new
or unfamiliar situations.

Step Three: Set the Goal

Once *DIY financial planners* know what they have and where it might get them, they're ready to answer the question "Where do I want to go?"

Goal setting can be motivational and beneficial in personal finance, and many of the employees that I help embrace it. But some refuse to do it, even though they admit to doing so elsewhere in their lives, like dieting, hobbies, and careers.

In light of differences that I find in people's viewpoints, I encourage those that want to build and preserve wealth to view their efforts in broader terms, such as being better parents or employees, and to set goals that'll be mean-ingful to them. It also helps when their goals are distinct, realistic, measure-able, and time-based, and mutual if others (like spouses) are involved.

This step typically concludes with aspirational statements that answer four related questions: "Who?", "What?", "When?", and "Why?" Following is an example.

"My goal is to increase my average credit score by at least 30 points in the next 180 days because I want to reduce my future borrowing costs."	
Who?	*Me, credit bureaus, financial partners*
What?	*Increase my average credit score from 700 to 730*
When?	*Within 180 days*
Why?	*To reduce my future borrowing costs*

Small financial goals typically don't require a lot of time, energy, or forethought. Large ones tend to be harder to accomplish because they're usually complex. Before committing to the latter, it's wise to thoroughly investigate them and to talk to people that will provide honest and valuable feedback. At minimum, the additional effort allows for abandoning or modifying the aspirations before getting too invested in them.

Finally, I urge employees to embrace 5 to 10 consequential financial goals each year, and to prioritize them based on their needs and timeframes. The following table is an example of what a list might look like for someone who's in their late-twenties.

Sample Personal Financial Goals		
Priority	Time Horizon	Goal
Immediate	Zero to 90 days	Reduce expenses Improve credit scores Create a Living Will
Short-Term	90 days to 2 years	Eliminate high interest debt Fully fund an emergency account
Mid-Term	2 years to 10 years	Increase contributions to tax-preferred retirement plans to 15% of income Buy my first home or condominium
Long-Term	Over 10 years	Have enough wealth to do my own thing

NOW IT'S YOUR TURN
Set 5 to 10 financial goals for the coming year

Take 15 minutes now to create a list of financial goals that you want to focus on during the coming year. Choose 5 to 10 that are immediate, short-term, mid-term, or long-term.

Step Four: Create a Plan

With the first three steps complete, *DIY financial planners* should be able to answer "What will I do to make it happen?" The question seems clear-cut, but can still get them stuck. Fortunately, there are simple planning principles that can keep things moving. Ironically, the ones that I advocate don't come from the financial services industry.

My late-uncle was a proud union operating engineer who invested four decades of his life erecting buildings that occupy urban skylines and industrial sites. He was a selfless, patient, and smart individual who taught me how to plan basic home improvement projects with simple rules-of-thumb that I believe are transferable to personal finance.

The first is *plan your work*. Whether they're drafted on napkins, white boards, or iPads, dependable plans reflect stated goals, pre-empt the actual work, and anticipate challenges. They identify and outline tasks that must be completed, and establish the order in which they should or must occur.

The second is *use the right tool for the right job*. Having taken inventory already, it will be clear that many resources are available, and that some are missing. People must decide which ones they'll need, where they'll find them, when they'll be required, and how to activate them. And wherever possible, they should try to delegate tasks to their financial partners.

The third is *measure twice, cut once*. This is where the plan is carefully evaluated before it's executed. *DIY financial planners* should confirm that they and those that are engaged to help: understand the goals; can perform their assigned tasks; and will adhere to their plans. More, to increase the likelihood of success, they should explain their intent to their financial partners and ask for feedback before proceeding.

Finally, it's wise to prepare alternative plans in case their initial efforts fail to produce their desired results.

NOW IT'S YOUR TURN
Create a plan to achieve at least one of your financial goals

Take 15 minutes now to create a plan to achieve at least one important financial goal that you want to accomplish in the coming year. You can use your own planning worksheet, something that you find online, or the one in **Appendix E**. Once completed, keep it in a place that you're likely to see it and be reminded of it.

Step Five: Execute the Plan

The final step relies on follow-through. This is where *DIY financial planners* learn if their plans will work, or if they'll require adjustments.

Based on my experience, the employees that are more likely to build and preserve wealth in the workplace excel at execution. They're people that consistently do what they say they'll do, and they don't take results for granted. Once their plans are in place, they remain on track by:

✓ Automating their decisions and actions using easy-button solutions provided by their financial partners.
✓ Confirming that delegated tasks are completed in their preferred timeframes.
✓ Scheduling specific times to review progress and adjust plans if needed.
✓ Communicating results with people that have stakes in the outcomes.

Anecdotally, 2-in-3 of the employees that I encounter either execute their plans perfectly or quickly abandon them. The rest want to do it, but need help and encouragement. Here's an example of how it can work...

An older employee approached me following a workplace seminar. She told me that she wanted to set a big goal, but was convinced that her husband wouldn't buy-in. She said, "He hates goal-setting and planning, but I think we need to do it." I invited her to share more of her story and she obliged.

She explained that her husband and she were in their 60s, and dreamt for many years about retiring and traveling around the country in an RV. She concluded with "But all we do is talk! We never do anything about it, and I'm beginning to think that it won't happen." I asked "Does he really want this?" and she replied "Absolutely! He's just not sure that we can afford to do it the way he wants to."

We talked a bit more. Then I said, "I think I get it. In his defense, retirement is a big deal. But to your point, you could miss your chance if you wait for perfection. Let's spend 15 minutes sketching out the first four steps. Then you can show him your plan." When we finished, she said, "This is great! I'll do it tonight."

A year later, I returned to the location to conduct additional seminars. The employee didn't attend, but she made the effort to find me during a break to share wonderful news. Her eyes sparkled and her voice was giddy as she said, "Tony, we did it! We bought an RV that we absolutely love. We've taken a couple trips already, and here's the best news: just today, we notified our employers that we're retiring. We'll be footloose and free in a few weeks!"

This individual's follow-up reveals an important tendency that I regularly witness among resourceful employees, and it seems to be a secret ingredient to success. Whether it's reporting in with an elated "Mission Accomplished!" or sheepish "I didn't get to it yet," they voluntarily make themselves accountable to others for their execution, or lack thereof.

NOW IT'S YOUR TURN
Schedule your annual financial review

Your odds of success increase when a conscious approach and unrelenting devotion lead to strong mindsets. Take a minute to schedule time in the coming year, possibly coinciding with your annual workplace benefits enrollment, to review your progress, set new goals, modify your plan, and to decide if going-it-alone is getting you the desired results (see **Section VI**).

Bonus Step: Adopt Role Models

When asked about their paths to fame and fortune, musicians often exalt the role models that inspired them. Interestingly, some differentiate between two types: public influencers and personal mentors.

For example, The Beatles' influencers were reportedly Elvis, Carl Perkins, and Chuck Berry, and mentors included Little Richard,[7] Brian Wilson,[8] and

---

[7] Bill Harry, *The Beatles Encyclopedia: Revised and Updated* (London: Virgin, 2000, pgs. 140, 660, 856-858, 881).

[8] Charles L. Granata, *I Just Wasn't Made for These Times: Brian Wilson and the Making of the Beach Boys' Pet Sounds* (London: Unanimous, 2003, pg. 17).

Ravi Shankar.[9] P!nk credits Madonna and Janis Joplin as influences,[10] and describes Linda Perry, the leader of the band 4 Non Blondes, as a mentor.[11]

Adopting role models is an extra step that resourceful employees take to reinforce their strong mindsets and conscious approaches. It keeps them on track. They follow *public influencers* like money gurus, business leaders, or commentators that are renowned for their insights, advice, or achievements, via social media, videos, websites, and books. Or they engage *personal mentors* for tailored advice. These are people that have walked similar paths earlier in their lives, take active interests in their understudies, and freely share their perspectives in one-on-one settings.

NOW IT'S YOUR TURN
Request introductory conversations with potential personal mentors

Take 15 minutes to identify individuals that you admire and would hate to disappoint, and ask them if they'd mind a conversation about their approaches to personal finance. Since there's a chance that they won't have the time, interest, or much to offer, try to talk to a few different people.

---

[9] Peter Lavezzoli, *The Dawn of Indian Music in the West: Bhairavi* (New York and London: Continuum, 2006, pgs. 147, 150, 162, 169).
[10] Balasubramanyam Seshan, "P!nk welcomes baby Willow Sage Hart into the World" (International Business Times, June 3, 2011).
[11] P!nk, Behind the Music (YouTube, August 2012).

SECTION II

A SAVING MINDSET

CHAPTER 3

THE ANT, THE GRASSHOPPER, & THE CATERPILLAR

In the ageless tale, *The Ant and The Grasshopper*, the ant works throughout the summer to create a surplus while the grasshopper plays and enjoys the moment. When autumn arrives, the ant revels in the comfort of preparedness and the grasshopper grapples with its imminent demise.

But in the era of fanfiction, a period in which classic stories are rewritten to include alternative plot lines, what if this one's updated to include a very hungry caterpillar?

➢ The ant is ready for winter, but it requires exhaustive effort, thrift, and frugality. Maybe it's a workaholic, or it lives in continuous fear of starvation, ostracism from the colony, or the queen's wrath.

➢ The grasshopper isn't ready for winter, but it clearly has a different agenda during the summer. Perhaps it observes those that are miserable and chooses to have fun, or maybe it's motivated by a constant need to evade hungry predators.

➢ The caterpillar isn't concerned about winter, but it works very hard. It realizes that the only chance it has of escaping the leaf on which it was abandoned is to eat vigorously and pray that it miraculously morphs into something with wings.

The fable illustrates the benefits of working and saving, and the dangers of shortsightedness and folly. But it ignores the unique mindsets and circumstances of the characters, and different approaches. As such, some people appreciate the ant's eye toward the future, some cheer the grasshopper's zest for the moment, and some wish there were other options.

You Must Choose

I believe that nearly everyone that I meet in the workplace is capable of creating a cash surplus that'll allow them to manage typical household expenses, weather occasional financial storms, and sweep more into other wealth-building endeavors. Similar to the ant, the grasshopper, and the caterpillar, they must answer the question "What will I do to do to make it happen?"

For a moment, let's reprise the role of financial advisors and imagine that we're trying to assist the ant and the grasshopper, two clients that are likely to experience major life events in the near future. It's unclear whether their circumstances will be good news or bad, but they're certain to need significant amounts of cash to navigate whatever's on the horizon. As their advisors, which client's saving mindset is more likely to help them survive and thrive?

The Grasshopper	*"Sorry, but I want to enjoy life now. I certainly don't want to worry about unknowns, budgets, or work! I know that makes me 'irresponsible,' but who knows if I'll make it to winter, right? Besides, I'll lean on friends or delay paying some of my bills if things get tight. It's just not worth it to get anxious like some others do. There'll be plenty of time for that later. Assuming there is a 'later...'"*
The Ant	*"I don't want to fret about money. I want to feel confident that I can pay my bills and be ready if a good opportunity arises. Having solid income, low expenses, and adequate surplus helps me sleep better. My secret is spending less than I earn, and ensuring that I can access my cash if I need it. It's ok if people think that's boring. I want my independence. That's exciting to me..."*

It's not a difficult choice. The grasshopper's free-spirited style might be undercut by the first sign of adversity, and it probably won't be able to seize upon future opportunities. Conversely, the ant's peace-of-mind approach gives it a better shot at confronting the unknowns on the horizon.

Very few of the employees that I meet are as obvious. While most claim to embrace beliefs and attitudes consistent with strong saving mindsets, too many exhibit behaviors and habits that are associated with weak or conflicted ones. They're aware of threats to their careers, but act indifferently toward job performance, pay raises, or promotions. They know that dollar bills don't grow on trees, but regularly spend as if they do. They hate losing money, but nonchalantly overpay for stuff. And they recognize the value of having extra cash in the bank, but lack the patience to leave it alone. These disconnects are problems that must be addressed.

Some of the happier individuals that I meet are those that put it all together, and they enjoy sharing their stories with colleagues because they feel "If I can do it, anyone can!" Contrary to what naysayers might think, these aren't necessarily people with big job titles and corner offices, or the penny-pinching misers; not even close. They're employees at all levels that consistently increase their value in the workplace, spend less than they earn, and build sleep-tight-at-night liquid savings.

When their peers ask "How did you do it?" most reply "It isn't always easy, but it's also never that hard." Like everyone else, they experience "roll the dice," "to hell with it," and "I want it now!" impulses. But in their weaker moments, they remind themselves that they'll be rewarded in due course for delaying or suppressing those feelings, it'll just take a little longer. For them, the key to strengthening their saving mindset is starting small, keeping things simple, and being patient.

Mindset Concept: Household Cash Flow

In their search for surplus, people should occasionally assess the money flowing into and out of their households (or *cash flow*). At minimum, the effort can help them rediscover missing income, identify wasteful spending, and anticipate future gains and shortfalls. It isn't a task designed to "drain the fun out of life" as an attendee in one of my seminars once asserted.

Positive cash flow creates euphoric feelings of getting or staying ahead. *Surpluses* occur in household budgets when people spend less than they earn, and it improves their ability to save for future needs, prepare for growth opportunities, and reduce financial stress. While it isn't always possible, it should be the norm; not the exception.

Negative cash flow fosters miserable feelings of falling behind. *Deficits* occur in household budgets when people spend more than they earn. It depletes their existing savings, and can potentially lead to borrowing, uncertainty, and insecurity. While it isn't necessarily bad, it should be the exception; not the norm.

Neutral cash flow occurs when household spending equals earnings. This situation is tricky to evaluate because it gives people, particularly those that are perpetually trapped in scenarios where they're neither getting ahead nor falling behind, any number of feelings (e.g., hapless, hopeless, happiness, relief).

Determining household cash flow involves two steps. First, total monthly earnings and expenses must be calculated. *Earnings* include money flowing into the household. *Expenses* include money flowing out. In both cases, some types are unchanging and predictable (or *fixed*), and others are continually changing in both amount and timing (or *variable*).

Second, total monthly expenses must be subtracted from total monthly earnings. The result is either a positive number (or *positive cash flow*), negative number (or *negative cash flow*), or zero (or *neutral cash flow*).

Monthly Earnings   -   Monthly Expenses   =   Monthly Cash Flow

Many of the employees that I help use homemade budget tracking tools to monitor their cash flow. Although useful, online tools are also easy to use, allow data to be compiled and analyzed over time, and potentially integrate with other digital tools and accounts. Before paying for or subscribing to any of them, I encourage people to explore the tools offered by their financial partners or the sample worksheet in **Appendix F**.

Mindset Concept: Household Budgeting

Few phrases in my workplace seminars lead gainfully employed people to tune me out faster than *household budgeting*. While invitations to occasionally review cash flow are perceived as nice reminders, most employees become noticeably irritated anytime conversations shift to this topic. But I also find some that are interested, either for themselves or others that they are trying to help, and the reasons that they cite for temporarily or permanently implementing household budgets involve:

> Building savings

> Paying for college

> Retiring without adequate savings

> Eliminating debt

> Suffering job loss or disability

> Practicing living on a fixed income

The effort to create a budget is similar to evaluating cash flow, but more tedious. It begins with efforts to assess consumption habits, identify cost reduction opportunities, and expose future shortfalls. It continues with other steps, like forecasting and synchronizing the timing of income payments and fixed expenses, distinguishing between essential and non-essential priorities, setting caps on certain spending categories, and monitoring daily cash flows. This process doesn't necessarily mean that people must eliminate the joy of life, but they're definitely putting limits on it.

There are many methods to household budgeting. For people that prefer low-tech approaches, they might manually allocate cash into jars, envelopes, or bank accounts for specific household expenses, and withdraw it as needed during the month. They do their best to run surpluses and deposit unused funds into savings accounts. For those that go high-tech, they might monitor and restrict their spending using: several dedicated debit cards (where each account is used for different spending needs); online budget tracking tools; or mobile apps that automatically limit spending based on anticipated expenses or income.

People that have experience living on budgets realize that it's difficult, especially if it's for prolonged periods. They're quickly reminded that some income sources are unreliable, some expenses are unpredictable, and some scheduling disparities between income and expenses must be strenuously managed to avoid compounding future financial hardships.

While finding new money isn't always an option, there are ways to deal with some of the most tenuous household budget issues. Some service providers, like utility companies, will grant discounts and subsidies, or eliminate the variability in monthly expenses, to customers that are experiencing financial hardships. Other service providers will offer planning tools, counseling services, and assistance applying for public financial support.

CHAPTER 4

THE ELEPHANT IN THE ROOM

I didn't know it at the time, but it was the first of countless glimpses of an elephant that's in nearly every workplace that I enter...

It was late on a weekday in May 1996. I'd been living out of a suitcase for several days, and had one final one-on-one 401(k) enrollment session to conduct before I could begin my 4-hour drive home.

The meeting was with an office assistant who'd sat within earshot of the room in which I'd held a dozen face-to-face discussions. I presumed that she'd enroll because she regularly interrupted my earlier meetings to urge her coworkers to sign up.

But once she sat down to discuss her own participation, it became apparent that she'd be my toughest customer. She revealed that she was divorced with two young kids, didn't receive any child support from her ex-husband, worked full-time to provide for her family, and was convinced that she couldn't afford to contribute.

Since she seemed to understand the plan's advantages, I recommended that we focus on looking for surplus cash in her household budget. She humored me and said "If you find it, I'll save it!" So, we spent an hour dissecting her expenses and brainstorming cost-cutting strategies, but she proved at each turn that she was using every trick to stretch a buck. As hard as we tried, we couldn't find a single spare dollar and ultimately agreed: the 401(k)'s biggest fan at that location couldn't afford to enroll.

During my long drive home, I lamented the futility of my effort to help. We both understood her real problem, but neither of us was comfortable addressing it.

One of the most common questions that employees ask in my seminars is "How can I earn more money?" Before answering, I occasionally wonder how things worked out for that hard-working individual and wish that I could share the insights that I've gained.

Increase Your Workplace Value

Every paycheck is a monetized expression of an employer's perception of an individual's value in the workplace. While there are many non-monetary perks to employment, none is more important to most *DIY financial planners'* efforts to build and preserve wealth than being paid.

In the prime of their careers, employees instinctively strive to increase their earnings; *this is good*. Unfortunately, their efforts are often passive, undisciplined, and unimaginative; *this is bad*. It's a paradox that produces herky-jerky ripple effects throughout their financial lives. In a bygone era, the impact of unconscious approaches might have been unnoticeable because the pace of change was slower, but it's hard to imagine that'll work in the future.

A case in point is an assertion made by the Institute for the Future that 85% of the jobs in 2030 didn't exist in 2017.[12] Coupled with gloomy forecasts relating to the impact of the expanding gig economy on traditional workplace earnings, perks, and security, it appears that many people in the current workforce are unknowingly in the crosshairs of significant financial upheaval.

Rather than bemoaning or ignoring the threat, employees that want to continue deriving the bulk of their economic vitality via traditional employment must commit to increasing their value at work, and do so in collaboration with their employers. That's a lot to ask those that already feel underappreciated, but it's better than waiting for cheap labor or technological innovations to make them, and their paychecks, obsolete.

---

[12] Institute for the Future for Dell Technologies, *The Next Era of Human Machine Partnerships* (Palo Alto, Dell Technologies, 2017, pg. 14).

First Insight: Learn from Employers

Unapologetic disruptors like Amazon, Google, and China, are hell-bent on expanding their financial interests around the globe. As they topple traditional market barriers and crush industry rivals, they send an unmistakable message: improve now, or find new work. To avoid becoming collateral damage in these global economic battles, employees must continually assess and refine their skillsets so that they can remain relevant and employed. Fortunately, most won't have to look far to find answers.

Having personally worked with hundreds of organizational leaders during my career, I find that the vast majority of them are well-suited to help their employees understand, anticipate, and navigate the chaos ahead. They're often bright individuals that are rewarded for their vision and compelled to see others' occupational attributes through wider prisms. So, when they share thoughts about the economy, industry, business, or competition, *DIY financial planners* should listen intently for insights into four general workforce characteristics that employers will value in the future:

- ➢ *Technical skills* apply to specific professions and aren't relevant to others.
- ➢ *Transferable skills* apply to most industries and include leadership, multitasking, teamwork, communication, and critical thinking.
- ➢ *Professional values* apply to nearly every profession and include attitude, energy, integrity, reliability, and productivity.
- ➢ *Network connections* are relationships with people that can be sources of relevant news, trends, best practices, and additional acquaintances.

NOW IT'S YOUR TURN
Seek industry, occupational, and professional attribute insights

Spend 15 minutes scheduling conversations with your mentors, supervisors, and leaders to gain insights into industry trends and best practices, career opportunities, and current and future workforce needs. Also, do your own research before these meetings, and share what you learn with them.

Second Insight: Think like Owners

Of the organizational leaders that I serve, business owners tend to think differently than others in the workplace. They often see themselves as stewards of and servants to entire industries, and their work is both their passion and pastime. Short-term issues garner some of their attention, but somehow they keep watchful eyes on long-term obstacles and needs.

I regularly hear them bemoan the dearth of qualified talent. When I ask them what they want, they often describe contributors at all levels that are as deeply committed to their industries and professions as they are. As such, employees that intend to build and preserve wealth in their chosen careers should strive to answer the types of questions that business owners ask:

- ✓ "Do I recruit new talent?"
- ✓ "Do I mentor others?"
- ✓ "Do I identify industry trends?"
- ✓ "Do I offer valuable ideas?"
- ✓ "Do I inspire improvement?"
- ✓ "Do I always go the extra mile?"
- ✓ "Do I think and act long-term?"
- ✓ "Do I ask 'what else can I do?'"

For people that are employed by organizations or bosses that can't, don't, or won't acknowledge the value of their contributions, I implore them to continue asking these questions and to realize that their efforts to do so might prepare them for exceptional opportunities elsewhere.

Third Insight: Adapt for the Future

Many *DIY financial planners* should be worried if employment predictions for the coming decade are accurate. While there will always be exciting opportunities for some, those that aren't prepared are likely to falter. It's therefore incumbent on employees to invest in relevant professional attributes. However, before fixating on specific programs, they're wise to answer the question "What must I do to improve my technical, transferable, and professional skills, and network connections?"

Some of the employees that I help presume that investments in formal education and training will automatically increase their future earning potential, but that's only true if the benefits will be valued by employers. As such, they should seek feedback from mentors, supervisors, and organizational leaders before setting their sights on these programs.

If they receive positive responses, that's great. Employers work hard to scrutinize these types of opportunities and might even subsidize them. Conversely, negative responses might suggest that the perspective programs are not valuable. Questions employees should answer are "How will this alter my value in the workplace?", "What must I sacrifice to complete the curricula?", "What do I need to earn in the future to recoup my outlays of time and money?", and "Can I realistically finish this program?"

There are also informal steps that employees can take to adapt. For example, some dutifully dedicate segments of their days to learning about their industries, professions, or trades, or focus on leadership, technology, and quality. Others search for ways to break bad habits, pull themselves out of ruts, or increase productivity by improving physical, mental, and emotional wellbeing. They read articles and listen to talks accessed via LinkedIn, YouTube, TED Talks, and news websites, or enroll in webinars, lunch-and-learns, and conferences offered by businesses, universities, community groups, or trade associations.

NOW IT'S YOUR TURN
Assess the costs and benefits of formal education and training programs

Take 15 minutes now to consider the value of pursuing a few formal educational and training programs that interest you, and compare the hard dollar (e.g., tuition, books, parking) and soft dollar costs (e.g., stress, time, missed opportunities) to potential long-term rewards. If it makes sense, investigate work and public-domain resources that might be in your reach, and talk about it with people that you trust.

Fourth Insight: Scrutinize Secondary Income Ventures

Some employees that I help look beyond their present full-time jobs for extra income, additional experience, and hedges against career disruptions. But these endeavors often generate unforeseen risks, expenses, and distractions, so it's wise to carefully scrutinize them before jumping in.

Active opportunities require ongoing personal involvement to generate income; this means that people must directly engage in the work to earn the money. Classic examples include employees that run side businesses like family farms or homebased franchises. Newer types (often called *side gigs*) are flourishing due, in part, to rapid growth of companies that rely heavily on independent contractors, such as Uber, DoorDash, and GrubHub. Unlike traditional employment, people engaging in these activities are frequently responsible for paying their self-employment taxes, buying liability insurance, and furnishing the necessary supplies, materials, and equipment.

Passive opportunities don't require ones' active involvement to produce income. With little or no ongoing participation, people profit from royalties, subscription fees, and other revenue streams. Timeless examples include licensing of patents and trademarks, selling published compositions, and entering silent partnerships. Modern examples are revenue producing websites, blogs, and podcasts, and products that others produce, market, and sell.

Employers view secondary income differently. Some encourage it. They might need employees during cyclic or intermittent surges, such as during tax season or rush hour, and believe those that earn income elsewhere aren't as transient. Or they believe that such ventures help workers develop skills that directly benefit their organizations. But others oppose these extracurricular activities because they compete for people's time, energy, and loyalty, and are potential risks to their organizations.

Moonlighting isn't new and it can be rewarding. But employees should thoroughly investigate these endeavors and answer critical questions before embarking on them. Here are a handful: "How will my employer feel about it?", "What are the legal, regulatory, and tax requirements?", "What are the risks and liabilities?", "What are the start-up and ongoing costs?", "What's the realistic likelihood of a profit or loss?", and "What types of scenarios could turn the part-time opportunity into a full-time nightmare?"

Fifth Insight: Get Serious about Personal Branding

Brands are words, symbols, or identities that differentiate products and organizations from their competitors, and owners and leaders care deeply about building and preserving them. They know that they're vital to success, and realize that it can take years to build strong ones and seconds to destroy them.

Employees should recognize that similar dynamics exist in labor markets. And every day, they distinguish themselves through their behaviors, actions, and results, and affect the value of their own personal brands. For this reason, I encourage them to become contributors that their teammates respect, create appropriate public images, and avoid damaging traits that might derail their future earning potential.

In my experience, employers value employees that cast positive shadows and spurn those that are known for undesirable behaviors, such as deceiving, gossiping, mistreating others, burning bridges, criticizing leaders, sabotaging teammates, missing work, arriving late, failing to finish tasks, and breaking promises.

Be Your Own Advocate

Sometimes I witness workplace scenarios where good people leave quality organizations, and neither party is happy about the separation. From my vantage point, it occurs most often when employees aren't comfortable advocating for themselves...

When a boy turned 11 years old, his dad kept a promise: he allowed his son to begin mowing the lawn every week and paid $20 per cut provided that the job was done right.

When the kid was 18, and had just finished the lawn for the last time before heading to college, his Dad gave him the customary $20.

In a light-hearted moment, the son asked "Dad, why didn't you ever give me a raise? You paid me the same $20 for seven years." The dad replied "Well, honestly, you never asked for one."

The son's demeanor turned serious. "What? Really? But you're my Dad..."

There was a pause, and then the dad said "Exactly. If you couldn't count on me to make sure that you were paid what you were worth, you shouldn't expect anyone else to."

The son wasn't happy, but he never forgot the valuable lesson.

Employees owe it to themselves, those they cherish, and their employers to embrace conscious approaches to this facet of their lives, but it helps to have some background before proceeding.

First, employers' compensation strategies are rarely arbitrary. They view pay as one piece of a larger array of incentives that are carefully designed to achieve multiple goals for each role, and they weigh many factors at multiple levels. For example, at the *individual level*, it might correspond with observed attributes such as skills, competencies, experience, credentials, and potential. At the *positional level*, it could be associated with duties, requirements, on-the-job risks, uniqueness of the roles, shift differentials, and available candidates. And at the *organizational level*, it might relate to regulations, industry, competition, location, size, and financial outlook.

Second, there are numerous forms of employee payment. *Fixed compensation* tends to be stable and thereby predictable, and it includes annual salaries and hourly wages. *Variable compensation* isn't fixed, but many people rely on it. It can change in amount, timing, and qualification, and examples include commissions, overtime, bonuses, and gratuities.

Third, the total cost of employee compensation is higher than the gross earnings that appear on paystubs. For example, $1000 in wages actually costs employers an extra $100 to $250 due to additional payroll taxes and Workers' Compensation. This might seem irrelevant to people that believe that they deserve more money, but the leaders that manage organizational finances know that every pay raise must be offset by higher revenue, lower profits, or concessions elsewhere.

And fourth, the "Who?", "What?", "When?", "Why?", and "How?" involved in compensation reviews is different in every organization. In some, processes are informal and decisions are made by immediate supervisors. In others, individual leaders have little or no discretion because pay is highly-structured and based on detailed market studies.

Phase I: Initiating

Employees that want to start discussions about their contributions to their organizations and desire for more money should begin by asking immediate supervisors for 15 minutes to discuss career development and professional fulfillment. This can be awkward, especially for those that haven't done it before or work in organizations that lack formal procedures.

When these meetings arrive, employees should begin by restating their purpose, propose brief agendas, and confirm their agendas are acceptable before continuing. It can be as simple as asking to spend 10 minutes discussing organizational needs and 5 minutes explaining their desire to schedule annual reviews or follow-up meetings. At a minimum, they should learn their employers' preferred approaches to discussing pay raises and attain commitments to subsequent discussions.

This interaction should be relaxed, but focused. Since everyone's time is valuable, the idea is to get in, pave the way for further dialogue, and get out quickly. For employees working remotely, phone or video conversations are less personable, but are acceptable if that's the employers' standard (or only) option. For those working onsite with their bosses, in-person is preferred.

Phase II: Assessing

Equipped with fresh insight, employees should proactively: create lists of their previous contributions; identify areas for personal growth; update their professional goals; determine average wage and salary ranges for comparable jobs in the area; and establish the pay raises that they'll request.

If they're confident that they're ready to take additional steps in their careers, they should assess opportunities for advancement. If they're uncertain, they should identify the professional attributes that are hindering their progress and offer their employers reasonable solutions. And if they're sure that they aren't ready or that their organizations aren't positioned to accommodate their desired promotions, then they're wise to focus on non-monetary improvements to their employment.

Phase III: Demonstrating

People have short memories. In preparation for the next discussions, employees should provide accurate, relevant, and concise summaries of personal contributions that they identified during the assessment phase. They can include: lists of assigned, pending, and completed tasks, and projects with applicable goals, deadlines, and outcomes; and synopses of relevant observations and suggestions for personal, team, and organizational improvement.

Sometimes it's difficult to pinpoint individual contributions. If it's because the work was performed as part of tightknit teams, then employees should highlight their contributions to team successes and describe their roles. If it's related to underperformance, then they should request training and support. If it's due to anxiety about taking fair credit, then they should ask mentors for ideas about advocating for themselves in ways that fit their personalities.

Phase IV: Confirming

Before moving to the negotiation phase, employees should confirm that their employers agree with their perceptions of the value that they provide and their potential for growth. Doing so can expose differences that might prevent progress in negotiations and reveal a need to validate statements made during the previous step.

There are a few typical outcomes related to this step. Best case, the employers will agree with most or all of the employees' assessments. That's the goal, and it's more likely to occur if everyone is honest. Worst case, the parties disagree. Here, employees should solicit feedback, and determine if they accept their employers' decisions and want to take another crack. And in some cases, employers request more information or time. In these instances, employees should be accommodating and respond professionally.

Phase V: Negotiating

The negotiation process might be straightforward in scenarios where the parties agree to the proposed terms. But employees might encounter partial or total rejection of their desired changes if questions or uncertainty linger for their employers. In these situations, they should be prepared to listen.

Perhaps they are asking for too much, their contributions don't merit the adjustments, or their organizations aren't financially able to award pay raises.

When employees receive disappointing responses, like legitimately negative feedback, they should honestly assess the input. At a minimum, they can ask for more training, opportunities, or mentoring, and aim for future financial rewards. Remember, employers need quality people, and negotiating professionally and respectfully is typically viewed favorably.

Phase VI: Accepting

When employees understand their employers' needs, demonstrate and confirm their value to the organization, and both parties negotiate in good faith, acceptance should be a natural conclusion to self-advocacy. But the process isn't complete until verbal agreements are solidified in writing.

Too many relationships are destroyed because people don't take this final step. Instead of waiting for employers to make this move, it's acceptable for the employees to send print or electronic correspondence thanking their supervisors for their time and feedback, summarizing the verbal agreements, and requesting written acknowledgement.

NOW IT'S YOUR TURN
Prepare for your next compensation review

Whether you intend to initiate a compensation conversation or prefer to wait for your next review, take 15 minutes now to assess your value in the workplace, prepare to demonstrate your contributions to your employer, and identify opportunities to improve (e.g., training, role, compensation).

CHAPTER 5

THIS IS PERSONAL

Ok, I admit it: I once clicked on one of those "Try This Simple Trick" Internet ads that offer to share a secret to weight loss. The idea that a life hack could pull me out of a fitness rut was intriguing, and overrode my fear of being victimized by malware and future solicitations. Luckily, the vendor was legitimate and delivered as promised, but only after coercing me to watch a 15-minute infomercial for a nutrition supplement.

Many of the people that I help are in similar situations with their spending. They lack the time, attention, or discipline to make the best use of their money, and don't know where to start. Fortunately, they're willing to try a spending trick that I teach. Here it is, as a short infomercial...

> Do you want to know a secret to giving yourself one of the biggest effective pay increases of your life? Do you work hard to earn a good living, but still struggle to get ahead? Have you tried money saving gimmicks that didn't work because whatever you set aside in one month disappeared the next? If you're like most people, the answer is "Of course!"
>
> The next time you're stressed about household finances, I want you to think of a simple acronym. "TEN" is short for "Trim Expenses Now" and it's worked for me and others, and it can work for you too.
>
> It starts by making a temporary written record of every purchase that you make in the next 30 days. If you're into paper, you can place your sales receipts and handwritten notes for every transaction in a basic folder or envelope. If you're into digital, you can make a note in a spreadsheet or budgeting app. Regardless, you need four bits of information for each occurrence: date, vendor name, expense type, and dollar amount.

After 30 days, you'll sort the records into general categories, and then tally the amount that you spent in each one. You can do your own thing, or you can use tools provided by your financial partners or the sample worksheet in **Appendix F***.*

Finally, you'll step back, review your spending, and pick 10 expense categories that you can reduce simply by becoming the household expert on containing the costs associated with those items.

Now, you might ask "What's the catch?" Well, there is one. "TEN" demands that you focus on trimming your chosen expenses for a full year. Wherever you go and whatever you do, you'll be conscious of applying "TEN" to those aspects of your spending. That's it!

Beginning in late-2004, my wife and I adopted this life hack. With purpose and commitment, we cut our annual spending by $7,000 in the first year. That was akin to a $10,000 annual pay raise. More, it was fun and the habits stuck. The next year, we added 10 more items and the savings accumulated. It got a lot harder to find easy cost-saving strategies in subsequent years, but we've continued to find new ways to improve our spending habits.

Since 2006, I've shared this idea with many others (minus the acronym) who have confirmed that it works. Some use it to build their emergency savings, and others use it to achieve different goals. As an employee once said "This isn't about being frugal; it's about living."

Spend Your Money Consciously

Spending is a powerful form of self-expression. From a distance, peoples' behaviors might seem stable and sensible, or erratic and senseless, or something in between; it's difficult to know what's truly happening without walking in their shoes. In that spirit, let's meet characters that embody some of the interesting employees that I help.

➤ Skylar Snowden is a commission-based sales rep from the East Coast who spends most of her workplace Paid Time Off benefit vacationing in a Colorado ski-town. She's there so often that coworkers openly gripe about her frivolous, wanna-be lifestyle and taunt her about leaving the city.

➤ Super Granny is an office administrator who lavishes memorable gifts and experiences on her two grandkids. Her neighbors feign concern that she's sacrificing too much of her future wellbeing to please them. In reality, they're jealous and wonder where she got the money.

➤ Benito Big Screen is a floor installer who pays a small fortune for home entertainment. He excitedly tells acquaintances that he can't live without his cable and pay-per-view television, and some think that he's squandering his money.

➤ Chuck Saver is a seasoned sales manager for a high-end retail department store. He was an executive for his company, but recently took a step back and transferred from Los Angeles County to a large city in the southern U.S. He's already earned a reputation among his new colleagues for being a bit miserly.

➤ Winnie Wanderlust is a 31-year-old customer service rep who's travelled to more exotic destinations than most people do in their lifetimes. She's always planning her next adventure, and some of her peers assume that she's a spendthrift.

Given the setup, it's natural to assume that these are origin stories for characters that spend their money irrationally and live beyond their means. It's also normal, as other characters in their midst might, to observe their lifestyles and ask "How do they do it?" or "What am I doing wrong?" In reality, they're reminders that purposeful spending isn't solely about financial wellbeing; it's also about achieving exciting and meaningful goals that serve equally important, if not greater, causes.

Reduce Housing Expenses

Skylar Snowden wasn't passionate about her job or life in the big city. In fact, most days she hated both, but she couldn't afford to leave because the money was too good. She knew that her coworkers gossiped about her frequent trips out west, and tried to ignore their jabs about being a ski bum.

49

Earlier in her career, she bought a two bedroom, two bath condo after a friend convinced her of the financial advantages of home ownership. It was supposedly the right thing to do, but it never translated into happiness. Frequent business travel and long workdays meant minimal time at home, and the tax breaks didn't seem adequate to justify the hassles. More, her heart wasn't in the city. To her, urban life was simply a work accommodation. She preferred the mountains, and spent a lot of her time and money escaping to Colorado.

Eventually, she questioned whether the advantages of owning the city condo trumped renting, especially given her lack of location attachment, minimalist needs, and local laws that held rent costs in check. She decided to step back and reassess her spending using the simple TEN trick. After tracking expenses for a month, she learned that she spent too much on the city condo: $1,925 for the mortgage; $710 for property taxes; $490 for condo association dues; $345 for a parking space; $300 for home furnishings; $210 for Private Mortgage Insurance; $150 for utilities; $150 for condominium insurance; and $125 on maintenance not covered by the association. In total, her housing costs exceeded $4,400 a month (or $52,800 a year), and that didn't include money she spent on getaway vacations. She was blown away and rhetorically asked "How is this 'conventional wisdom'?"

So, what did Skylar do? She reviewed her monthly expenses and determined that some could be reduced or eliminated if she sold the city condo and returned to renting. Other expenses, such as parking and insurance, were unavoidable. She found a deal on an apartment, sold the city condo, and combined the sale proceeds, savings on housing expenses, and cash previously spent on getaway vacations to buy a small house in Vail that became her refuge and qualified for the home mortgage deduction. When she wasn't there, she rented it through Airbnb to generate additional income and qualify for other tax breaks.

By the time the dust settled, the total amount that she spent to rent her city apartment, own the condo in the mountains, and travel to and from Colorado, was equal. But occasional rentals of her mountain condo netted her an average of $600 of extra monthly income; she was further ahead. More, she found her permanent getaway without leaving her good paying job in the big city.

Reduce Utility Expenses

Super Granny could not explain the drug addiction that led her daughter to abandon her two young children. She was relieved that her son and daughter-in-law adopted them, but felt that she needed to help. She wanted to give them occasional gifts, ensure that they had nice clothes, and take them on at least one fun vacation every year. Unfortunately, she didn't earn much and knew that she had to set money aside for her retirement.

Granny decided to use the simple TEN trick to see if there was any extra money in her household budget. It was an activity that she'd hoped to postpone until later in life, but the family situation forced her hand. After tracking her spending for 30 days, she tallied her expenses and realized that she spent a lot on utilities: $180 for gas and electric; $180 for bundled phone, Internet, and cable; $115 for her cell phone; $45 for pest control; and $20 for sewer, water, and trash. It totaled $540 a month.

So, what did Granny do? She told a few people what she wanted to do and asked for advice. They went beyond offering ideas; they helped. Her son installed a smart-thermostat that lowered her energy bills by $25 a month. Her niece got her a better mobile service package for $55 a month. And her colleague convinced her that she could cancel her landline, and showed her how to get Internet and cable for $60 a month. She sweet-talked her pest control company into dropping her monthly fee to $25, and didn't bother investigating sewer, water, and trash fees.

In just one month, Granny's monthly utility bills dropped from $540 to $315. To some, $225 per month (almost $2700 a year) in reduced expenses doesn't sound like much, but it was enough to give her grandkids better birthdays, holidays, and back-to-school experiences. Plus, it funded one amazing 4-day road trip, just her and her grandkids, each year. She became super without undermining her need to take care of herself.

Reduce Food Expenses

Benito Big Screen maintained tight relationships with his parents, siblings, and friends. He loved them and felt that those bonds made him a better man. But he realized that time spent with them was at the expense of his wife Paquita and their four children, and it was creating marital friction.

One day, he had an epiphany. He imagined hosting frequent gatherings that would bring those he cherished together for sporting events and his famous paella. He hoped it would solve his problem and shared the idea with Paquita. She was receptive provided that it didn't affect the family budget or the kids' college savings. "Things are tight, Benito, but it's worth a try."

They agreed to use the simple TEN trick before making a decision. After tracking expenses for 30 days, they saw that their food budget had gotten out of hand. In their effort to juggle full-time jobs, and the kids' activities and growing appetites, they spent $710 for meals at home, $340 for convenience meals-out, and $390 for entertainment meals-out.

Benito studied the numbers and asked Paquita if she would allow him to manage the family's food needs. She secretly loved the idea because it was one less thing for her to do, but played coy. "Sure, you can be 'Food Boss,' as long as you keep everything we need in the house." To her surprise, he embraced the job and soon devised a formal food-bill-reduction strategy.

He began by declaring a hiatus from fast food and convenience store purchases. While they were helpful, they were also expensive. For Paquita and him, it meant brown-bagging lunch at work. For the family, it meant switching to ready-to-eat meals that Paquita and he prepped on the weekends. He allowed for one or two emergencies, but otherwise cut the expense entirely.

Next, he identified healthy and affordable at-home meals that everyone in the family would eat, even as leftovers. These family favorites became mainstays in the household meal plan, and he committed the ingredients to memory. This produced a second benefit: it reduced the temptation to buy items that might go to waste or blow the budget.

Then, he learned to price shop. After studying grocery store ads and apps, he noticed that two stores regularly featured the lowest prices on 90% of the items that he needed; the others were consistently overpriced. He then visited them and knew that he could cut his costs without compromising quality. He also looked for coupons and considered in-store brands for key items, but those steps were lower priorities.

Finally, he focused on efficiency. He limited himself to one shopping trip a week and stocked up on ingredients when he found good deals. He maximized his freezer, and created additional storage for non-perishable items that didn't fit in the kitchen. It became an in-home mini-grocery store that Paquita called "Benito's Grocery Store."

With a conscious approach, Benito reduced his family's average monthly food bill by $420 and actually improved their eating habits. And he created enough surplus in the household budget to cover the costs associated with a new big screen TV, a robust cable package, major pay-per-view events, and the hosting of large gatherings that made everyone he cherished happy.

Reduce Financial Service Expenses

Chuck loved his career in retail. He'd been doing it for over 30 years, and had been in senior management for many years. The industry suited his personality and natural skillset, and it allowed his wife Camie and him to live a lavish lifestyle. They owned a large home in a nice L.A. suburb, drove newer-model luxury vehicles, belonged to a club, and always dined out.

Life was blissful for the couple until their wake-up call came; the day that several of Chucks' longtime peers were unexpectedly laid off in a corporate restructure. He wasn't impacted, but he suspected that he'd be included in the next round of cuts. At Age 54, he was suddenly terrified about the future.

Chuck and Camie lived on the financial edge for decades. They knew that it was time to change and embraced the simple TEN trick. After tracking their household expenses for 30 days, they spotted numerous opportunities to reduce their spending, but two categories infuriated him.

First, their monthly insurance premiums were hefty. They included: $475 for medical; $80 for dental; $25 for vison; $30 for cancer and accident; $470 for auto, home, and liability; $45 for life insurance that was packaged with their mortgage; and $25 to insure their two smartphones. Ironically, the costs didn't include anything spent on insurance deductibles or copays. They were in good health and had unblemished driving records.

Second, their monthly debt payments were high. They included: $7,730 for their 30-year fixed rate home mortgage and property tax escrow; $910 for a loan on his fully loaded SUV; $660 for a lease on her car; and $195 for minimum payments on the $25,000 unpaid balance of their Home Equity Line of Credit (HELOC). Fortunately, they didn't have any credit card debt.

In total, these two types of expenses accounted for $10,645 per month ($127,740 per year). They were items that Chuck had always claimed to be managing, but that he'd flippantly dismissed when his $400,000 annual salary felt secure. He'd been too busy to pay attention.

What did the couple do next? They divided the household budget, so that each of them could search for practical ways to reign in their spending. Her focus was on lifestyle-related items. His was on insurance and financing.

Chuck looked into making immediate changes to his workplace insurance, but learned that, unless his wife or he experienced life changing events, they had to wait until year-end before he could do anything. He also asked their insurance agent and their accountant for cost-saving suggestions.

When Chuck and Camie regrouped to discuss their ideas, they chose to do something completely unforeseen: they relocated to a less expensive part of the country. He requested and was granted a transfer to one of the company's stores in a lower-taxed state. It was a step back in some ways, but they felt that the change could prolong his career and help them shed their spend-thrift ways.

They sold their home in L.A., and some of the proceeds were used to re-pay the balance on their HELOC and to make the down payment on an equally nice house in their new city. This led to markedly lower mortgage payments and property taxes. They waived the life insurance that their home lender tried to sell them and avoided the PMI because they paid 20% of the home sales price upfront. And, as their insurance agent predicted, their auto, home, and liability insurance premiums dropped substantially.

Finally, because of the relocation, Chuck was able to break from the lease on Camie's car and change his workplace insurance elections mid-year. Since they remained in good health, he elected the low-cost High Deductible Health Plan, and cancelled the vision, cancer, and accident insurance. And he got rid of the insurance on their smartphones.

The couple missed the West Coast's excitement and beauty, but they understood and appreciated the value of feeling financially unburdened.

Reduce Convenience Expenses

Winnie Wanderlust was raised in a family that couldn't afford to travel, but that didn't deter her as a child from dreaming about visiting exotic destinations or from obtaining an international business degree as a young adult. Unfortunately, her passion for adventure was replaced by practicality when she graduated college and began working for a small local business. Before she knew it, five years had passed and she hadn't gone anywhere.

Winnie wanted to change without compromising her saving and investing efforts, so she tried the simple TEN trick. After tracking expenses for a month, she noticed that she spent a small fortune on convenience. She realized that she'd unconsciously replaced a desire to see the world with quick-fix creature comforts: $145 at the coffee shop; $135 for cigarettes; $120 for lunches; $85 for an underutilized hot yoga club; $30 for unused online subscription services; $55 on healthy snacks purchased at a minimart near work; $40 for food delivery; and $15 on bank ATM fees. In total, she spent $625 a month on items that she could buy cheaper or completely live without.

So, what did Winnie do? With a little time, effort, and discipline, she reduced her convenience expenses to $50 a month, and redirected the rest to a travel fund. She studied low-cost travel (e.g., Groupon, Rick Steves) and learned that planning ahead, being flexible, and avoiding tourist traps were keys to using the money that she saved for two fantastic trips each year. Over the next 6 years, she became the globe trekker that she always wanted to be.

NOW IT'S YOUR TURN
Try the simple TEN trick to reduce your household spending

Schedule a 30-day period in which you can track your household spending and identify 10 expense items that you can tighten for one year without a lot of hardship. To find ideas, ask your financial partners, read books, visit websites, watch YouTube videos, or talk to your peers.

Control Your Unconscious Spending

In my work with employees that struggle with their spending habits, it seems that many exhibit common self-defeating behaviors.

➢ *Lack of Discipline.* Some lack a purpose that's sufficient to keep them energized and focused. They postpone or dismiss steps to control spending, to a point where they knowingly overpay for items or maintain unused subscriptions. Wasting money means nothing to them, and they ignore its ability to help them achieve bigger dreams. It's okay if that's what they want, but most admit that it isn't. In these scenarios, it helps to stick to shopping lists, visualize goals, and use technology that limits spending.

➢ *Lack of Judgement.* Some individuals aren't concerned about their current and future wellbeing. They don't fear excessive spending as others might, and describe feeling exhausted or depressed, or exhibit signs of mental or physical illness. It's as if they can't find the strength to slow down or say "No," and they spend their money without knowing whether purchases are affordable, necessary, or worthwhile. In these situations, it helps to confirm that other aspects of their lives are OK by engaging mental health professionals via their workplace Employee Assistance Programs, health insurers, or public-domain organizations.

➢ *Lack of Patience.* Before credit cards and online shopping became ubiquitous, people tolerated the inconvenience of delaying gratification until they had the money (or at least until the store opened). Today's shoppers are accustomed to immediately satisfying their needs and wants, and are easily frustrated and stressed when they can't. In these cases, it helps to understand the impulses that trigger decisions, practice taking a mental pause before acting, and recognize the potential to do better things with the money.

➢ *Lack of Practicality.* It's normal for people to want the nicer, newer, and enhanced versions of the products and services that they already have, especially when the companies serving them are happy to sell them what they want. But this leads some to underappreciate the values of utility, repurposing, splurging, and dollar-stretching. Before engaging in unnecessary spending, it's prudent to quantify the benefits of postponing purchases, or to search for ways to derive extra use from items that are already owned.

➢ *Lack of Foresight.* Some people seem unable to anticipate the future impact of current spending decisions. While most understand that creating surplus today means avoiding belt-tightening tomorrow, a handful spend as if there is no tomorrow. They can't or don't imagine other uses for their money, and are distracted by whatever's in front of them. In these situations, it helps to seek examples of others whose lives were enhanced by foresight or derailed by the lack of it.

➤ *Lack of Teamwork.* Some people are in relationships with partners that have different financial mindsets, or are mentally unable to control their spending. This is the most difficult scenario because success requires synchronicity. Here, I encourage couples to engage professional counsellors. They may not relish the experiences and often rebuff the suggestions, but it may be their only options to succeed together.

NOW IT'S YOUR TURN
Improve your household spending habits

Take 15 minutes now to identify your counter-productive spending habits. Use free or low-cost expense tracking tools that might be offered by your financial partners, or the Cash Flow Assessment worksheet in **Appendix F**. And, if you feel that it's necessary, engage the assistance of professional counseling services that might be in your reach.

CHAPTER 6

REMAINING ON CLOUD NINE

At some point during childhood, people learn the value of having cash in their pockets. They discover what it feels like to be on Cloud Nine when their parents or grandparents give them a few bucks, or when they earn it for baby-sitting or doing yard work. With bright futures and no obligations, they quickly spend their spoils on new treasures and only spare coins remain from the windfall.

And as adults, they're continually reminded of the necessity of having it. They rediscover Cloud Nine whenever new money arrives, but pressing needs and prior commitments erode the potency of their earnings. From the moment it hits, the euphoria of payday begins dissipating and the countdown to the next one begins.

For most of their lives, people inherently recognize that money is transient. When they aren't careful, it slips through their fingers as fast as it lands in their hands. That's not necessarily bad if more is on the way, but it can be problematic when their next paycheck is insufficient to pay unexpected bills or capitalize on opportunities, or when it's the last one they'll see for a while.

Regardless of what people earn or spend, there are times that their ability to remain on Cloud Nine is endangered. To maintain peace-of-mind in the most unsettling scenarios, they need to set adequate amounts of cash aside.

Build Your Sleep-Tight Savings

According to the money gurus and public service announcements, the act of saving money is a no-brainer: spend less and leave the surplus alone. But the *DIY financial planners* that I help realize that there's more to it. They want insights into how much they should keep and where it should be stored because they know that there are different reasons for doing so like:

➤ Short-term cash flow	➤ Home down payment	➤ Education
➤ Financial emergencies	➤ Gratification and luxury	➤ Healthcare
➤ Debt elimination	➤ Home improvements	➤ Retirement

It would be simple if all savings needs were equal; every surplus dollar could be stored in one-size-fits-all accounts. But they aren't, and people are compelled to choose from an array of so-called "savings" options. While each allows them to store money, they're designed for different purposes. Some safeguard cash for immediate and short-term needs, some support investment and depository functions, and some do other things. Generally, there are two primary reasons to save.

The first is for *liquidity.* Money that'll be necessary for short-term needs, like paying typical household expenses, funding known future bills, and navigating financial emergencies, should be readily accessible. This means storing it in accounts, such as savings, checking, and money markets, that present little or no risk of loss of deposited amounts (or *principal*) and can be retrieved within a few minutes, hours, or days.

The second is for *investment.* Money that doesn't need to be accessed in the short-term can be held in accounts or assets that are harder to convert to cash, but allow people to earn higher rates of return. Some perceive these vehicles (e.g., retirement accounts, collectibles) to be savings, but they aren't ideal for liquidity because it can be harder to retrieve the principal.

Savings Goals

There are many suggestions about saving for liquidity, and the employees that I help often want to know how much they should set aside. In response, I offer two time-tested rules of thumb.

The first is for *typical expenses.* Everyone has predictable living expenses. Whether they're paid with cash, credit card, or digital apps, people breathe easier when they know that they can pay their bills from accounts that are accessible, without penalty, within 24 to 48 hours. They should strive to maintain 10% of their gross annual household earnings, or the equivalent of 5 to 7 weeks of their typical monthly household expenses, in these accounts.

The second is for *emergency expenses.* Eventually, people encounter unexpected events that inflict financial pain. Worse, sometimes multiple hardships arrive in rapid succession (within weeks or months). Regardless, people have better chances to survive when they can draw from their own sources of liquidity. As such, they should strive to maintain at least 3 to 4 months of their gross annual household earnings in separate, hands-off emergency-only cash accounts. But if they believe other disruptive events are inevitable, like a prolonged illness or job loss, they should aim for up to 12 months of income.

Combined, the two should equal at least 5 to 6 months of people's *annual household income*, or more if additional hardships are imminent. Some money gurus argue that's excessive since funds can often be withdrawn tax-efficiently from tax-preferred accounts for emergencies, but premature use of these assets increases the likelihood of future problems. Others feel liquidity goals should be based on annual household expenses. That's a mistake too since expenses frequently go up when financial hardships arrive; not down.

The logic for creating sufficient liquidity is to remain on Cloud Nine, especially when income temporarily decreases or evaporates due to unforeseen circumstances. For those that are on tight budgets, I urge them to start small. Setting $50, $100, or $200 aside monthly using automatic sweep features on bank accounts quickly creates breathing room. Once there's enough to handle their typical monthly expenses, they can redirect the sweep feature toward their emergency accounts.

NOW IT'S YOUR TURN
Adopt your liquid savings goals

Spend 15 minutes taking inventory of your liquid savings, assessing where it might take you if you experience multiple financial calamities, and set goals to improve your situation.

Appropriate Accounts

The bulk of people's liquid savings should be safeguarded in depository accounts at reputable and insured financial institutions. Although it's wise to keep small amounts of cash at home, solid banks and credit unions are better. They offer minimal risk of loss. Accounts are typically insured up to $250,000 if the institutions fail [via the *Federal Deposit Insurance Corporation* (*FDIC*) for banks and the *National Credit Union Share Insurance Fund* (*NCUSIF*) for credit unions]. And they give people access to their deposits within 72 hours.

➢ *Savings accounts* are used for storing cash that has immediate use. They allow periodic deposits and withdrawals, and offer nominal interest.
➢ *Checking accounts* are used to efficiently deposit and withdraw cash as often as needed. They allow check-writing, debit, and ATM transactions, and offer nominal interest.
➢ *Money market accounts* are used to store larger amounts of cash that need to be available quickly, but not necessarily immediately. They typically offer higher rates of interest than savings accounts because account holders agree to maintain larger balances.
➢ *Certificates of Deposit* (*CDs*) are used to store money for longer terms. They offer better rates because savers let institutions hold their cash for specific time periods and must pay penalties for premature withdrawals.

For those seeking higher returns on liquid savings, but don't want to forfeit FDIC or NCUSIF protection, online financial institutions generally provide better rates of return than traditional retail banks because they don't maintain local branches or offer traditional in-person services.

NOW IT'S YOUR TURN
Verify that you are using accounts that are appropriate for liquid savings

Take 15 minutes now to confirm that your liquid savings are held in cash deposit accounts that are accessible within 72 hours. While you're at it, ensure that they're low- or no-risk, secure, and insured accounts, and that you understand applicable terms and conditions.

Institution Strength

During The Great Recession, almost 500 banks across the U.S. failed.[13] It doesn't sound bad today, but at the time it felt like federal regulators entered a new bank or credit union weekly, seized its assets, and transferred management to temporary custodians. It was scary, and many of the people that I helped regularly sought validation that theirs were safe.

As people accumulate liquid savings, the strength of their chosen financial institutions should weigh as heavily as other criteria, such as rates, fees, service, and accessibility. They shouldn't forget the lessons of the last decade, the names of some of the biggest failures (e.g., Wachovia, Washington Mutual, National City Bank, Commerce Bancorp), or operate under the delusion that it won't happen again. To this day, many banks and credit unions remain unhealthy, and it wouldn't take much for closures to begin anew.

While the FDIC and the NCUSIF release data about each institution's financial health, they don't provide easy-to-use lists of unstable and weak ones. Luckily, third-party *industry rating agencies* fill the void with free, online tools that consumers can use. For example, *Weiss Ratings* grades banks and credit unions with a user-friendly A+-to-F system. *Bankrate* assesses key indicators with its Safe & Sound scoring program and uses a 5-star approach. And *Bank Tracker*, run by The American University's Investigative Reporting Workshop, provides summaries of relevant financial metrics in its searchable database.

NOW IT'S YOUR TURN
Verify the strength of your depository institutions

Take 15 minutes now to verify the financial strength of your bank or credit union. If your institution receives low grades, spend extra time investigating solid alternatives and consider making a permanent change.

---

[13] Federal Deposit Insurance Corporation, *Crisis And Response: An FDIC History, 2008-2013* (Washington, DC, FDIC, 2017, pg. xiii).

Boost Liquid Savings

During workplace seminars, employees often describe liquidity-building strategies that fit in two categories. *Old School* ideas have been around for ages. At their core are conscious efforts to live on fixed household budgets and direct newfound money into savings. Those that do this say that they "act as if the money's not there" and manually transfer the money into their accounts; it's not automatic. They diligently save in their cash accounts until their liquidity goals are met, and thereafter steer new surplus into longer-term growth accounts.

For most of these people, newfound money includes pay raises, bonuses, refunds, rebates, inheritance, gifts, and investment dividends. Some use the proceeds generated by reselling their unused and unwanted items to build liquidity. Instead of automatically donating non-cash goods to charities, they try to sell them at rummage sales, to consignment shops, or on popular websites. It's extra work, but this might be better than itemizing deductions for charitable goods donations given changes that were made to the federal tax code in 2017.

New School ideas are technology-enabled. The goals are the same, but the employees that embrace them openly admit that they won't save otherwise, or at least the money will never reach their liquidity accounts. So, they automate the acts of saving, and there are plenty of resources to assist them, such as: automatic sweep features on bank accounts; debit and credit cards that direct small amounts of money based on spending activity into interest-bearing savings accounts; and mobile applications that personalize automatic savings based on weekly or monthly spending.

A growing number of employers are helping employees increase their liquid savings rates. Some organizations allow individuals to direct portions of their paychecks into different depository accounts via payroll deduction. And others offer formal workplace plans that allow their people to contribute to short-term interest-earning savings (or *sidecar*) accounts that are linked to their existing workplace retirement plan accounts.

Remain Vigilant

DIY financial planners often talk about sleeping better when they know that their liquid savings is sufficiently funded. But their work isn't finished. They must continue to monitor and cultivate these accounts to ensure that their surplus keeps pace with their personal circumstances and broader inflation, and that withdrawn funds are replenished. Eventually they may need it, and it's then that their discipline will be rewarded.

A BORROWING MINDSET

CHAPTER 7

A DOUBLE-EDGED SWORD

In the 1946 film, *It's A Wonderful Life*, the Academy Award-winning actor Jimmy Stewart portrays a character named George Bailey, the son of a well-intentioned founder of a small community bank that uses customers' savings deposits to extend residential loans to borrowers.

When his father unexpectedly dies, George dutifully volunteers to run the institution until its board of trustees can decide its fate. Upon learning that they're considering shutting it down, he delivers an impassioned defense of the business and pleads to keep it open. He argues that it helps patrons raise their children in nicer homes, live in safer neighborhoods, and become better citizens. Here's an excerpt of his oration about the utility of borrowing:

> *"Just remember this, Mr. Potter, that this rabble you're talking about, they do most of the working and paying and living and dying in this community. Well, is it too much to have them work and pay and live and die in a couple of decent rooms and a bath?"*[14]

In many ways, the movie masterpiece captures the double-edged nature of borrowing. First, it introduces viewers to characters that are helped and harmed by debt. Second, hidden in its rich history is the anecdote of Bedford Falls, the fictional town that's been indelibly etched in the minds of countless people spanning many generations. The effort to bring this place to life ensured the film's immortality and earned it an Academy Award, but the cost to do so caused the production to run over-budget and likely forced the fledgling studio to draw heavily from a line of credit that it had established with a lender months earlier.

---

[14] *It's a Wonderful Life*, directed by Frank Capra (1947, Los Angeles, CA, Republic Entertainment, 2007), DVD.

It's A Wonderful Life is a testament to perseverance and hope, and it reveals important aspects of borrowing. Namely, George's inspired speech underscores the personal and social value of credit and debt, and Bedford Falls symbolizes the risk and reward inherent in every endeavor that's financed, in part or whole, with someone else's money.

You Must Choose

I began teaching credit and debt management in 2006; at the peak of a national housing bubble and in the midst of a multi-year consumer-spending spree in which the average borrower had substantially more credit card debt than they had cash in the bank. For a few years, it was a popular topic because so many employees were over-extended, and their interest intensified as the Great Recession deepened. But as the economy recovered and household finances improved, their attention gradually shifted to other priorities.

Given recent events related to the Coronavirus pandemic and persistent uncertainty about the future, it's time for *DIY financial planners* to permanently commit or recommit themselves to strong borrowing mindsets. They must answer the question "What will I do to make it happen?"

Let's reprise our role as financial advisors and imagine that we're helping Violet and Mary, two clients that are approaching exciting life stages that coincide with dubious economic trends. While their futures are unpredictable, they need to be ready for the opportunities and challenges that they might face. As their advisor, which one appears better suited to utilize this tool?

Violet	*"All borrowing's the same to me: it's money that I don't have and others want to lend me. Since I'm gonna be rich someday, why shouldn't I get what I want now and pay for it when I've got the cash. And worrying about the fine print is a waste of time! I can't compete with their lawyers, so I'll just file bankruptcy if I can't repay. Seriously, there's no point sweating this. You only live once, right."*

> *"There are valid reasons to use debt and I've seen it do a lot of good for people. But I also don't think that borrowing money should be treated lightly because it can affect so many aspects of life. I want a be smart about it, and will do whatever's necessary to make proper use of it. You never know when it might come in handy."*

Mary possesses the stronger mindset. Provided that she manages credit and debt wisely, she'll have occasions to leverage it in ways that can accelerate her security and prosperity. Violet is naïve. She underestimates the financial damage that she can potentially cause to herself, and will likely miss unforeseeable opportunities to get ahead.

The vast majority of employees that I help generally understand this aspect of personal finance. Those that demonstrate abilities to manage it wisely aren't familiar with every detail, but they keep it on a tight leash and strive to become savvy consumers. During one memorable exchange with a group in Minnesota, an employee described her mindset this way: "My husband and I might borrow for things that'll get us ahead, but that's only if the rest of our financial house is in order."

Conversely, those that find themselves on the wrong side of the debt equation usually confess to:

- ✓ Assuming too much about their future income
- ✓ Forsaking prudence in crucial moments
- ✓ Ignoring their credit histories
- ✓ Abandoning their obligations
- ✓ Working with questionable lenders
- ✓ Failing to make timely debt payments
- ✓ Neglecting to read the fine print
- ✓ Listening to the wrong people

When circumstances are such that improvement seems impossible, I implore the people that I help to scrutinize this aspect of their lives, and to leave no stone unturned as they search for better ideas, actions, and resources. Based on my experience, their efforts to strengthen their borrowing mindsets are frequently rewarded.

Mindset Concept: Good and Bad Borrowing

Many money gurus profit by espousing the virtue of debt-free living. They share brink-of-ruin stories that are often rooted in unbridled spending sprees or highly-leveraged real estate ventures to warn others of the dangers of indebtedness. And occasionally their teachings are echoed in my workshops by their ardent disciples.

In ways, I empathize with the never-again sentiment. Borrowing holds the potential to accelerate peoples' financial demise and shouldn't be dismissed. But I caution against mindlessly consuming one-size-fits-all advice dispensed by the attention-seeking charlatans that dramatize their tales of self-inflicted wounds.

Based on years of work with employees at all levels, I'm confident that the vast majority don't need to stand on the edge of steep cliffs to realize that falling off will hurt. They're smart enough to know that borrowing isn't the enemy; an unconscious approach to doing so is. At the risk of provoking the wrath of the anti-debt evangelists, I believe that it's acceptable to admit that it can create prosperity that would otherwise be inaccessible to most, but it also requires discernment between good and bad reasons for doing so.

Good borrowing can catapult people toward wealth creation. Examples shared by employees that I help include using: reasonable college loans to obtain degrees that increase their lifelong earning potential; fixed-rate mortgages to build *equity* (or *ownership*) in appreciating properties or raise their kids in safe neighborhoods; low fixed-rate auto loans to secure vehicles that reliably get them to and from work for many years; loans to finance secondary income opportunities; no- or low-interest loans from their healthcare providers; tax-advantaged loans to help them bridge temporary financial gaps; and high-quality credit cards for protection and valuable perks.

Bad borrowing can send people hurtling toward financial destruction. Examples listed by those that I help include: spending sprees that can't be fully repaid before the next credit payment date; high-interest loans used to purchase rapidly depreciating items like furniture or computer equipment; loans to finance vacations that end years before the debts will be repaid; loans used to buy vehicles that exceed the need for quality, reliability, or income creation; mortgages for properties that might be difficult to sell; student loans for degrees in professions that aren't likely to provide dependable, long-term earning potential; and loans from predatory lenders.

Ultimately, potential borrowers must answer the questions "Is this good or bad borrowing?", "What else is happening in my life (e.g., career, family, health)?", "What are the terms of the lending agreement?", and "How will I repay the borrowed money if my cash flow gets tight?" If they have doubts about the answers, they probably shouldn't act.

Mindset Concept: Secured and Unsecured Debt

According to Nitro College, it's estimated that nearly 80% of American adults rely on one or more types of debt to finance current consumption.[15] Unsurprisingly, their use of different lending instruments, like credit cards, auto loans, and residential mortgages, corresponds with common opportunities and challenges encountered during various life stages.

Secured Debts

Sometimes, people will borrow money that's tied to tangible assets that they use as deposits (or *collateral*). Known as *secured debts*, borrowers agree to give the lenders legal and binding rights to repossess or withhold specific assets, like real estate, vehicles, or cash, if they don't repay their loans. In exchange, the borrowers gain favorable lending terms and conditions.

---

[15] Nitro College, "The Details of Debt: How Debt Impacts Americans' Quality of Life" (2020, www.nitrocollege.com, Web, June 28, 2020).

In my work with employees, *residential mortgages* are the most often discussed type of secured debts. Homebuyers use them to buy residential property when they lack surplus savings or perceive other financial advantages for borrowing, such as to preserve their cash for other purposes, spread payments over many years, or to maximize tax breaks. Since it's a big decision, many people that I help are uncertain about the terms and options.

Fixed-rate (or *conventional*) *mortgages* offer fixed interest rates and flat monthly payments during the lives of the loans. The most common duration is 30 years, but 20 year, 15 year, 10 year, and 5 year options are available. Generally, borrowers that expect to remain in their dwellings for many years and prefer predictable payments choose these mortgages. In exchange, they agree to higher interest rates and pay more over time relative to other types of mortgages.

Adjustable-rate mortgages (*ARMs*) offer fixed interest rates and flat monthly payments during special introductory periods that should be significantly lower than competitively priced fixed-rate mortgages. However, the attractive rates may only last between 1 and 7 years; after which, the interest rates reset based on current market rates and loan features (subject to limitations) for the remaining lives of the loans.

Balloon mortgages blend features of fixed-rate mortgages and ARMs. Similar to the former, they offer fixed interest rates and payments during introductory periods. However, after the introductory periods end, unpaid balances are due in-full. Borrowers are then forced to repay the full amounts, or to finance the debts under new terms (or *refinance*) based on the lending environment at the time the balloon rates expire.

ARMs and balloon mortgages are often used by homebuyers that anticipate selling their dwellings before their introductory periods expire. It can be a useful wealth-building tool, or a weapon of financial destruction if the borrowers remain in the properties beyond the introductory periods, are unable to refinance the mortgages before the introductory interest rates expire and market rates rise, or fail to experience income growth that they hoped would offset increases in the mortgage interest rates and payments.

In residential mortgages, borrowers that fail to pay 20% or more toward the purchase prices are required to buy *Private Mortgage Insurance* (*PMI*) to protect lenders against the chance that they abandon the loans (or *default*).

PMI doesn't directly help borrowers, but it does help lenders feel more comfortable about working with homebuyers that have little or nothing invested in financed properties (and are therefore more likely to default).

Home equity loans and *home equity lines of credit* (*HELOCs*) are forms of secured debt that are attached to existing residential mortgages. They permit homeowners to borrow extra cash, either in fixed amounts or as revolving lines of credit, against the equity that they've accrued in the properties.

Reverse mortgages are similar to home equity loans, except that the borrowed amounts aren't repaid by borrowers. Instead, the accumulated equity in their homes is used for repayment. These loans are used as wealth preservation tools by older Americans, particularly as pension plans disappear and growing numbers of retirees scramble for reliable income to satisfy personal consumption needs. To be eligible, homeowners must be at least Age 62 and satisfy additional IRS requirements.

Unsecured Debts

Sometimes people borrow money that isn't guaranteed with tangible assets. Since lenders lack the right to repossess or withhold assets if the debts aren't repaid, they take bigger risks on these types of agreements because their only recourse is to legally settle them. It's for this reason that unsecured debts typically feature provisions that are more restrictive. Examples include credit cards, student loans, and medical bill loans negotiated with health care providers.

Based on my interactions with employees, *credit cards* are the most frequently used form of unsecured debt. They offer convenience, theft protection, expense monitoring, spending rewards, and other value-added services, but they also become very expensive when mismanaged. Of all of the horror stories that people share, these account for most (e.g., dubious special offers, hidden fees, confusing interest rates, mystifying rewards programs).

Student loans are also increasingly common. Generally, the borrowed amounts must be repaid with interest, although some jobs in government and non-profit organizations qualify for debt forgiveness if specific criteria are met. Typical advantages include deferral of payments and interest, fixed interest rates, minimum monthly payments, and streamlined application rules. The most common government-backed student loans include:

- ➤ *Perkins Loans* are for those who demonstrate exceptional financial need. Although they're set to be discontinued, they remain attractive because the federal government pays the accrued interest while students are enrolled in qualified institutions at least half-time, and borrowers are given 9 months to begin repaying their loans after graduating or failing to meet minimum enrollment requirements.
- ➤ *Stafford Loans* are the most common, and they're either unsubsidized or subsidized. All students qualify for the former and can access funds and defer payments while they're enrolled in qualified institutions. However, those in the latter don't pay interest that accrues while they're attending school. Students can qualify for one or both types based on their household incomes, and repayments start 6 months after graduating or failing to satisfy minimum enrollment requirements.
- ➤ *Parent Loans for Undergraduate Students* (*PLUS*) are used by parents that borrow on behalf of students. They aren't based on financial need or subsidies. Rather, they're based on parents' credit worthiness. More, they are limited to the cost of attending the university minus any financial aid that's awarded, and repayment schedules begin 60 days after the funds are disbursed.

Mindset Concept: Consumer Lending Agreements

It's important to acknowledge that lending agreements are created by seasoned professionals and profit-oriented organizations. For that reason, consumers should always strive to gain clear understandings of key contract provisions before formally entering these relationships.

There are generally two parties named in these agreements. First, there are *lenders* that offer to loan their money out. Second, there are *borrowers* that ask to use lenders' money and promise to repay it. There are always *primary borrowers*, but sometimes there are *secondary borrowers* (or *cosign-*

ers) that consent to accept legal responsibility for repaying the unpaid portions of loans if the primary borrowers abandon their responsibilities.

The amounts loaned are called the *principal*. In return for the privilege to borrow the money, borrowers agree to pay lenders the principal plus additional amounts known as *interest*. The interest charged is expressed as a percentage (or *interest rate*), and it's influenced by factors, such as the default risks, loan durations, inflation rates, lender profits, market forces, regulatory restrictions, and other allowable adjustments.

Typically, lenders will base their interest rates on predetermined indices like the *Prime Rate* which is the most favorable interest rate charged by commercial banks for short-term loans. Lenders add amounts (or *margins*) to the indices before establishing the interest rates that they'll charge, and disclose both to give borrowers confidence that the interest rates won't arbitrarily change during the life of the agreements.

There are three basic types of consumer lending agreements that people that I help use to finance their debts.

➤ *Revolving credit accounts* are loans that allow borrowers to draw money from the lenders at any time, up to predetermined limits. It's as if lenders tell borrowers "take what you need up to the limit, repay it as you're able, and take more if needed up to the limit." Borrowers can repay the principal in full within a specified period to avoid interest, or repay portions of the principal and carry unpaid amounts forward with interest applied. Examples include credit cards, payday loans, and HELOCs.

➤ *Installment credit accounts* are loans made in fixed amounts that borrowers must repay in periodic, regular, and fixed installments over predetermined time periods with interest, until the principal and interest are fully repaid. Here, it's as if lenders give borrowers set amounts of money to use and repay. Examples include residential home mortgages, student loans, and auto loans.

➤ *Open credit accounts* are loans that involve balances that must be repaid monthly. Lenders give borrowers the ability to draw whatever they need, interest-free up to predetermined limits, with the understanding that the debts will be paid in full by a specific day of the next month. Examples include company credit cards, charge cards, and service credit for utilities, phones, and health care providers.

In some loan agreements, interest rates may be temporarily locked at low levels, but will rise in the future. The short-term (or *introductory*) rates may apply to balance transfers on revolving credit accounts, or on certain types of installment loans like ARMs and balloon mortgages. For other types of loans, lenders might provide *interest rate caps* to assure borrowers that the costs won't change, at least during specified periods.

Lenders typically use *billing cycles* of 20 to 40 days, and give borrowers adequate time to make their payments. The period might be 20 or 30 days from the monthly statement closing dates in revolving credit accounts, or fixed monthly maturity dates in installment accounts. The unpaid amounts are known as *principal balances*, and lenders stick to repayment schedules in which portions of future payments are applied to both principal and interest. The settlement (or *amortization*) is final and loans are fully amortized when principal balances equal zero.

In most lending agreements, lenders charge other *fees* and *penalties* that can increase the costs. For revolving credit, they might levy annual fees, cash advance fees, check-writing fees, and customer service fees. For installment credit, they might impose loan origination fees and processing fees. In both cases, they also enforce penalties, such as for late or missed payments, and for bounced checks.

Because lending agreements are notorious for being convoluted, federal policymakers passed the *Truth in Lending Act* in an attempt to standardize them. For example, it forces lenders to furnish their *annual percentage rates* (*APRs*) so that perspective borrowers can gain clearer insights into actual loan costs and conduct apples-to-apples comparisons of competing offers. Lenders are also prohibited from engaging in specific *predatory practices* like charging excessive fees, failing to disclose contract terms and conditions within required timeframes, and convincing borrowers to refinance when it's not in their best interests.

CHAPTER 8

FLEX YOUR MUSCLE

S ince the end of the 19th Century, New York City's sewers have been rumored to provide refuge to a colony of large alligators.[16] Given the Big Apple's bitter winters, it's not a natural habitat for such animals. But local officials have removed a few specimens over the years (presumed to be forsaken pets or fugitives that arrived on visiting cargo ships), and that fuels the fairytale and stifles some people's ability to discern between fact and fiction.

Similar myths and confusion abound in the world of consumer credit. In theory, it should be a simple concept. It's the *trust* that exists between parties entering agreements whereby one can borrow from the other with a promise to repay later. But in practice, it's complex because trust is often fickle: borrowers aren't always reliable; lenders aren't always ethical; both operate out of self-interest; and policymakers, regulators, court officials, and lawyers intervene to keep the peace.

In my experience, organizational leaders tend to understand credit and are good at leveraging it. Conversely, their employees are more likely to be confused by it, abstain from using it, or use it improperly, to a point where it impedes them. This is where I believe they need to be on the same page, so that both can prudently flex their credit muscles.

---

[16] Corey Kilgannon, "The Truth About Alligators in the Sewers of New York" (February 26, 2020, www.nytimes.com, Web, June 26, 2020).

Manage Your Credit Profile

In the past, consumer credit markets were a mess. Lenders lacked standard methods for gathering, sharing, and analyzing information, and borrowers lacked fundamental rights, knowledge, and resources to secure financing. However, today they're integrated, efficient, and reliable, and thereby easier for all parties to navigate.

Credit Characteristics

Just as consumers evaluate products and services based on what they see, hear, and read, lenders do their best to assess potential borrowers' *suitability* (or *credit worthiness*) before proposing the conditions in which they'll lend money, if at all. Generally, they gather information relating to what is known as *The Four C's* of peoples' credit worthiness.

➤ *Character* refers to applicants' experience managing credit and debt, and it includes their financial stability, payment histories, open lines of credit, unpaid debts, and frequency of seeking new sources of credit.
➤ *Capacity* refers to applicants' ability to repay current and future debts based on other financial attributes like future earnings, living expenses, existing debts, and savings.
➤ *Collateral* refers to property that applicants pledge to hand over to their lenders in the event they fail to repay their debts.
➤ *Capital* refers to money that applicants contribute upfront (or *down payments*) to the total cost of financed items.

Since there isn't a single, all-purpose tool that lenders can use to assess credit worthiness, they must obtain some information on their own via personal interviews, reference checks, proof of financials, appraisals, etc., and other information from reports and scores generated by third parties.

Credit reports are historical summaries of people's credit-related activities and include personal identification, residential addresses, prior credit applications, account details, legal judgments, and bankruptcy filings. They are created, maintained, and distributed by businesses referred to as *credit bureaus* (or *credit agencies*) that warehouse data collected from creditors, lenders, and government institutions. Experian, TransUnion, and Equifax are the three largest, and they supply the reports used in most consumer inquiries.

Lending institutions are the most frequent users of these reports. Positive information generally leads them to offer favorable lending terms, and negative information usually results in prohibitive lending conditions or outright declinations. But non-lending institutions, like cell phone carriers, property landlords, insurers, and utilities, also use them to evaluate consumers. For example, some auto insurers believe that insureds' credit reports are indicative of their driving habits and correlate with the risk of filing claims, so they tie their policy premiums to credit worthiness.

Given the wide-ranging impact of credit information, it's important for *DIY financial planners* to regularly review their reports and ensure that their credit worthiness isn't being diminished by:

➢ *Outdated Information.* Most negative items are legally required to be removed over time if they're resolved. In cases related to common infractions like excessive credit applications, they should go away after 2 years. Missed payments vanish between 2 and 7 years. Complex matters, such as civil judgements, foreclosures, and charge-offs, should clear after 7 years from the trigger dates (e.g., date fulfilled, date of delinquency). And bankruptcies disappear 7 to 10 years from settlement dates, and unpaid tax liens should be purged once they're paid.

➢ *Erroneous Information.* Inaccurate information can cause many financial and non-financial problems. Sometimes it's harmless or inadvertent, and other times it's the result of identity theft. Examples include incorrect residential addresses, inaccurate reporting by creditors, unfamiliar credit accounts, and inexplicable activity in various types of credit accounts that were previously closed.

Bad credit information can be costly to borrowers and non-borrowers alike. For this reason, federal law requires the top three credit bureaus to furnish free copies of their reports at least once every 12 months to consumers that request them. Upon receipt, recipients should review them, notify the reporting agencies of any discrepancies, demand reexaminations of disputed items, and expect written explanations for accepting or denying their appeals within 30 days. Their contact information is found on the following page.

Credit Agency	Website	Phone
Equifax	www.equifax.com	800.685.1111
Experian	www.experian.com	888.397.3742
Transunion	www.transunion.com	800.916.8800

The employees that I help frequently raise common credit report myths. One goes like this: "I heard my credit report includes annual earnings, bank account information, and my 401(k) and investment accounts." In fact, some credit bureaus attempt to gather that type of data for unrelated purposes, but it's never included on people's credit reports. Another is akin to: "I heard that married couples have combined credit reports." As easy as that is to imagine, it's not true. Everyone that's applied for credit has their own credit reports, even in situations where they applied for credit jointly.

NOW IT'S YOUR TURN
Adopt a strategy to periodically review your credit reports

Spend 15 minutes obtaining free copies of your credit reports by visiting www.annualcreditreport.com. After you confirm your identity and access the site, consider adopting one of the following ongoing review strategies:

✓ Print all 3 reports simultaneously so that you can review them side-by-side. This helps you identify differences and discrepancies, but will also prevent you from using the service for the next 12 months.
✓ Print one and delay receipt of the others for 4 to 8 months. This allows you to spread the opportunity throughout the year, but it's difficult to consistently manage.

Credit Scores

Credit bureaus assign three-digit numbers to consumers to help various institutions efficiently and reliably assess their suitability for credit, insurance, employment, and other opportunities. These "scores" condense individuals' credit-related behaviors based on information found in their credit reports.

The most common versions of credit scores are variations of the Fair Isaac Corporation FICO® scoring models, which consist of five general components including:[17]

> *Payment history* quantifies borrowers' histories of repaying their debts on time and in full. It accounts for 35% of the total FICO® score.
> *Outstanding debt* quantifies borrowers' use of lines of credit that are already available to them. It accounts for 30% of the total FICO® score.
> *Length of credit history* quantifies borrowers' historical access to credit. It accounts for 15% of the total FICO® score.
> *Recent credit applications* quantifies borrowers' recent applications for new lines of credit. It accounts for 10% of the total FICO® score.
> *Type of credit used* quantifies borrowers' mix of secured and unsecured debt. It accounts for 10% of the total FICO® score.

While some credit scoring systems reference points as low as 100 and as high as 900, traditional FICO® scores range from 300 to 850. In all cases, lower scores suggest greater risk of default and higher scores suggest lower risk of default. Since the bureaus receive different data at different times, and use their own modified versions of the FICO® formulas to produce multiple scores for varied purposes, consumers often discover that they have many scores in use at any given time. More, they find that their scores can diverge by 20, 30, 40 points, or more.

The institutions that assess applicants' credit scores take their own unique approaches to secure and analyze them. Some obtain and review separate scores from each bureau, or they procure all three and create their own single average score. Others use only one bureau's score. This might not seem to be relevant, but it results in higher charges and extra hassles for some consumers. As such, *DIY financial planners* are wise to maintain a sense of the range of their scores and to ask potential lenders which one(s) they use.

Let's imagine a colleague, Abigail, is ascending in her career and wants to buy a new sport utility vehicle. Rather than withdrawing money from existing savings and investment accounts, she prefers to borrow the money that she

---

[17] Fair Isaac Corporation, "What's in my FICO® Scores?" (2020, www.myfico.com, Web, June 26, 2020).

needs for the purchase. But before negotiating the price or discussing financing options, she does her homework and discovers that her FICO® scores with the three credit bureaus are 751, 738, and 717.

The SUV that Abigail chooses will require a $30,000 loan that she intends to repay over 6 years. Using the following table, she sees that a credit score of 720 or better qualifies her for the lowest interest rate, and anything below 720 results in higher rates. A lender that reviews all three scores or uses an average of the three scores will likely offer her a loan at the 4% rate. But a lender that uses the lowest of the three scores, or only relies on the bureau that reports her score of 717, will likely demand 6% interest. That might not sound too bad, but the difference results in $2,003 in additional interest payments during the life of the loan. That's an extra $28 of her monthly budget going toward her auto loan.

Total Interest on $30,000 6-Year Car Loan (Compounded Monthly)			
Score	Interest Rate	Monthly Payment	Total Interest Paid Over 6 Years
720 to 850	4%	$469	$3,794
700 to 719	6%	$497	$5,797
675 to 699	8%	$526	$7,872
620 to 674	12%	$587	$12,228
560 to 619	18%	$684	$19,265
500 to 559	No Loan		

Now, let's pretend Abigail's scores are much lower, and the one used by a lender to evaluate her credit worthiness is only 600. She might qualify for a loan, but at the 18% rate. In this scenario, she'll pay a whopping $19,265 in interest payments over the life of the loan. That's $15,471 more than what she'd have paid with the highest score, and it's an extra $215 per month. Imagine what she could do with that money if it wasn't spent on interest!

The separate situations demonstrate that, like all consumers, Abigail's past credit-related behaviors can reward or haunt her, and she'll owe it to herself and those she cherishes to improve or maintain higher scores. Even in dire financial situations, she can make big improvements in a year or two if she's patient, diligent, and commits to the following steps:

- ✓ Pay bills on time
- ✓ Maintain a small number of accounts
- ✓ Refrain from opening new accounts
- ✓ Raise limits on current accounts rather than open new accounts
- ✓ Avoid carrying revolving balances
- ✓ Repay debts in-full rather than moving them to other accounts
- ✓ Tell lenders in advance about late or missing payments
- ✓ Review credit reports regularly and report erroneous entries

It's important to realize that some derogatory marks count more than others do. For example, the impact of a missed payment on a person's credit score is bigger than a new credit application. It's also worth noting that some negative characteristics can be mitigated by negotiating with a lender and creditor, but it must be done proactively and honestly.

It's equally important to avoid credit improvement tactics that can back-fire. Some people think that cancelling all of their credit cards is wise, but the bureaus equate this to admissions that they can't manage credit. As such, it might be better to preserve accounts with one or two banks, and one or two retailers. Others believe that cancelling pricey or unused accounts is wise, but it may be advantageous to maintain the accounts with the longest histories to boost the length of the credit history portions of their scores. And, a small group use gimmicks like consolidating credit card debts on single cards, dis-puting all derogatory marks, and engaging disreputable credit repair clinics.

People that need professional help should look to their financial partners. This might include: workplace programs like Employee Assistance Programs; personal service providers like banks; non-profits such as the National Foun-dation for Consumer Credit at www.nfcc.org or the Financial Counseling Asso-ciation of America at www.fcaa.org; or government agencies like the Con-sumer Financial Protection Bureau at www.consumerfinance.gov.

Common credit score myths are also raised by the employees that I help. One that I first heard during a workplace seminar in 2006 goes like this: "I've heard that reviewing my credit report causes my credit scores to drop." It still comes up, but it's not true. The bureaus want those closest to the information to validate the information so that it's reliable. Another myth is: "I was told decreases in my scores will be quickly fixed if I pay off all my debt." The truth is that the credit scoring formulas are complex and slow to replace unfavorable activities. And finally, there's this one: "I hear that placing fraud alerts on credit reports hurts peoples' FICO® scores." Rest assured, alerting bureaus and creditors about potential fraud doesn't have negative effects.

Flex Your Credit Muscle

Rather than dismissing the importance of credit worthiness and adopting shortsighted attitudes like abstention or abuse, *DIY financial planners* should strengthen their credit so that they can proactively and profitably leverage it. Those that prove that they can manage debt, maintain healthy credit reports, and achieve higher credit scores will solidify future opportunities to flex their credit muscles in ways that might help them build and preserve wealth.

Lending

As credit improves, consumers should demand better terms and conditions from their current lenders, like lower interest rates, higher limits, and waived fees. It's possible, assuming that they're working with reputable financial partners, that they can significantly improve their situations without terminating long-standing relationships.

Similarly, they should periodically shop for better offers. But rather than waiting to be solicited via mail, email, or the Internet, it might be beneficial to use companies known as *credit matchmakers* to identify, compare, and apply for credit. Contrary to another myth, visiting these sites doesn't automatically affect people's credit; applying for credit will.

But there are reasons to be cautious. For example, consumers should recognize that a single application submitted through a matchmaker can result in multiple new hard inquiries on their credit reports. They should also realize that lenders pay these businesses for attracting and vetting applicants. Finally, they should know that these organizations aren't legally required to act in consumers' best interests.

Regardless whether people seek to work with existing lenders or engage new ones, they should always confirm their understanding of all terms and conditions before applying for new credit. This means answering questions like those that follow.

Interest	What's the Annual Percentage Rate?
	How could the rate change over time?
	How will changes be communicated?
Fees	What fees might the lender charge?
	How are variable fees calculated?
Transfers	What are the terms and conditions for balance transfers?
	What fees and costs are charged?
	How are transferred amounts paid and retired?
	How does the agreement change if transfers remain unpaid after the introductory period expires?
Calculations	How are balances calculated?
	How is interest on advances and transfers calculated?
Grace	What is the grace period for late or missed payments?
Billing	Can billing cycles be adjusted upon consumer requests?
Limits	What's the maximum credit limit?
	Under what conditions can the lender adjust the limit?
Changes	How are changes to the agreement communicated?

Housing

Improved credit can expand people's housing options. For example, it can mean that renters have new opportunities to renegotiate their existing agreements, qualify for nicer units owned by fussier property owners, or secure affordable residential mortgages that are necessary to purchase homes or condominiums.

Entrepreneurship

Improved credit can be instrumental to entrepreneurial opportunities. For people looking to start or expand businesses, open franchises, or buy investment properties, it can mean the best borrowing terms and conditions, and qualifying for exclusive business ventures.

Rewards

Improved credit can result in better rewards. Credit card companies offer attractive perks like cash back, gift cards, and travel deals to consumers with solid credit, and many reserve the best deals for those with stellar credit. For consumers that pay their monthly balances in full, this is a nice way to supplement other wealth building efforts.

Insurance

Improved credit can qualify for lower insurance premiums. For current or potential homeowners whose down payments are less than 20% of the purchase price, better credit can be leveraged to reduce Primary Mortgage Insurance costs. Similarly, in states that permit auto and life insurers to penalize applicants for poor credit, it can be used to renegotiate premiums for current coverage or to shop for lower cost coverage offered by other companies.

Utilities

Improved credit might merit better agreements with utility providers. For people that are penalized for poor credit by service providers like their gas or electric company, it can mean qualifying for reduced fees, and avoiding sur-charges and up-front deposits. Or, in the case of cell phones, it means having the ability to shop for better deals with other carriers.

Jobs

Improved credit can also impact job opportunities. Some employers re-quire external job candidates to undergo credit checks before they'll be con-sidered, and others ask current employees to submit to the same scrutiny for internal promotions. Those with poor credit may lose out to applicants whose credit characteristics are more favorable.

NOW IT'S YOUR TURN
Opt out of unwanted solicitations

As you take proactive steps to shop for better credit and lending agree-ments, take extra steps to opt out of unwanted solicitations.

Start by reducing the credit solicitations that you receive by signing up for the Federal Trade Commission's Opt-Out Prescreen program. You can do this by visiting www.optoutprescreen.com or by calling 888.567.8688.

Next, reduce the direct mail solicitations that you receive by registering for the Data & Marketing Association, formerly the Direct Marketing Asso-ciation and now part of the Association of National Advertisers (ANA), mail preference service at www.dmachoice.org.

Finish by helping someone that you cherish take the same steps. It's a nice gesture, and it could save both of you time in the long run.

CHAPTER 9

A BET ON TOMORROW'S GOOD FORTUNE

Debt is a financial tool that allows individuals and couples to bet on tomorrow's good fortune. Whether it's used to satisfy immediate consumption needs or make long-term investments, the potential for gain or loss is amplified by the total amount that they borrow, the cumulative interest paid, and any extra fees that are incurred. Guess right, it's *"Yay!"* Guess wrong, it's *"Rats!"*

The people that I help span the borrowing spectrum; some have healthy relationships with debt, and others struggle. Regardless, I find that most equate indebtedness to having monkeys on their backs and eagerly await the day that they're rid of them...

Nick Lane was paralyzed by debt. Exasperated, he called his employer's Employee Assistance Program, explained his problem, and was referred to Daisy Liu, a professional debt counsellor. Before reaching out to her via Skype, he read her blog and decided that he liked her philosophy, approach, and tag line "I get debt monkey$ off your back™."

He felt relief when Daisy answered his video call with a warm greeting. She said "Hi, I'm Daisy! I'm a professional..." but then halted as she noticed the caller's obvious symptoms. Referring to a group of debt monkey$ practically smothering the poor soul, she said "Whoa! You're covered in debt monkey$!"

Nick was clearly aware of his situation and dejectedly replied "I know. It's bad. I used to think they were cool. Now, I hate 'em." He added "By the way, I'm Nick Lane."

She smiled and said "Well, Mr. Lane, no worries. I've seen worse. Do I see five?" He raised his hands so they were visible and indicated "six" with his fingers and a thumb.

"Wait..." She paused to count and said "I see 'seven." He bowed his head slightly, then nodded affirmatively. "That's ok, Nick. It's easy to forget" she said reassuringly.

"Ok, it looks like you've got at least three different types. Two big ones that seem pretty tame, and several small ones that are clearly out of control. Is that correct?"

"Yes! The big ones are fine. They're easy to manage and help a lot" he exclaimed. "One helps me to get to and from work, and the other helped me go back to school so that I could earn a better living. I had a bigger one in the past that made it easier to raise my kids in a nice neighborhood." He took a breath and said "It's the little ones. They're killing me!"

Daisy asked "Where'd the little ones come from?" He started to say "I have no idea..." but she didn't let him finish. "Mr. Lane, debt monkey$ are never uninvited. At some point, you adopted them." Her rebuke was met by silence, but she smiled and said "Try again."

Nick cleared his throat and said "I 'adopted' them before I divorced my Ex. I was miserable. I wanted to have some fun, but it didn't last." He paused, but Daisy didn't interrupt. "Look, I was at a place in life where I didn't dawdle on details. When the party ended, instead of being happy, I wanted to give up. But I couldn't. My kids needed me. Now, I just want to breathe again and be a good dad! I want my life back."

"Alright, Nick. You've definitely seen the double-sided nature of these creatures. Some can be really good, and others horrible. Either way there's always a risk of losing control, and they never vanish on their own." Then she said "It sounds like you're ready to conquer your debt monkey$, so let's get started."

Some people, particularly those that have been or are currently mired in debt, can empathize with Nick, but those that know how to use it realize that the tool isn't the problem.

Inventory Your Debt

In my experience, borrowers that struggle typically don't know enough about their debts to accurately share basic information. They lose track of the amounts that they owe and the prices that they're paying; a dangerous symptom of an unconscious approach that afflicts many people.

I encourage those that I help to create lists of their unpaid IOUs. In Nick's case, Daisy asks him to create one as he attempts to climb out of debt. Once finished, his initial draft looks like this...

Nick Lane's Debt Worksheet						
Creditor Name	Debt Type	APR (%)	Balance Due	Monthly		Time to Maturity
				Minimum Payment	Due Date	
2nd Wind Motors	Auto Loan	6.99%	$13,500	$300	10th	5 years
Freedom Bikes	Auto Loan	13.99%	$8,500	$370	12th	2 years
Reputable Capital	Credit Card	19.49%	$3,000	$50	9th	N/A
Big Perks Club	Credit Card	15.49%	$800	$30	20th	N/A
Gimmick Travel	Credit Card	21.95%	$250	$30	12th	N/A
New Day Cash	Credit Card	38.99%	$1,000	$175	1st	N/A
US Dept. of Education	Student Loan	6.35%	$15,000	$185	24th	N/A

Once completed, the two can identify the good and bad aspects of his debts, and outline steps that he can take to improve his situation. It also creates reasons to evaluate his needs, rationale for borrowing, and ability to repay his IOUs.

Assess Your Indebtedness

There are many reasons that people evaluate their indebtedness. Among them are two that I often encounter in the workplace: the need or desire by some to apply for new lines of credit; and the need to evaluate the degrees to which bad debts are impacting them.

Applying for New Credit

Before finalizing loan agreements, it's wise for involved parties to assess the likelihood of repayment. Lenders want to avoid applicants that are prone to default, or at least charge enough interest and fees to justify their risk. Conversely, borrowers want to avoid getting too far into debt and prove that they're good risks so they can secure their loans on the most favorable terms.

In the application process, lenders use a version of a mathematical formula known as the *debt to income* (*DTI*) ratio to assess applicants' overall debt burdens. Expressed as percentages, DTI estimates the portion of potential borrowers' projected monthly incomes that'll be needed to repay existing debts. The equation is expressed:

$$\text{Monthly Debt Payment} \quad / \quad \text{Monthly Income} \quad = \quad \text{\% of Monthly Income Used for Debt}$$

Monthly debt payment is the total combined amount of payments from traditional lines of credit that aren't likely to be repaid in the coming 6 to 12 months, as well as personal loans, alimony payments, tax liens, court-ordered payments, and separate maintenance payments. *Monthly income* is the total combined amount of W-2 wages or salaries, alimony income, child support, pension income, and social security income, or annualized average amounts related to bonuses, commissions, investments, and rental income.

Some lenders, such as high interest credit card companies or payday lenders, aren't constrained by DTI, but others are. For example, traditional mortgage lenders are prohibited from extending qualified loans to applicants with DTIs over 43%,[18] and will probably require considerably lower ratios. The following illustrates how they might perceive borrowers' DTIs.

DTI Ratio	Mortgage Lender's Assessment
Below 30%	Acceptable risk | Likely to approve
30% to 43%	Questionable risk | May not approve
43% to 50%	Bad risk | Most can't approve
Over 50%	Horrible risk | Won't approve

Returning to Nick, let's say that he laments not having a home. He realizes his situation isn't good and hasn't started to unwind his debt problem, but is open to financing a purchase if he can find a dwelling that's nice and affordable. Fortunately, he talks to Daisy before he initiates the pre-approval process. She thinks "He still doesn't get it," but she understands his urge and uses the inquiry to open his eyes.

---

[18] Consumer Financial Protection Bureau, "What is a debt-to-income ratio? Why is the 43% debt-to-income ratio important?" (November 15, 2019, www.consumerfinance.gov, Web, June 26, 2020).

Daisy begins by calculating his DTI. She divides his gross monthly income of $7,000 by the sum of his minimum monthly debt payments ($1,140) and other required payments ($900 for alimony and child support), or $2,040. Using the formula, she initially determines that his DTI is 29.1%.

$$\$2,040 \quad / \quad \$7,000 \quad = \quad 29.1\% \text{ DTI}$$

She shows Nick where his ratio lands on the table and he's pleased. As unpleasant as his situation is, he's happy that he still has a chance to purchase a home that'll give his kids a nice place to stay when they visit. "The radio ad was right, Daisy. This isn't so bad. I can totally do this."

In response, Daisy says "I'm sorry, Nick. What I'm showing you is referred to as your *front-end DTI*. A good lender won't stop there. They'll use an alternative version of DTI that won't leave you feeling as good." She then runs him through *back-end DTI*; a version of DTI that assesses his ability to handle the combined burden of his current and potential debt payments, including principal, interest, required insurance, and applicable taxes.

For the sake of illustration, she assumes a monthly payment of $1,100 for the home mortgage, PMI, and property taxes. This shows him that, given his monthly income and current debt payments, his back-end DTI is a mammoth 44.9%. Due to mandatory lending requirements, she explains that traditional lenders are thereby prohibited from offering him a qualified home loan. The formula follows:

$$(\$2,040 + \$1,100) \quad / \quad \$7,000 \quad = \quad 44.9\%$$

She explains that he can probably find a lender, but it's likely to compound his problems. "Nick, traditional lenders can't help you. There are smaller ones that'll lend you the money, but at high interest rates. That's not good for you or your kids." She helps him see that it's in his best interest to repay his current IOUs and delay a home purchase until he can afford it.

Evaluating the Impact of Bad Debt

Ideally, *DIY financial planners* should borrow in ways that build and pre-serve wealth; not create pain and mediocrity. As such, they're wise to period-ically assess the extent to which bad borrowing is inhibiting their efforts to get ahead; something reputable debt counsellors and wealth planners might do before making recommendations.

There are different approaches that they can take to complete this exer-cise. I prefer to divide the total amounts of their outstanding consumer debts by the total amounts of their disposable incomes. The equation follows:

Monthly Bad Debt   /   Monthly Disposable   =   % of Monthly Income
        Payment   Income   Used for Bad Debt

Here, *monthly bad debt payments* include credit cards, payday loans, and other IOUs that appear on credit reports, but they specifically exclude student loan debts and residential mortgages. *Monthly disposable income* includes household income that remains after paying their taxes.

Returning to Nick, Daisy divides his monthly consumer debt payments of $955 by his monthly disposable income of $1,800. She concludes that his bad debt ratio is 53.1%. The formula is:

$955   / $1,800   =   53.1%

Then, she uses a table to show Nick the precarious nature of his problem and to explain that he has less disposable income available because so much of it is needed to repay debts that are tied to bad borrowing. "Nick, you used bad debt to feel good, and I get that. I see it all the time. But now you have no wiggle room. Imagine if your insurance or transportation costs go up, or you experience a financial emergency. There's no doubt in my mind that this has a lot to do with the stress that you constantly feel."

Bad Debt as % of Disposable Income	Counsellor's Qualitative Debt Assessment
Less than 5%	Desired | No concerns
5% to 15%	Decent | Take small steps to shed debt
15% to 30%	Distress | Take moderate steps to repay debt
30% to 60%	Dangerous | Take big steps to repay debt
More than 60%	Dire | Begin bankruptcy discussions

She emphasizes the need to unravel his bad debt and avoid further adversity. Otherwise, the next step in his financial recovery might require bankruptcy protection.

NOW IT'S YOUR TURN
Assess your current debt load relative to your current income

Spend 15 minutes calculating your bad debt load ratio to determine the extent to which you might have a problem.

Unravel Your Debt

In my seminars, I generally focus on four keys to avoiding or reversing extreme indebtedness.

First Key: Search for Help

DIY financial planners that believe that they need help should enlist good debt counsellors. On a basic level, these professionals offer valuable education and guidance. But on a deeper level, they can help secure lower interest rates, eliminate late fees, and improve other aspects of lending agreements.

In severe cases, they can negotiate settlements whereby they collect and forward payments to creditors.

Debt counselors can be found in many places. I encourage the employees that I help to begin their searches at work because their employers often provide reputable and confidential counselling services via Employee Assistance Programs, and some offer debt management, consolidation, and refinancing solutions. They should also investigate non-profit organizations, like the National Foundation for Credit Counseling (NFCC) and the Financial Counseling Association of America (FCAA), and government agencies like the Consumer Financial Protection Bureau (CFPB) and the Federal Deposit Insurance Corporation (FDIC).

But they should remain guarded. There are bad actors that prey on those seeking help. They tend to be fly-by-night organizations that mispresent their services, use deceptive repair tactics, charge high fees, and make promises that they can't keep. Before retaining counsellors, people should ask detailed questions (see **Appendix G**) and investigate complaints by contacting their State Attorney General's Office, or by visiting the Federal Trade Commission (FTC), Better Business Bureau (BBB), or CFPB websites.

Once engaged, it's important to realize that creditors might perceive the use of these professionals and their services as symptoms of deeper financial problems, and the degree to which they're involved will adversely impact consumers' short-term credit worthiness. Ultimately, distressed borrowers must decide what's more important.

NOW IT'S YOUR TURN
Investigate helpful debt management resources in your reach

If you're struggling with debt, spend 15 minutes investigating free or low-cost debt education, counselling, and management resources that might be in your reach at work or in the public domain. At minimum, ask them to help you identify techniques to reduce your borrowing costs and eliminate your bad debt.

Second Key: Stop the Bleeding

Whether borrowers choose to go-it-alone or enlist help, they must stop the bleeding. In addition to regaining control of their spending, they need to decide how to attack their IOUs. Some adopt a *smallest-to-largest* method whereby they repay debts that have the smallest unpaid balances. This reduces the number of creditors, avoids potential penalties, and creates quick results. Others use a *highest-to-lowest* approach in which they repay debts with the highest interest rates. This eliminates IOUs that disproportionately affect their credit. Both strategies require them to make minimum monthly payments on all of their accounts.

Let's say Daisy Liu subscribes to smallest-to-largest. She'll tell Nick to use his $1800 of monthly disposable income to make all of his minimum monthly payments and apply the excess to his smallest unpaid IOUs (e.g., Gimmick Travel and Big Perks). In the second month, he has more disposable income and she instructs him to make minimum monthly payments and apply the remainder to the smallest of his unpaid IOUs (e.g., Big Perks and New Day Cash). By the third month, he's eliminated three creditors. This will continue until all of his bad debts are repaid.

Another debt counsellor, Jen Smyth, believes in highest-to-lowest. She'd tell Nick to use his $1800 of monthly disposable income to pay the monthly minimum on each IOU and apply the remaining amount to his most expensive account (e.g., New Day Cash). In the next month, she'd suggest using his disposable income to make the minimum monthly payments, and apply the rest to the accounts with the next highest interest rates (e.g., Gimmick Travel and Reputable Capital). By the third month, he's repaid his two most expensive creditors.

After adopting repayment strategies, distressed borrowers should send collectors written explanations of their plans. The effort might not satisfy all creditors, but it's a good start. More, they should realize that federal and state laws offer them some protection. For example, collectors can only discuss the issues with them, their spouses, or their legal representatives, and can't have anyone thrown in jail, garnish wages without legal court orders, or file lawsuits without legitimate rights.

In situations where borrowers dispute owed amounts, they should immediately inspect their credit reports. If legitimate lenders are seeking questionable amounts, written responses from the borrowers explaining their dis-agreements should be sent within 30 days of the collections notice. If lenders' claims are erroneous or fraudulent, written notices of the disputes should be sent to the credit agencies and collectors should be asked to provide more information.

Third Key: Find the Money

When distressed borrowers become convinced that getting out of ext-reme debt is impossible, they're prone to abandon obligations, snub lenders, hide assets, and pursue bankruptcy. While that can seem like an easy path, it causes serious and long-term damage to multiple facets of their lives. Before reaching that point, they should consider other sources of money that might be in their reach.

Post-tax options might include refinancing existing debts, requesting pay raises, securing additional work hours, or finding part-time jobs or side gigs. It can also include selling assets, such as real estate, collectibles, investments, company stock, annuities, permanent life insurance, and big-ticket items that are still being financed. These options may not feel good, but they're better than waiting for the courts, lawyers, and law enforcement to intervene.

Pre-tax options might include funds held in tax-preferred accounts, like 401(k)s, IRAs, and HSAs. While some of the money might not be accessible, like employer matching contributions that aren't fully vested, employees may be allowed to withdrawal some of it. The distributions will likely be subjected to tax withholdings and penalties if they don't meet long-standing or special hardship rules, but the setback to their retirement might be preferable to the disastrous effects of steep interest payments, stiff penalties, bad credit, and bankruptcy proceedings.

Perhaps a better option than retirement plan withdrawals, if allowed by employers, are loans from their 401(k) or 403(b) plans. Relative to high inter-est personal loans, these tend to be quick, easy, and affordable. Plus, the loan repayment is made via payroll deduction, which helps people avoid missed payments and incurred penalties. Where permitted, account owners can bor-row up to half of the account balance up to statutory or plan limits, but it must be repaid within specified periods.

The biggest drawback to these types of loans is that they erode retire-ment nest eggs. Another is that, in situations where employees are termin-ated before fully repaying their unpaid principal, the loans must typically be repaid within 30 days of the last day of employment. While account assets can be used for this purpose, problems arise if there's not enough money in the accounts to cover the outstanding balances or if the borrowers aren't pre-pared for the corresponding tax liabilities.

For homeowners that have accumulated equity in their primary residen-ces, they can also apply for HELOCs to consolidate their debts. If approved for the loan, interest on the principal might be tax deductible, but they should ask their tax advisors before assuming that they automatically qualify.

Another option that can provide cost-saving relief is to consolidate unse-cured debts into single loans that offer better lending terms. In addition to reducing their borrowing expenses, it helps people simplify their payments so they can make them on time and avoid missed payments and associated fees. The disadvantage is that it might be viewed negatively by future lenders.

Fourth Key: Seek Bankruptcy Protection (If It's Really Bad)

When severely distressed borrowers' voluntary efforts to satisfy or rene-gotiate lending agreements fail, federal and state bankruptcy laws give them avenues to restructure or abandon many of their debts while protecting cer-tain assets like earnings, primary residences, and retirement accounts.

Chapter 13 Bankruptcy (or *restructuring bankruptcy*) is where courts in-tercede to allow borrowers to settle their debts in reasonable timeframes by implementing meticulously detailed repayment plans. This option does less damage to their credit and permits them to hold onto their assets during the process, but it requires verifiable proof of steady and reliable income.

Chapter 7 Bankruptcy (or *liquidation bankruptcy*) is where courts assign trustees to sell defaulting borrowers' assets that aren't exempt from liquid-ation and use the proceeds to settle debts with creditors that have properly filed claims. Similar to Chapter 13, some individuals aren't eligible, like those that earn sufficient income to repay. This is the simplest and most common form, and it has the most significant and lasting impact on peoples' future credit.

These laws lessen peoples' fears of oppressive penalties and retribution for pursuing financial opportunities that involve the risks of default, and give borrowers that fail to repay their IOUs second chances. But it's a highly specialized aspect of personal finance that requires deep expertise and knowledge of relevant rules, requirements, and procedures. It's for this reason that people in these situations are encouraged to engage reputable and local debt management experts, like counselors and attorneys, as soon as possible.

NOW IT'S YOUR TURN
Accelerate the repayment of your unpaid debt

If you're drowning in debt, take 15 minutes now to identify steps that you can take to stop the bleeding, find the money, or engage experts who will help you accelerate the repayment of your unpaid IOUs.

SECTION IV

AN INVESTING MINDSET

CHAPTER 10

A WORTHY SUBSTITUTE

Many of the *DIY financial planners* that I help acknowledge that it'll take more than the sweat of their brows to get ahead. They half-jokingly tell me that the only way they'll financially succeed is by winning the lottery or trying something unconventional...

It's late-morning on a sunny day in early-September. A married, middle-aged couple is driving on a rural, two-lane highway in western Ohio. They're heading to her parents' house to celebrate her dad's 65th birthday, but it's without their kids because her mom doesn't want them to see their grandpa in such rough shape. On the bright side, it gives the two some uninterrupted time together.

They talk for a bit, but eventually drift into their own worlds when the dialogue becomes the same-old-same-old. Then, without a word, their thoughts converge as they pass dozens of rows of ripe and ready apple trees, and observe a flurry of related activity; a tractor is pulling a trailer into a barn; crates are being loaded onto a truck; and a dozen workers are bustling about the place.

Breaking the silence, she says "Where did the summer go? It's already harvest time."

"I don't know. It seems like time goes faster as we get older," he says. Then he adds "You know, we really should eat more..."

She smiles and interrupts him. "Oh, my God! Do you remember how excited the kids would get when we'd put apple juice in their sippy cups? Life used to be so simple."

"It was! I can still see their expressions as they'd eat your dad's applesauce? They were so cute as babies. What the heck happened?" he asks as he snickers.

With the scene quickly disappearing behind them, she redirects the conversation and asks "Honey, what were you thinking about earlier?"

"The usual: money. Your folk's situation makes me worry about our future." Then he asks "Why? What were you thinking about?"

"Same. But that apple orchard got me daydreaming again" she says. "Wouldn't it be a fun way to earn extra income? And seriously, how hard can it be to grow trees and pick fruit? The money we've set aside would be plenty to get us up and running..."

"You've been itching to do something for years, but seriously?" He continues, "What do we know about apple orchards? And where will we find the time?" He pauses to let the reality of the question sink in, and then finishes "That's a huge step, and it's probably harder than people like us realize. Babe, are things really okay for you at work?"

She replies "Sure. Everything's fine. I love my job, and you're good at what you do. But I feel like we've got to try something else so we can move faster. Without some kind of a boost, I don't think we'll ever do the things we dreamed about..."

She shakes her head. He redirects his attention to the road ahead. The discussion dies, and both continue searching for answers.

Similar to the couple in the story, most people contemplate these types of entrepreneurial adventures, but eventually conclude that they don't have what it takes to go all-in. Fortunately, there's another option.

You Must Choose

Investing is a passive income generating activity that allows employees at all levels to circumvent obstacles that constrain their efforts to build and preserve wealth. Moreover, given the shift by employers toward participant directed investment plans, it's imperative for them to strengthen their investing mindsets. The question they must answer is "What will I do to do to make it happen?"

Once again, let's reprise the role of financial advisors and imagine that we're trying to guide two clients. Both are dual-income couples that have young kids, adequate cash surplus, and the desire to accumulate adequate funds to address future college, health care, and retirement expenses. Based on the following mindsets, which is more apt to be prepared for the opportunities and challenges on the horizon?

The G. Smiths	*"We've known since the dot-com crash that the only people that make money investing are the crooks on Wall Street. They get away with murder while the little guys get burned. It happens so often that it can't be coincidental. Heck, even 401(k)s are scams! So, when it comes to playing investment roulette, our chips are always on 'hard work' and 'cold cash.' What's there for us to discuss?"*
The Honeycrisps	*"Our kids and our careers demand 110% of our attention, so we're not able to work side jobs or start a business to earn extra money. But we do believe that wisely investing in the profitable work of others is a worthy substitute for time and energy that we lack. And with discipline and diligence, we think it'll help us achieve some of our long-term goals. The sooner we start the better."*

The G. Smiths espouse beliefs and attitudes that are held by people that focus on disasters that vaporized investor capital and eroded public trust, like the Enron scandal, the Great Recession, and the Coronavirus pandemic. Their apprehension might be justified, but it prevents them from letting their money work for them. Conversely, the Honeycrisps are honest about their limitations and avail themselves to a wider range of wealth building options.

In my workplace discussions, it seems that most *DIY financial planners* exhibit weak or conflicted investing mindsets. Some won't invest under any circumstances. Others only do it because they fear that they'll miss out or feel strong-armed by enthusiastic colleagues. They volunteer explanations like "I didn't want to look dumb" and "My friend told me that I couldn't lose..."

And frequently, I find that these people are driven by the assumption that *gambling* and *investing* are the same thing; they aren't. Both activities involve expectations of being rewarded for accurately anticipating future outcomes, but investing requires the additional step of taking owners' or lenders' stakes in enterprises and people.

In response to these admissions and insights, employees that have strong investing mindsets often show empathy, offer reassurances, and share some of the common sense lessons that they learned like:

- ✓ Treat every decision seriously
- ✓ Stick to your stated objectives
- ✓ Don't hesitate to ask for help
- ✓ Don't do it if it doesn't feel right

- ✓ Do your own homework
- ✓ Mind your portfolio
- ✓ Avoid wishful thinking
- ✓ Use incentives if they make sense

Mindset Concept: Investment Alignment

In simple terms, investments (or *assets*) are tangible and intangible things that might be valuable in the future.

But that description isn't very practical because it's too broad; it can literally include anything. Therefore, investors rely on narrower definitions that require assets to satisfy three criteria: they must possess periodic rates of return; their rates of return must vary over time; and they must have the ability to be bought and sold with relative ease.

Assets are categorized in two ways that are meaningful to the employees that I help. First, they're divided into groups (or *asset classes*) that are based on common attributes and behaviors. Asset classes, like cash, fixed income (e.g., corporate bonds, government bonds, treasury bills), equity (e.g., company stock, preferred stock), and real estate, generally relate to broader investing goals (or *objectives*) such as:

➤ *Preservation of capital* is for investors that don't want to lose the money that they initially invest (or *principal*), or don't want their principal to lose its value due to inflation.

- ➤ *Produce current income* is for those that need their principal to produce income that they can live on in the near term.
- ➤ *Produce future growth* is for investors that want their principal to grow so that they'll potentially have significantly more money in the future.
- ➤ *Speculation* is associated with high-risk-high-reward investing, and it's for those that are willing to lose substantial amounts of their principal in exchange for the opportunities to achieve lucrative gains.

Second, assets are regulated or unregulated. Those in the former group are referred to as *securities*. They're traded on convenient and highly efficient platforms like the New York Stock Exchange, NASDAQ, and Over-The-Counter markets, and two types serve as the core of most investors' portfolios: *bonds* allow them to act as lenders to institutional borrowers; and *stocks* permit them to be bona fide owners of enterprises. And those in the latter group are known as *non-securities*. They include items like precious metals and gems, artwork, and real estate, that are typically bought and sold via auctions or private listings.

NOW IT'S YOUR TURN
Confirm that your assets and objectives are aligned

Schedule time to confirm that the assets in your investment portfolio align with your needs and circumstances. Ask your financial partners to help you answer self-assessment questions like:

- ✓ "What are my investment objectives?"
- ✓ "What are the time horizons for my goals?"
- ✓ "How do my existing assets align with my objectives?"
- ✓ "How should my current financial situation alter my goals?"
- ✓ "What changes should I make?"

Mindset Concept: Investment Performance

Once acquired, assets can grow in value and be sold for more than their purchase prices. Or they can lose value and be sold for less. Along the way, some provide additional monetary benefits like bonds that pay *interest* and preferred stocks that make periodic cash or stock payments (or *dividends*).

The simplest tool used to measure changes in performance is known as the *rate of return*. I find that most employees are familiar with the concept, but some need a refresher on how it works. A basic equation that's used to calculate it (for assets that don't produce dividend or interest payments) is:

[(New Price – Old Price)   /   Old Price]   x   100   =   Rate of Return

To demonstrate, let's assume that the Honeycrisps buy a single share of Apple Orchard, Inc. stock for $10. If they sell the asset for $15 one year later, they'll realize a 50% *gain* in the value of their investment.

[($15 – $10)   / $10]   x   100   =   50%

Conversely, if they sell the share a year later for only $5, they'll take a 50% *loss* on the value of their investment.

[($5 – $10)   / $10]   x   100   =   -50%

As good as it feels to take gains (or to cut losses), investors can potentially amplify their wealth-building efforts by consistently reinvesting their principal and earnings so that the funds can continue growing together (or *compound*). Over long periods of time, the accumulation effect can be sizeable.

Given that compounding is critical to wealth creation, I urge investors to learn two performance-related formulas that'll help them assess its impact. The first, the *Rule of 72*, is for quick mental calculations and the equation is:

72 ÷ Annual Rate of Return   =   Number of Years to Double in Value

The Rule of 72 can be used to quickly estimate the time that's needed for asset values to double at given rates of return (assuming that earnings are reinvested). So, if Apple Orchard, Inc. maintains an 8% annual return, and the Honeycrisps consistently reinvest their principal and profits, then it'll take 9 years for their initial investment to double.

$$72 \div 8\% \qquad = \qquad 9 \text{ Years}$$

It can also be used to estimate the rates of return that are necessary for assets to double in value within given periods of time. If the Honeycrisps want their investment in Apple Orchard, Inc. stock to double in 6 years, then a 12% annual return is required.

$$72 \div 6 \text{ Years} \qquad = \qquad 12\%$$

The second performance-based method is the *future value formula*. This requires some math acumen, but it permits investors to estimate the future values of assets. Calculations can be adjusted to reflect the principal investment, the assumed interest rates, and the periods of time for which both the principal and earnings will be invested. Here's the basic equation:

$$\text{Money Invested} \quad \times \quad (1 + \text{Interest Rate})^{\text{No. of Periods}} \quad = \quad \text{Future Value}$$

Continuing with the example, if the Honeycrisps buy one share of Apple Orchard, Inc. stock for $10, hold it for 5 years, and the annual rate of return is 8% during the time that they own it, then the future value of their share is projected to be $14.69.

$$\$10 \qquad \times \qquad (1 + .08)^5 \qquad = \qquad \$14.69$$

Finally, investors should compare assets' rates of return to relevant and standard measuring sticks (or *benchmarks*). For example, cash-related assets are compared to the *30-Day U.S. Treasury Bill*, U.S.-based large capital stocks to the *Standard & Poor's (S&P) 500 Index*, and international equity and global stock funds to the *Morgan Stanley All Country World Index* (*MSCI ACWI*).

Whether performance is real or relative, actual gains and losses are only realized once assets are sold. As such, the Honeycrisps shouldn't view their investment in Apple Orchard, Inc. as a victory or defeat until they sell their share.

Mindset Concept: Investment Risk

Conceptually, *investment risk* refers to the potential that investors will be disappointed by investment performance. Their assets might lose some or all of their value, or increase in value but fall short of expectations.

The term describes different types of risk that affect rates of return. Some are system-wide (or *market*) and are typically unavoidable. Others are specific (or *business*) and can potentially be mitigated like: *sector risk* which involves underperforming industries; *credit risk* which involves bond issuers that default on loans; *interest rate risk* which involves assets that are impacted by changing interest rates; *liquidity risk* which involves assets that are hard to sell; and *timing risk* which involves investing at the wrong time.

Periodically, investors are invited to complete questionnaires that help them pinpoint their risk tolerances. Their answers are used to plot them on spectrums that usually correlate with suitable investment recommendations. On one end are people that prefer little or no risk. They're conservative because their sole concern is protecting their principal. On the other end are those that very comfortable taking substantial risk. They seek opportunities to earn higher rates of return and are considered to be very aggressive. And in between are those that are deemed moderately conservative, moderate, and moderately aggressive.

In practical terms, investors can see investment risk in the historical fluctuations of assets' rates of return, and use the insight to decide the degree to which they can tolerate the highs and lows. Analytical indicators that tend to be useful in this process include:

➢ *Standard deviation* reveals the range of fluctuations in an asset's rates of return, and it identifies *typical* (or *average*) and *atypical* (or *outlier*) performance.
➢ *Beta* compares fluctuations in individual assets' rates of return to appropriate benchmarks, and indicates whether individual assets are more or less risky that similar assets.
➢ *Sharpe Ratio* compares fluctuations in an individual asset's rates of return to those that have virtually no chance of loss (or are risk-free). It helps to determine whether, given the risk, investors are adequately rewarded for their investment decisions.

Perhaps the biggest risk to employees are rapid or significant increases in the general prices of goods and services (or *inflation*). That's because most of them are investing for long-term objectives, and inflation can be devastating when it outpaces the returns generated by their investments. Several reliable indicators can be used to assess it including:

➢ The *Consumer Price Index (CPI)* tracks changes in the prices of consumer goods and services from buyers' perspectives.
➢ The *Producer Price Index (PPI)* measures changes in the prices of consumer goods and services from sellers' perspectives.
➢ *Inflation-adjusted* (or *real*) *rates of return* shed light on the net effects of inflation on assets' rates of return.
➢ The *Rule of 72* provides an estimate for the time that it'll take for the cost of living to double based on assumed inflation rates.

Mindset Concept: Investment Allocation

I periodically meet *DIY financial planners* that believe that they have what it takes to consistently profit by timing their trades and concentrating their investments in smaller numbers of assets. They idolize famous investors that accumulated incredible wealth by anticipating market moves or were the first to invest in the next big thing, and they are convinced that they can do it too. While a handful seem to be good at it, they're the exception; not the norm.

The vast majority of people that I encounter prefer a different approach. For various reasons, they accept the timeless maxim "don't put all your eggs in one basket" and adopt allocation strategies that spread their investments among diverse arrays of assets (or *diversify*). Their decisions to do so are validated by numerous studies that find that this should result in lower volatility and higher rates of return over longer timeframes. These individuals also compensate for their lack of time, interest, knowledge, skills, and purchasing power by investing in professionally managed portfolios (or *pooled products*).

Mutual funds are the most popular type of pooled products. They use investor capital to buy, hold, and sell securities, and are commonly found in retail and workplace investment accounts. Lesser-known alternatives include: *collective investment trusts* (which are run by banks) and *segregated accounts* (which are managed by insurers or employers) are used in larger retirement plans because plan managers view them to be more flexible and less expensive than mutual funds; and *exchange-traded funds* (*ETFs*) are used at times because they function like mutual funds, trade like individual securities, and might be less expensive than other types of pooled products.

Generally, pooled products stick to one of two investment management philosophies.

➤ *Active* reflects a belief that markets aren't random, and that prudent investors can profit by using information to invest in companies, sectors, and countries that are more likely to outperform their peers. This strategy tends to work well in markets that are less efficient.

➤ *Passive* implies a belief that changes in asset prices are unpredictable. As such, most investors can't consistently outperform the rates of return for common market indices, especially when expenses and capital gains are subtracted. This approach tends to mirror common indices and results in lower investment expenses.

Although many pooled products attempt to maximize investor returns by reducing the effects of certain types of risk, some add age-based (or *maturity*) constraints to their objectives. Known as *Target Date Funds* (*TDFs*), these investment portfolios regularly reset (or *rebalance*) so they gradually shift from more risk to less risk as predetermined maturity dates approach. TDFs are very popular, and many employers use them in their workplace plans as the *default investments* for employees that decline to make their own choices.

Annuities are pooled products that guarantee future benefits to insureds (or *annuitants*) or their beneficiaries in exchange for paid premiums. These can be similar to other pooled products, except that the managers accept the risks associated with underperformance, and the insurers distribute fixed or variable payments that are tied to the performance of the underlying assets.

Investors that use these products should occasionally verify that the portfolio allocations align with their personal objectives, and they should increase the frequency of these assessments as their withdrawal dates approach. This is because professional managers sometimes deviate (or *drift*) from previously stated objectives.

Since most investors aren't able to time their buying and selling activities in manners that consistently produce optimum rates of return, they're urged to apply a strategy known as *dollar-cost averaging*. This requires them to buy assets in fixed increments at recurring intervals, and it limits their exposure to market risk and the impacts of their timing decisions. While the effectiveness of this technique is debated by some experts, it tends to work for many of the people that I help because the consistency of automatic purchases reduces the emotional aspects of investing.

Mindset Concept: Investment Expenses

With few exceptions, investment performance is diminished by expenses. The first type that employees are likely to encounter are fixed fees that cover the overhead costs associated with maintaining cash and securities accounts (or *administrative expenses*). Some are billed regularly, like periodic record-keeping fees in 401(k)s or HSAs, and trading fees in brokerage accounts and IRAs. Others are paid as they're incurred, such as extra fees for account balances that fall below required thresholds and for special investor inquiries.

The second pertain to professionally managed portfolios (or *investment fees*). Pooled products charge *management fees* that are portions of the total portfolios that must be liquidated to pay the professionals that manage them. These can also include sales charges (or *loads*) that are collected when shares are bought (or *front-end loads*) or sold (or *back-end loads*), and advertising and distribution expenses [or *12(b)-1 fees*] that are used to pay expenses that are associated with attracting new shareholders.

And the third is tied to products like annuities and permanent life insurance. In addition to management fees and sales charges that are found in other products, they include *mortality charges* to pay for guaranteed benefits, *surrender charges* to discourage policy cancellations and early withdrawals, and *rider fees* that pay for additional features and benefits.

Some investments are low-cost, but many (even some claiming to be low-cost) are outrageously expensive. Ultimately, it's incumbent on investors to know what they're paying and to determine if they're receiving adequate value. This isn't easy, but a measure known as *total expense ratio* provides useful insight. It's expressed as a percentage of the total assets being managed, like 0.1%, 2.0%, and 3.4%, and it makes it easier to compare options. Similarly, some financial partners have the abilities to create personalized portfolio expense ratios for their clients.

NOW IT'S YOUR TURN
Assess the amounts that you are paying for your investments

Take 15 minutes to schedule time to assess the costs associated with your work-related and personal investments. This can get tedious, so ask your financial partners to help you secure the necessary information. And once you know how much it's costing you to invest, you can determine whether you're satisfied with the status quo, or are ready to consider alternatives.

Mindset Concept: Investment Return Incentives

Some investments feature enhancements (or *incentives*) that potentially increase the final (or *net*) rates of return realized by investors.

In the workplace, employers (or *plan sponsors*) that I support use incentives in conjunction with certain investment-related benefit plans, like 401(k) and 403(b) retirement plans and HSAs. They might deposit funds that are con-

119

tingent on employees' deferrals. These are known as *elective* (or *matching*) *contributions*. Or, they might put money in that's not tied to employee participation (or *non-elective contributions*). And publicly-traded stock companies might give employees periodic opportunities to buy shares of organizational stock at legally permissible discounts.

Typically, employees are required to satisfy specific criteria before they'll reap the benefits of these incentives. They might not be allowed to enroll in applicable plans, qualify for employer contributions, or take ownership of the money (or *vest*) until they meet pre-established age, hourly, or service requirements. But there are situations where they immediately and fully vest in their employers' incentives, like HSAs and retirement plans in which the sponsors forego all vesting requirements.

In the public domain, investment earnings are normally taxable. But policymakers at all levels sometimes use their jurisdictional authority to alter tax codes in ways that reward investment in assets that serve community interests. For example, they might: bestow tax breaks on those that invest in civic projects; reduce capital gains taxes on the sale of certain assets; or grant tax deductions or credits to those that invest for future education, health care, and retirement consumption.

NOW IT'S YOUR TURN
Determine if you are leaving money on the table

Take 15 minutes now to ask your financial partners, particularly your employer, tax advisor, or wealth planner, to identify incentives that might be in your reach. If you aren't making the best use of them, then take steps to decide if it's in your best interests to take advantage of them.

CHAPTER 11

A GROWING CONCERN

From their kitchen tables at home to the Zoom calls for work, many of the employees that I encounter are debating the value of higher education. They're a microcosm of a conversation that's occurring elsewhere in society.

On one side of the argument are people that consider it a prerequisite to success. They're convinced that it translates to higher earning potential, lower risk of unemployment, and better physical and mental wellbeing. In my workplace seminars, attendees that support higher education refer to studies suggesting that those with Bachelor's degrees, on average, are paid more and remain employed longer than those that have high school diplomas only.

On the other end are those that believe it's a waste of most people's time and money. They feel the upshot doesn't justify the investment. They'll point to billionaire non-graduates like Oprah Winfrey and Mark Zuckerberg, apocalyptic employment forecasts for degreed individuals, and graduates that they know can't find work in their fields of study but are drowning in student loans.

Since there's legitimacy to both viewpoints, I find that many people will relax their views about the value of higher education in situations that involve someone that they cherish. Those that favor it will downplay its importance when it's financially unfeasible, and those that are against it will laud it as the acceptance letters arrive. That's ok. As the following story reveals, it's normal to rationalize...

Deena's in her late-20s. She's looking into the beautiful eyes of her three-week old infant and whispers: "Isabelle Marie, I'm already proud of you. I can see that you're smart and I promise to help you be your best. I'll give you everything that I wish I'd had." She briefly imagines her daughter as a young woman graduating from college, and turns her attention back to the present and says "Mommy will make it happen, but first I need to look at those tiny little toes again…"

And then she blinks.

Deena's in her early-30s. She just watched the school bus drive away; Isabelle's on it. It's the first day of kindergarten. The instant her daughter's out of view, Deena panics because she's not ready to let her baby go. She's late for work, but hurriedly races to her car, jumps in, and catches up to the bus so she can watch her daughter arrive at school. During the drive, she recalls her promise and scolds herself: "Deena! You haven't saved a dime to help your little girl with college! You've got to do this." Then her smartphone rings. It's her boss, and her attention quickly shifts to her job…

And then she blinks.

Deena's 11 years older. Isabelle just finished sophomore year of high school on the honor roll and says to her mom "Lexi and her mom are planning a college campus tour in October, and they asked if we want to go." Deena smiles and calmly replies "I'm so proud of you, Isabelle. Tell Lexi 'we're in.'"

But in actuality, Deena's terrified because she hasn't saved anything for Isabelle's education. She thinks "There's still time, but it's so confusing. I've got to figure this out…"

And then she blinks.

Isabelle's a high school senior. She gets a 25 on her ACT, has a solid GPA, and is accepted by her dream school. It's a wonderful achievement, but she doesn't have the money. Instead of getting sad or going into debt, she decides to wait a year before enrolling. She tells her Mom, "Don't worry. It's called a gap year. Lots of kids do it."

It's Deena's day of reckoning, but sadly her daughter will pay the price. She admits that she blew it and responds "I'm so sorry, Isabelle. Since you were a baby, I promised that I'd help you go to college. You did your job. Now somehow, I've gotta do mine."

Mother and daughter embrace in a hug…

And then they blink.

It's also normal for parents to feel deep and irreversible regret when they fail to deliver on big promises to the children that they love.

122

Lay Your Foundation

Occasionally, I meet people like Deena. They'll politely introduce themselves, tell their stories, and invariably ask "Does it make sense to withdraw money from a 401(k) to help a child pay for college?"

The financially prudent response is "No, as much as you want to help, you can get loans for college but not for retirement." But that answer ignores the overriding emotions that are involved. Since most of the people that ask are parents that would literally die for the children they're trying to help, taking cash from retirement accounts must seem like no-brainer decisions.

I hate these types of scenarios because they didn't need to happen. The people could have avoided the heartaches created by their inabilities to help their loved ones capitalize on potentially life-altering educational opportunities, but it would've required different choices earlier in their lives. By the time they're talking to me, it's too late to use some of the best tools.

Like planning elaborate family vacations, *DIY financial planners* increase their odds of being ready to support their perspective students by beginning to prepare as soon as possible. First, they must anticipate the timeframes in which their assistance will be needed. This answers one of the key questions in the process: "How long do I have?"

Then they need to solidify their funding philosophies. Irrespective of the costs that they'll incur or backing that they'll provide, this can be summarized by simple statements whereby their beliefs and attitudes help guide future decisions about the purpose, scope, limitations, and distribution of their gifts. They need to answer questions like "Who'll pay for what?", "Will I make my gift conditional on certain criteria?", and "How will the proceeds be disbursed?"

The employees that I help tend to lean toward one of four philosophies. The first is to make it clear to their children that they won't offer any financial support. It reflects beliefs that there are many paths to success, and that higher education is a personal endeavor for those that pursue it. The second is a *front-end* approach. It commits in advance to providing a degree of funding that ranges from some to all expenses, and assures the future students that they'll receive something to make the experience more affordable. The third is a *back-end* approach. It stipulates that related expenses will be reimbursed if specific goals are met, like maintaining minimum grade point averages, volunteering, or graduating, and it reinforces beliefs that there are no free rides. And the fourth combines front-end and back-end approaches.

Estimate Your Costs

Then, *DIY financial planners* should estimate the future costs to attend 2-year vocational (or technical) schools, or 4-year public or private universities. Luckily, countless websites have been designed by government, non-profit, and for-profit institutions to assist with this task. However, parents and students should always read the fine-print disclosures.

Review the Assumptions

The pricing that's disclosed on school websites and in independent third party comparisons rely on generic assumptions that don't apply to everyone. For example, the majority of students that enroll in 4-year programs do not graduate on time, state reciprocity is usually ignored, and projected tuition increases aren't accurate. Although the figures aren't necessarily intended to deceive people, they can certainly mislead those that aren't aware.

Understand the Expenses

Schools distinguish between two types of expenses. *Direct* are automatically paid to the institutions (e.g., tuition, mandatory fees), and *indirect* aren't or don't need to be (e.g., books, phones, transit). Some, like room and board, depend on students' personal situations. The distinction is relevant because direct expenses tend to be highly-inflationary and some types of aid can alleviate them, and indirect expenses can be easier to control when students are enrolled.

Look Beyond Advertised Prices

Similar to car dealers and furniture stores, advertised (or *list*) prices that are found on school websites and in third-party comparisons aren't the actual prices that most students will pay. These figures include direct and indirect expenses, but exclude financial support that the institutions might offer. *Net prices* are the list prices minus the institutional money. They're more accurate, and are usually provided once perspective students share detailed information about themselves.

NOW IT'S YOUR TURN
Use online tools to estimate future college or vocational school costs

Spend 15 minutes asking financial partners, high school guidance counselors, or financial aid experts at local universities for insights and resources that'll help you estimate the cost of different types of higher education.

Search for Your Financial Aid

Many employees assume that personal assets and student loans (or *self-help aid*) are their only vocational school or college funding options. Although that's often the case, I encourage them to become familiar with public financial support that doesn't need to be repaid (or *gift aid*).

Scholarships are gift aid that are based on merit. They're awarded to students that have excelled in academic, athletic, or civic activities, maintained membership in sponsoring organizations (e.g., church, clubs, non-profits), or demonstrated interests in specific career fields. Each one is characterized by distinctive features that are ultimately determined by donors. Some are large enough to fully fund entire degrees, but most are small and designed to help ease the overall financial burden.

Unfortunately, scholarships aren't easy to obtain. The application process can be onerous because donors want to give their gifts to the worthiest students and require social security numbers, cumulative grade point averages, course lists, reference letters, acceptance letters, family financial information, and descriptions of awards, activities, and associations before they'll be considered. They might also demand adherence to ongoing restrictions and obligations, and the competition can be fierce since there's no limit on the number of scholarships that candidates can apply for.

Ultimately, fewer than 1-in-10 undergraduate students receive private scholarship money and less than 1-in-50 earn enough to cover 100% of the costs to attend (as of the 2015-16 academic year),[19] so it's unwise for most parents and students to bank on them. But they shouldn't automatically dismiss them either. Households that are likely to enroll someone in colleges or vocational schools should begin researching opportunities at least two years prior to applying, and to focus on awards that the students have the highest probabilities of winning.

Grants are gift aid that are based on need. They're usually distributed on a first-come-first-serve basis by governments, schools, and private organizations. The most common types are Federal Pell Grants offered by the U.S. Department of Education and they're generally awarded to students pursuing 4-year bachelor's degrees. They're based on criteria such as tuition costs, enrollment status, and abilities to pay, and the maximum amounts ($6,345 in 2020-2021)[20] are adjusted annually. Recipients don't repay or pay taxes on the money as long as it's used for qualified education expenses incurred during the periods for which the funds are awarded.

There are plenty of other grants. The federal government provides them for supplemental education, teacher education assistance, and Afghanistan

---

[19] Mark Kantrowitz, "College Scholarships Statistics" (October 23, 2019, www.savingforcollege.com, Web, June 26, 2020).

[20] Office of Student Financial Aid, "Federal Pell Grants are usually awarded only to undergraduate students" (www.studentaid.gov, Web, December 14, 2020).

and Iraq war veterans. Federal and state agencies offer them for minorities, online programs, and distinct service-oriented disciplines that are experiencing personnel shortages. And private colleges offer them either as one-time-only or renewable discounts to entice students to enroll.

Finally, *schoolwork programs* (or *work-study*) are gift aid that helps students pay their expenses while working on campus, in communities, or in government in their desired fields prior to graduation. The earnings don't affect their eligibility for future aid, and it offers valuable work-related experiences, references, and exposure to careers that they might choose.

People that are interested in gift aid, particularly grants, should proactively assess the impact that their personal funding efforts might have on it. Those that won't enroll for several years should talk to financial aid experts, and those that are within a year or two of applying should complete the *Free Application for Federal Student Aid* (*FAFSA*). Both steps facilitate meaningful conversations and provide useful insights into financial aid eligibility.

NOW IT'S YOUR TURN
Seek insight into your eligibility for financial aid

If someone that you cherish is likely to pursue higher education, spend 15 minutes soliciting a financial aid expert's insights into gift aid eligibility. A quick visit to the U.S. Department of Education federal student aid website at www.studentaid.gov can also be valuable.

Close the Gap

After completing the aforementioned steps, parents and their perspective students are positioned to identify the financial gaps that exist between their funding philosophies and the anticipated net price of the education options that they're considering.

First, they should quantify their funding philosophies. For some, this can be as simple as setting specific financial goals, like $2,500 for each year students are enrolled, or $20,000 to be used as needed during the course of their studies. For others, it demands decisions about the types of schooling and expenses that they'll fund, like paying: direct costs during fixed timeframes; percentages of annual total costs; or upon the achievement of specific goals.

Let's return to Deena and Isabelle, but imagine an alternative path where Deena doesn't procrastinate. Instead, she takes steps early in Isabelle's life to help pay for her future higher education costs. Regardless of the gift aid that might be possible, she decides that she'll fund 100% of the total cost of two years of schooling at a 4-year in-state public university, and her daughter will pay for at least one year with her own money and another year with student loans. She selects a front-end approach because she wants to provide reassurance along the way.

Second, parents must subtract potential gift aid from the expected list price for the projected enrollment period. This is relevant for students that live in lower income households or hope to receive scholarships, but it can be challenging for those that won't attend for many years. For that reason, many people don't want to count on it and will assume that they won't receive any. The equation is:

List Price   -   Gift Aid   =   Net Price

In Deena's case, she can't predict the gift aid Isabelle will receive because she's starting the process early, but she does assume that her daughter will earn a modest scholarship worth $500 per year and a work-study that'll generate $4,000 per year. In the course of a 4-year degree, that's $18,000. More, she enters required information in a free online college planning calculator and learns that the list price of a 4-year degree from an in-state public university in 18 to 20 years will be $100,000. She calculates the estimated net price by subtracting the gift aid from the list price.

$100,000   - $18,000   = $82,000

Deena's initial reaction is "$82,000! Oh my word!" She realizes that this is the total outlay for a 4-year degree. She divides the net price of $82,000 by

4 years to determine the annual amount ($20,500), and then multiplies it by the number of years that she'll fund. Given her philosophy and the goal, that means that she needs roughly $41,000 set aside in 18 to 20 years. "That's still a lot" she says, but she'd rather make the sacrifice than take the chance that her daughter might miss a great opportunity.

Third, parents must decide the frequency of their contributions. Most college savings plans allow lump sum contributions to be made at any time, and regular and periodic transfers from personal bank accounts via *Automatic Investment Plans* (*AIPs*). For those that prefer AIPs, the following is helpful:

$$\frac{(\text{Amount Needed} / \text{Years Until Needed})}{\text{Periodic Contributions Per Year}} = \text{Periodic AIP Amount}$$

Here's what the equation looks like given Deena's circumstances.

$$\frac{(\$41,000 / 19 \text{ years})}{12 \text{ months}} = \$180 \text{ per month}$$

Although this means that Deena needs to save an average of $180 per month, she realizes that it doesn't account for tax breaks or investment gains. So she uses an online college planning calculator and determines that she can probably achieve her goal by saving as little as $150 a month (for the 19 years) via an AIP. She says, "I can totally do this!"

Choose Your Investment Vehicles

Occasionally, I meet employees that talk about the creative approaches that they take to fund future higher education costs for their kids. Some put money into investment accounts at brokerage firms like Charles Schwab and E*Trade, and require their future college students to invest it. Others buy rental properties or small businesses for their kids to manage. However, most appear to prefer conventional set-it-and-forget-it solutions that make the process simple and efficient.

Many people rely on *Section 529 College Savings Accounts* (*529s*) as their main funding vehicles. 529s allow them to invest money that's intended to pay future qualified school expenses (e.g., tuition, books, computers, room and board) that might be incurred by beneficiaries that enroll in eligible primary, secondary, and post-secondary educational institutions (and, as of late 2020, apprenticeships that are registered with the U.S. Labor Department).

529s are popular for many reasons. First, they're easy to use. Second, the amounts that can be contributed often exceed $300,000 (state rules dictate). Third, the impact of these accounts on eligibility for financial aid is relatively low if they aren't owned by the future students. Fourth, there are no income limitations or age restrictions on contributions. Fifth, beneficiaries can use up to $10,000 to repay student loans. And sixth, donors can redirect the assets to others if the primary beneficiaries don't use it, or rescind their gifts.

However, the biggest reason is tax-related. While contributions aren't deductible on federal income taxes, many states either allow contributions to be taken as deductions or they offer credits on taxpayers' annual filings. Plus, growth on investments held in the accounts are tax-free on federal and most state tax returns if future distributions are for qualified educational expenses. The clearest drawback is a 10% penalty on earnings when withdrawals aren't used for qualified expenses. Since tax rules can vary, *DIY financial planners* are wise to consult professional tax advisors before funding these accounts.

There are two types of 529s. The first, *education savings plans*, are the most common. They help beneficiaries pay for qualified expenses wherever they attend, including public, private, and parochial elementary or secondary schools, and some non-U.S. colleges and universities. They also give account owners control of the assets and allow them limited investment flexibility.

In most states, 529 investment menus are overseen by government appointed experts that strive to provide account owners with diverse portfolios that simplify the act of investing and are appropriate for the investment objectives. They usually offer pooled products, like mutual funds, TDFs, and ETFs, that are managed by reputable investment firms, and cash-equivalent options.

Given the oversight, that's generally good for account owners. However, they should still assess their options in light of their goals, time horizons, risk tolerances, tax incentives, and other financial circumstances. If residents feel that their state's 529s don't meet their needs, they're permitted to participate in other states' 529s but will likely lose applicable in-state tax breaks.

The other type of 529s, *prepaid tuition plans*, are increasingly rare and have limited availability. They allow people to reduce the impact of inflation on future direct college expenses at participating universities by prepaying at today's prices. From an investment perspective, there's nothing to do once the money's contributed. But these are less appealing options because they limit school choices, don't cover many indirect expenses, and can create a risk of loss or potential taxation if the intended beneficiaries don't enroll.

Some people rely on *Education Savings Accounts* (*ESAs*). Similar to 529s, ESAs allow them to fund qualified education expenses for beneficiaries on a tax-preferred basis without significantly impacting future students' eligibility for financial aid, and they can change beneficiaries to other family members if desired.

ESAs allow greater investment flexibility than 529s, but their income and age limitations are more restrictive. First, ESA contributions must not exceed $2,000 per year per beneficiary from all sources. Second, contributions must be made before the beneficiaries are Age 18, and the assets must be used for qualified expenses by Age 30. And third, funds that aren't used or transferred to other family members become the beneficiaries' property and can't be refunded to the donors.

Sometimes, the employees that I meet rely on alternatives to 529s and ESAs that aren't as straightforward. A small number use *Uniform Gifts to Minors Act* (*UGMA*) and *Uniform Transfers to Minors Act* (*UTMA*) accounts. These accounts, if permitted by their state laws, give them abilities to permanently transfer assets like cash, securities, and real estate to minors. The potential tax breaks can be appealing to some people, but they're problematic because they can undermine eligibility for financial aid, can't be transferred to other beneficiaries, and don't require beneficiaries to use the assets as intended after they take ownership of the accounts at Age 18 (or Age 21 in some states).

On rare occasion, I meet people that use *Roth IRAs* for college expenses. That's because these accounts offer greater investment flexibility than 529s, higher contribution limits than ESAs, and withdrawn earnings can potentially be excluded from taxation. More, there's no statutory requirement that the money must be used for schooling. But they're not ideal since the earnings are only tax-free if they're withdrawn after five years in the accounts. And potentially worse for some people, Roth IRA withdrawals can impact students' eligibility for financial aid.

Similarly, small numbers of individuals use two other options. Some buy *Series EE* and *Series I U.S. Savings Bonds* and hold them to maturity. The proceeds might be tax-free if used for higher education (and the holder meets other qualifying criteria) and won't affect financial aid, but the rates of return are historically inferior to typical Section 529 and ESA investments. And some use consumer *loyalty* (or *affinity*) *programs* that reward purchases of qualifying products and services with rebates at participating universities or contributions to 529s.

Finally, *workplace perks* are offered by some employers that realize that higher education expenses create burdens on many of their employees. For this reason, they might offer scholarships, work-study options for dependents of employees, debt repayment subsidies, and non-elective contributions to qualified retirement plans for those that are working to repay student loans.

NOW IT'S YOUR TURN
Take inventory of your college saving and investing resources

Take 15 minutes now to ask your financial partners to identify and recommend helpful college saving and investing resources. Then, visit websites like www.morningstar.com and www.savingforcollege.com to learn more.

Before You Enroll

In my prior role as an adjunct professor, it was disheartening when students couldn't complete their degrees or struggled to find jobs in their chosen fields of study after they graduated. It wasn't the outcome that they or their parents envisioned when they embarked on their journey years earlier, and I wished that I could have shared three thoughts with them before they enrolled.

First, 4-year degrees can open doors to lifelong career and income generating opportunities. But they're expensive endeavors that increasingly require five or six years to complete. As such, students that have serious doubts about giving their best from start to finish are wise to consider alternatives, like vocation school, military service, or union apprenticeships, or enrolling for a year or two in less expensive community and online programs.

Second, many universities are quick to publicize their strengths and slow to reveal their weaknesses, and they typically don't give refunds to unhappy customers. As such, perspective students should thoroughly vet these service providers before completing their applications. This means investigating attributes for degrees or majors that are most likely to appeal to them, such as:

- ✓ Student-to-teacher ratios
- ✓ 4-Year graduation rates
- ✓ Post-graduation earning data
- ✓ Acceptance rates for post-graduate studies

- ✓ Full-time versus part-time faculty ratios
- ✓ Post-graduation time to first job
- ✓ List of career counselling events and services
- ✓ Names of employers that participated in campus job fairs during the past 3 years

Finally, they should seek input from experts that are in their reach. Before applying, they should ask local business leaders, HR professionals, and current and former instructors for their thoughts about the institutions that are being considered. They can also investigate the services offered by fee-based college planning coaches referred to them by guidance counselors, financial partners, and friends, or found via the for-profit National Institute of Certified College Planners at www.niccp.com.

CHAPTER 12

HEED THE WARNING SIGNS

Like drivers slowing their vehicles to view the wreckage from a recent traffic accident, some of the employees that I help are interested in the circumstances of coworkers that admit that the only reason that they're working is to maintain their health insurance. The onlookers' responses range from empathy to annoyance, and their curiosity is justifiably based on varying degrees of self-interest. They want to know how to avoid similar fates.

Surprisingly, I often find that the ill-fated colleagues will share their stories with anyone who'll listen; they hope that others will learn from their experiences. Some openly admit during my seminars that they'd request leaves of absence to get healthy or seek job opportunities elsewhere, but they know that they can't survive financially without their work-based health benefits. Others proclaim that they'd retire immediately if they were 100% confident that they could afford to pay their future medical and pharmacy bills.

To varying degrees, the bystanders understand. They're aware of studies, like one issued by the Henry J. Kaiser Family Foundation, that estimate the average point-of-coverage costs for health insurance to exceed their abilities to pay (it was $7,188 for self-only plans and $20,576 for family plans in 2019.[21] Or they hear reports that health care inflation continues to skyrocket. And all know, or can reasonably guess, that health-related hardships can force most people into the ditch.

And yet, somehow, the flawed assumptions that led others to unenviable predicaments persist in the workplaces that I visit, such as:

➢ *The Ability to Continue.* Many employees assume that, in light of benefits continuation laws, they can keep their plans following job terminations.

---

[21] Kaiser Family Foundation, "2019 Employer Health Benefits Survey" (September 25, 2020, www.kff.org, Web, June 26, 2020).

But that's not a certainty because some people work for organizations that are exempt from such rules, others are let go for reasons that nullify their rights, and most that are eligible waive their rights when they realize that the insurance is unaffordable without employer subsidies.

➢ *The Ability to Work.* Many can't fathom being unable to work. But national studies suggest that 1-in-4 20-year-olds will be disabled for a year or longer by the time they reach Age 67,[22] and 56% of older workers experience at least one involuntary job loss after Age 50.[23] Similarly, many pre-retirees indicate that they intend to remain employed until they're eligible for Medicare at Age 65 or Social Security at Age 66 or 67, but research from the Employee Benefits Research Institute reveals that the median retirement age is actually 62.[24]

➢ *The Ability to Pay.* Many suffer under the delusion that their health care costs will go down when they retire. In reality, they'll probably pay more. As evidence, a 2020 report by the Association of American Retired Persons found that individuals covered by traditional Medicare paid an average of $5,800 for premiums and out-of-pocket expenses in 2017,[25] and the Employee Benefits Research Institute reported that the average 65 year-old couple that retired that year needed $273,000[26] set aside to be highly certain that they could pay their healthcare bills during retirement.

There are plenty of signs warning *DIY financial planners* of possible trouble ahead. Like drivers that find detours to avoid possible misfortune, it's time for them to grip the steering wheel and answer the question "What can I do now to avoid problems down the road?"

---

[22] Social Security Administration, "Fact Sheet: Social Security" (2020, www.ssa.gov, Web, June 26, 2020).

[23] Kelli B. Grant, "This job challenge should scare older workers" (January 5, 2019, www.cnbc.com, Web, June 26, 2020).

[24] Tim Parker, "Planning on Retiring Later? Think Again" (October 31, 2019, www.investopedia.com, Web, June 26, 2020).

[25] Claire Noel-Miller, "Insight on the Issues: Medicare Beneficiaries' Out-of-Pocket Spending for Health Care" (June 2020, Washington, DC, AARP Public Policy Institute).

[26] Employee Benefits Research Institute, "Savings Needed for Medicare Beneficiaries' Health Expenses Declines" (May 28, 2020, www.ebri.org).

Close the Gap

The employees that I meet give the impression that they understand that health care and insurance are expensive. And they frequently acknowledge that they're unlikely to receive meaningful help with it at vulnerable times in their lives, like when they become unemployed, disabled, or retired. As such, they inherently know that there's a chance that they might not be able to afford either later in life.

Some of them don't proactively address this potential gap. Typically, it's for the simplest reason: they don't have the money to do anything about it. But sometimes it's because they don't trust those that are trying to alert them to the problem, don't know what's necessary to fix the problem, or they can't forecast their needs that far in the future. All of these reactions increase the likelihood that they'll be unprepared.

And some of them increase their deferrals to workplace retirement plans for the express purpose of earmarking portions for their future health-related needs. This is better than doing nothing because 401(k)s and 403(b)s are tax-efficient and convenient, and presumably offer menus of solid investment options, but there are problems.

First, using the median 401(k) account balances (meaning that half of all accounts have less than the amount) in early 2020, the fact that people Ages

137

40 to 49 had $39,200 and Ages 50 to 59 had $65,300 saved[27] suggests that many will fall short. Second, the value of these assets might be diminished when the taxes come due. And third, there's a steep price to pay for using them for non-retirement needs, like paying for COBRA premiums when they are unemployed or medical bills while they're on disability.

Some fund alternative tax-advantaged accounts. For example, *Roth IRAs* provide investment flexibility, the principle can be withdrawn penalty-free at any time, and earnings can be taken penalty-free (at least at the federal level) prior to Age 59½ to pay for qualified health expenses. Similarly, the cash value accrued in *permanent life insurance* policies can be used for these expenses.

Finally, some buy *variable health care annuities*. These products feature guaranteed minimum withdrawal benefits that commence at specified points in time and continue to pay annuitants for fixed periods like 5 years, 20 years, or life. They can be useful, and annuity riders can be purchased to make them more appealing. But the money is difficult or impossible to access for health-related events that occur before their maturity dates. Worse, the annuitants might not live long enough to derive the benefits that they paid for.

While it's always encouraging to discover *DIY financial planners* focusing on this need, there's a financial tool that's ideally suited to close the gap and might be in their reach.

NOW IT'S YOUR TURN
Assess your potential sources of future healthcare coverage

Take 15 minutes now to assess likely sources of healthcare protection in the event that you (or your spouse) lose your job, become disabled, retire before you're eligible for Medicare, or retire after you're eligible for Medicare. Your financial partners can provide valuable insight into benefits, options, costs, and the amount you should save.

---

[27] Barbara Whelehan, "The average 401(k) balance by age" (March 13, 2020, www.bankrate.com, Web, June 26, 2020).

Health Savings Accounts

By choice or default, a growing number of employees are insured in *High Deductible Health Plans* (*HDHPs*). While most appreciate the lower point-of-coverage costs (compared to traditional health plans), they loathe the higher point-of-claim exposure. Fortunately, HDHPs that satisfy mandated requirements give them opportunities to use *Health Savings Accounts* (*HSAs*) to fund a wide array of current and future health-related needs.

Upon enrolling in qualified HDHPs, insureds are eligible to open HSAs and defer income that's exempt from federal payroll and income taxes, and income taxes that are levied by many states. This is valuable since the tax savings on contributed money can be sizeable. Plus, employers often contribute funds to workplace HSAs that immediately belong to the account owners.

The beauty of participating in HSAs at work is that contributions are taken from employees' gross earnings (usually per paycheck). This means that their deferrals automatically avoid Social Security, Medicare, and income tax withholdings, and they get the pre-tax benefit immediately. Unfortunately, those that make deposits outside of payroll deductions, buy personal HDHP policies, or are S-Corporation owners, won't realize the favorable impacts until they file their tax returns.

The total amount that can be contributed to HSAs by employers and employees is adjusted by the IRS annually. In 2021, the maximum is $3,600 for self-only coverage and $7,200 for family coverage.[28] There's also a catch-up feature that allows individuals that are Age 55 or older to defer an additional $1,000 per year (per spouse for covered couples). Regardless how the money is deferred, it must be deposited into the accounts by account owners' tax filing deadlines.

Although people want HSA contributions to be simple, it's important for them to recognize that there are pitfalls to avoid. For example, they must pay taxes and penalties on contributed amounts exceeding the annual IRS limits. Similarly, those that are approaching retirement should understand the tax implications associated with making HSA contributions in the years that they plan to begin receiving Social Security benefits.

---

[28] Internal Revenue Service, "26 CFR 601.602: Tax forms and instructions" (2020, www.irs.gov, Web, June 26, 2020).

Once money is in HSAs, it can be used in the current year or carried into subsequent years, and it can remain there throughout the lives of the account owners. Even better, any growth on invested account assets is tax-free at the federal level and in most states. This creates special opportunities that compel account owners to ask "Will I use my HSA for shorter-term health care needs, or for a wider range of longer-term needs?"

For those that are new to these accounts and aren't sure how they'll use them, it's rarely crucial for them to make immediate investment decisions. That's because initial contributions are held as cash in FDIC insured accounts, and administrators typically require minimum balances ranging from $1,000 to $2,500 before they'll allow account owners to invest their excess amounts in riskier assets.

However, after minimum thresholds are met, account owners can invest more aggressively. Menus typically include higher yielding cash-equivalent assets, and pooled products such as mutual funds, TDFs, and ETFs. This is the point at which investment decisions should tie back to the intended shorter-term and longer-term use of the funds.

HSA owners that lack sufficient liquidity to address potential or known short-term health-related needs should focus on investment options that involve less risk, at least until they have enough cash to cover at least a year of point-of-claim costs, or a year of point-of-coverage costs if they anticipate other related needs. Interest-bearing FDIC insured cash and cash-equivalent assets are better in these situations because they ensure that the principal is readily available. Conversely, those that have ample liquidity or longer time horizons might prefer to invest in riskier assets that offer them potentially

140

higher returns. It gives them opportunities to prepare for longer-term health care needs, non-health needs, or supplemental retirement income.

Since employers often establish HSAs for their employees, some people are less than enthusiastic about their accounts. They might dislike the investment options, performance, or fees. For this reason, they're free to transfer their assets to other HSAs. However, before doing so, they should identify and assess costs associated with these decisions.

NOW IT'S YOUR TURN
Assess your opportunities to maximize HSA investing opportunities

If you are or expect to be an:

✓ *HSA Spender*, take 15 minutes to assess your spending habits and use tools offered by your financial partners that might help you make better use of your account
✓ *HSA Investor*, take 15 minutes to assess your current investment objectives and asset allocation, and decide how they need to change so that they're aligned.

Also, if you're uncomfortable investing, determine if your HSA vendor provides fee-based advice services that'll make it easier to manage your account.

HSA withdrawals are generally tax-free provided that they're used for:

➢ *Qualified expenses* like medical services, prescription drugs, travel expenses that relate to essential care, premiums for Long Term Care insurance and COBRA coverage, and Medicare point-of-claim costs.
➢ *Covered individuals*, like primary insureds, spouses, some domestic partners, and dependents that are claimed on federal tax returns (even if they weren't covered under the policy at the time the account owners made their HSA contributions).

Withdrawals for non-qualified expenses like over-the-counter drugs, nutritional supplements, elective cosmetic surgery, and premiums for some types of insurance (e.g., disability, cancer, Medicare Supplement) are subject to taxation. Those under Age 65 should anticipate 20% income tax withholdings and 20% penalties for early withdrawals, and those that are Age 65 and older should expect to pay ordinary income taxes on their distributions.

Although HSA vendors typically offer valuable guidance and support via a host of services, the account owners ultimately bear the burdens to confirm and demonstrate that withdrawals are qualified. Wherever they have questions or doubts, particularly in advance of any major decisions, they should consult professional tax advisors or refer to *IRS Publication 969*.

HSA payment methods vary, but vendors standardly allow account owners to pay via telephonic and online payments, debit cards, and cash reimbursements, and some allow electronic funds transfers and check writing (for extra fees). Ironically, there's no requirement that expenses be reimbursed in the years that they're incurred. For that reason, some account owners use non-HSA dollars to pay qualified expenses and delay their account reimbursement requests until they retire. Known as *shoeboxing*, they prefer to leave these assets untouched for as long as possible, so that they can grow tax-free and create the largest possible non-taxable distributions.

Finally, IRS rules prevent employees from contributing to *Flexible Spending Accounts* (*FSAs*) and HSAs in the same year, but do allow them to contribute to *Limited Purpose FSAs* (*LPFSAs*) provided that their employers offer them, and they're enrolled in both HDHPs and HSAs. This allows them to pay their dental and vision expenses with non-HSA dollars, and thereby preserve their HSA dollars for other purposes. Similar to traditional FSAs, LPFSAs are use-it-or-lose-it accounts, except where the plans permit participants to carry up to $500 of remaining account balances into subsequent plan years.

Prioritize Your Tax-Advantaged Accounts

As more employers adopt HDHPs, a growing number of employees are stumbling into paint-by-the-numbers life hacks that they hope answer "How do I prioritize my pre-tax contributions to my HSA and workplace retirement accounts if I can't afford to maximize both?" A common one sounds like this:

> First, contribute whatever's necessary for you to qualify for your employer's 401(k) or 403(b) match. Never pass on free money! Next, defer the maximum amount allowable to your HSA so that you realize the full impact of its triple-tax advantage. If you're Age 55 or older, contribute another $1000 using the catch-up feature. And once you have maximized those opportunities, resume your contributions to your 401(k), 403(b), or other tax-preferred assets.

Unfortunately, this one-size-fits-all advice isn't right for everyone. In fact, a surprisingly large number of the *DIY financial planners* that I help might be further ahead doing something else.

✓ *Short On Cash?* Some people lack liquidity and worry about their abilities to confront financial emergencies. In these scenarios, they should consider fully funding their 401(k)s or 403(b)s (before their HSAs) if their plans allow loans or hardship withdrawals. That's because the penalties for prematurely withdrawing money from these accounts might be lower than those associated with taking cash from HSAs for non-qualified expenses.

✓ *Not Staying Long?* Some employees know in advance that they'll terminate their current employment before vesting in the employers' 401(k) or 403(b) contributions. If they can contribute to HSAs, they should consider doing it first because the funds might be necessary to maintain insurance coverage during their pending job transitions. This is especially true when employers contribute substantially to employees' HSAs since those funds are fully and immediately vested.

✓ *Savers' Credit Eligibility?* Some people in low-income tax brackets must contribute certain amounts of their earnings to 401(k)s, 403(b)s, or IRAs to maximize the federal *Savers' Credit* (a tax incentive available to lower income tax payers that save money in qualified retirement plans). If they defer the minimum needed to secure employer matching contributions and use the excess income to fund their HSAs, they might fail to reap the full benefits of their tax credits.

✓ *Serious Health Issues?* Some people anticipate that they or their dependents will experience major health events during the year that could result in leaves of absence, loss of earnings, or drains on liquidity. If they don't have adequate cash in their HSAs and aren't substantially vested in their employers' contributions to their 401(k)s or 403(b)s, they should consider maximizing their contributions to the former to ensure that they can pay their pending medical bills.

✓ *New Participants in HDHPs?* Some people are new to HDHPs and haven't accumulated cash in their HSAs. If they're uncomfortable with the higher point-of-claim exposure, they should consider fully funding their HSAs before deferring money in their retirement plans. This is particularly applicable in situations where employers offer year-end *true-up contributions* to employees that missed out on 401(k) or 403(b) matching contributions earlier in the year.

People that are able to fund both types of tax-preferred accounts should consider their personal circumstances before prioritizing their contributions. The process might include discussions with professional tax advisors, or the use of savings illustration and optimization tools.

NOW IT'S YOUR TURN
Take steps to optimize your tax-advantaged accounts

Spend 15 minutes asking your financial partners about tools and guidance that they might offer to help you identify the best approach to optimizing the tax-advantaged health and retirement accounts in your reach. Then, work with them and your tax advisor to execute and adhere to your plan.

Hurry, Act Now

A generation ago, well-meaning federal policymakers attempted to curb runaway healthcare inflation by legislating the creation of HSAs. They felt that coupling generous tax incentives with HDHPs and other consumer-oriented innovations would help solve the problem.

Although people that champion HSAs can legitimately argue that these accounts achieved their stated goals, ongoing trends in participation and utilization give critics ammunition that threatens the long-term viability of these financial tools. For example, reliable data suggests that account owners that report adjusted gross incomes of $100,000 or more are significantly better at contributing to and accumulating money in these tax-preferred assets than people in lower income brackets.[29]

Given that both major political parties have shown an openness to dilute the tax preferences granted to people that contribute to tax-deferred retirement plans like 401(k)s and 403(b)s, it's easy to imagine that future policymakers will attempt to water-down or repeal current HSA tax breaks.

If this too-good-to-be-true incentive proves too-good-to-last, it might be wise for *DIY financial planners* to maximize it before it's too late.

---

[29] Office of Tax Analysis, "HSA-Tables.pdf" (January 6, 2017, www.treasury.gov, Web, June 26, 2020).

CHAPTER 13

~~THE GRADUAL SUNSET~~ A FRESH START

From 2006 to 2010, I authored a series of articles for *DIY financial planners*. One edition that was originally distributed in 2008 began:

> *The setting of the sun is neither spontaneous nor immediate. Rather, it's predictable and gradual. As life spans increase and quality of life improves for the average retiree, that image is increasingly applicable to this stage of life.*

The piece was a reaction to research that indicated that the vast majority of future retirees would survive for decades after retiring from their full-time jobs, and its purpose was two-fold. First, to convince readers to financially prepare for multiple post-retirement phases, like earlier retirement and later retirement. And second, to get them to realize that common challenges associated with longevity, such as inflation, health issues, and long term care expenses, could force them to prematurely drain their nest eggs.

Although the information that I conveyed withstood the test of time, I regret using the sunset as a metaphor for retirement. It's partial and uninspiring given the profound contributions that are routinely made by retirement-aged and officially-retired Americans. They demonstrate that, with proper preparation and good health, this can also be a fresh start.

The retirement dreams that employees share with me are many things, but they're never boring. Since my focus is on helping those that should be or are in the process of accumulating wealth, I encourage them to set two types of spending-related goals (see **Appendix E**).

One type of goal is the *continuation* of aspects of the pre-retirement life-styles to which they become accustomed. This reflects who they currently are and typical examples include: "I want to be certain that I can pay my bills, even in emergencies;" "We want to stay in our house for as long as possible;" and "I want to be there to help my kids and grandkids when they need me."

The other type is *transformational*. This is where they aspire to become who they hope to be. It might translate to lifestyle changes and bucket lists, and sometimes these goals are akin to: "I want to travel to all of the places that I couldn't when I was working;" "We want to build a cabin on a secluded piece of land;" and "I want to leave a lasting legacy for my community."

Once these people know what they hope to do during their fresh starts, I urge them to regularly answer four questions that their resourceful peers ask. [Note: These questions are less helpful to those that are very near or already in retirement.]

Estimate Your Spending

The first is "How much will I spend during retirement?" Contrary to the unconscious approach used by many of the *DIY financial planners* that I meet, the initial focus isn't on current savings rates; it's on future consumption.

The U.S. Bureau of Labor Statistics (BLS) offers a ballpark figure that some people use. It states that the average annual spending for households headed by someone Age 65 or older in 2019 was $50,220.[30] Adjusted for a 3% annual rate of inflation, this implies that these households will cumulatively spend an average of $1,390,000 over the next 20 years (2020 to 2039).

While the BLS amount is a useful yardstick for some employees, this isn't true for all. For example, those that have higher standards of living, reside in pricier locations, or adopt expensive transformative goals are almost certain

---

[30] U.S. Bureau of Labor Statistics, *Consumer Expenditure Survey, 2019* (September 9, 2020, www.bls.gov, Web, November 18, 2020, Table 1300).

to exceed it. As such, it's wise for everyone to periodically generate their own personalized estimates.

A logical place for people to start is to make educated guesses about *life expectancies* for them, their spouses, and adult-dependent children. Many public-domain tools exist to help with this, like the Social Security Administration's life expectancy calculator at www.ssa.gov/cgi-bin/longevity.cgi and the Society of Actuaries' longevity illustrator at www.longevityillustrator.org. And they might add extra years if longevity runs in their families, as evidenced by multiple parents or grandparents who live(d) into their 80s, 90s, and beyond.

Next, they must identify the ages at which they and their spouses (if applicable) hope to retire. Here, they should be mindful of credible research that suggests they'll retire several years earlier than they anticipate. For instance, the Society of Actuaries found that pre-retirees planned to retire at a median age of 65 (half of the respondents gave ages that were above and half gave answers that were below), but actual retirees reported being out of the workforce by a median age of 60.[31]

Once people settle upon their estimated life expectancies and projected retirement ages, they can gage the number of years that they'll be retired. They can do this using the following equation:

$$\text{Life Expectancy} \quad - \quad \text{Retirement Age} \quad = \quad \text{Years in Retirement}$$

Then, they must assign dollar values to their specific retirement goals and estimate their future annual expenses. This can be a daunting task, but there are multiple methods that they can use to complete it. I typically discuss two basic options during workplace conversations.

The *more refined method* is for people, like those that are nearing retirement, that desire accurate estimates. They frequently use software programs or personal spreadsheets to closely track their spending for many months or several years before retiring.

I notice that many of these individuals distinguish between essential expenses (e.g., food, taxes, housing, emergencies) and discretionary expenses

---

[31] Greenwald & Associates for Society of Actuaries (SOA), *Aging and Retirement: 2019 Risks and Process of Retirement Survey* (Schaumburg, Illinois, SOA, 2020, pgs. 56-58).

(e.g., gifts, entertainment, vacations). One reason that they do this is to fore-cast their future consumption needs in best and worst case scenarios. But I also find that some lump all of their pre-retirement expenses into monthly or annual amounts; they're comfortable assuming that their spending habits will not change substantially.

Regardless, those that choose this method need to apply the future value formula to their annual spending amounts to reflect inflation that'll likely oc-cur before they retire. If they move to the next step without doing this, their estimates will be low and unreliable.

The *more expedient method* is for people that aren't concerned with pre-cision. They can multiply the income they expect to earn in their final year of employment by a percentage known as a *steady spending ratio*. This method assumes that they'll spend amounts in each year of retirement that'll equal fixed portions of their gross pre-retirement earnings minus payroll taxes and other withholdings, like HSA and retirement plan deferrals. The formula is:

Pre-Retirement Income Amount	x	Steady Spending Ratio	=	Post-Retirement Spending Amount

Generally, the ratios that people use range from 60% to 90%. Those that think they'll be lower-income or higher-spending might use higher ratios (e.g., 80%, 90%) because they're likely to spend higher amounts relative to their pre-retirement incomes. Those that expect to be higher-income or lower-spending might use lower ratios (e.g., 60%, 70%).

This method is sometimes criticized. One reason is because it doesn't re-flect the gradually declining nature of retirement consumption. In response, some people apply higher ratios to earlier phases when they'll be more ac-tive, and lower ratios to later phases when they'll be less so.

Finally, they must enter their estimated years in retirement, annual ex-penses, and average annual rate of inflation into compound interest formulas to determine their total inflation-adjusted spending. Online calculators make this final step easier.

For illustration, let's imagine that Neville is a 45 year-old single coworker. He was a public school teacher early in his career and views retirement to be a chance to return to teaching, albeit on his terms. In a perfect world, he'd love to do it overseas. It's his notion of a fresh start.

But Neville is concerned. He was told by a financial advisor that he'd need millions of dollars set aside to live his dreams, and the idea that he won't have adequate wealth scares him. Ultimately, he dedicates time to estimating the amount that he's likely to spend in this stage of life.

Based on his current good health, lifestyle (he doesn't use tobacco), and family history, Neville thinks that he'll live to Age 85. He hopes to work to Age 67, but conservatively assumes that he'll do so until Age 65. If he's correct, that means that he'll spend 20 years in retirement.

$$\text{Age 85} \quad - \quad \text{Age 65} \quad = \quad \text{20 Years}$$

Neville doesn't feel that he has enough information to predict his spending habits that far in the future, so he uses a steady spending ratio to make a reasonable guess. He currently earns $70,000 a year and assumes he'll average roughly $100,000 in his last years of employment, and he chooses an 80% ratio because he hopes to be very active. Using the formula, he determines that his projected spending in his first full year of retirement will be $80,000.

$$\$100,000 \quad \times \quad 80\% \quad = \quad \$80,000$$

He finishes by keying in his estimated years in retirement, annual expenses, and average annual rate of inflation (in this case 3%) into a calculator that he finds on his bank's website. With the click of a button, his worst fear seems to be confirmed. The output says that his cumulative retirement spending will be about $2,149,600, and he begins to panic that he won't have enough.

NOW IT'S YOUR TURN
Estimate the amount that you'll spend during retirement

Take 15 minutes to ask your financial partners to identify resources that'll help you forecast your future inflation-adjusted retirement spending. This might include educational videos, expense tracking apps, future value calculators, and tools to anticipate your life span. Once you understand these resources, dedicate extra time to generating your personalized estimate.

Identify Your Income

For decades, the image of a 3-legged stool was used to answer the next question: "Where will the money that I spend during retirement come from?" Each leg depicted one of three primary sources of income that retirees would likely rely on to satisfy future spending needs: government programs, workplace pensions, and personal savings.

Sadly, the analogy is less reliable today, especially for many *DIY financial planners* employed by private sector employers, because Social Security and workplace plans don't offer the degrees of certainty they once did. As such, it's more fitting for many to view their sources as two sides of the same coin.

Institutional Sources

On one side is money that will come from public and private institutional sources. Here, individuals and couples have limited input and choices.

First, most employees and their employers contribute to *Social Security* via payroll taxes during the employees' careers. This funds future streams of retirement income that will replace portions of their pre-retirement earnings, keep pace with inflation, and provide spousal and survivor benefits.

Social Security benefits are determined by a formula that considers workers' earnings and ages. It assumes that they'll receive 100% of their standard benefit payments, or *primary insurance amounts* (*PIA*), if they begin drawing checks in the years in which they reach their *Full* (or *Normal*) *Retirement Ages* (*FRA*). The FRA for those born between 1943 and 1959 arrives sometime in the year in which they turn Age 66, and at Age 67 for those born after 1959.

Social Security offers flexibility with respect to claiming benefits that can substantially decrease or increase PIAs. For example, eligible individuals can begin receiving their PIAs as early as Age 62. This provides income that might be essential to survival, but payments will be substantially lower than their FRA amounts. Conversely, they can delay PIAs until Age 70. This will lead to payments that are significantly higher than their FRA amounts, but it'll also reduce the time that they'll receive benefits.

Future retirees should make concerted efforts to understand and consider their Social Security claiming strategies. This is especially true for those that expect to rely heavily on these payments because their abilities to spend, and to preserve and grow their nest eggs, will be affected. And for married couples because the scenarios and options can be extremely complicated (to the point where professional help often becomes advisable).

Fortunately, the Social Security Administration offers numerous helpful resources. It provides in-person and telephonic counselling, and online tools to help future beneficiaries estimate payments, determine optimum times to apply, and get answers to other questions. It also supplies benefit statements. Currently, paper copies are automatically sent to people that are at least Age 60 and aren't receiving benefits, and online versions are available to those below Age 60 via their mySocialSecurity accounts at www.socialsecurity.gov.

Second, some employees receive extra income from *defined benefit plans* (or *pensions*) that are provided by current and former employers. These plans promise to pay them, and possibly their beneficiaries, predictable monthly income when they retire. The amounts that they'll receive are based on formal qualification criteria and are calculated in accordance with pre-determined benefit formulas.

When people that accrue and vest in these benefits retire, pension plan administrators give them choices to receive their monthly payments. Options usually include: *life annuities* pay pensioners during their entire lives; *annuities with periods certain* either pay pensioners for their entire lives, or their beneficiaries for a limited time if the pensioners die while receiving payments during initial benefit periods; and *joint and survivor annuities* pay pensioners and their spouses for as long as either are alive.

Employers that promise pension payments are legally required to provide personalized statements to participants and beneficiaries. They have multiple options for complying with the requirement, but the documents are valuable because they: report accrued and vested benefits; and explain other relevant details, such as whether Social Security and other payments will be deducted in the final benefit calculations.

And third, some people come to possess other assets that produce guaranteed income throughout their lives or upon their retirements. Examples include inheritances and legal settlements that are held in trusts or other retirement-related products.

Once individuals identify their institutional sources of future retirement income, they need to determine the extent to which they'll face shortfalls. They can do this by subtracting the total amount of their estimated annual institutional income from their estimated annual expenses. The formula is:

Estimated Annual Expenses	-	Estimated Annual Institutional Income	=	Annual Retirement Budget Shortfall

Continuing with the example of Neville, he begins by confirming the institutional income that he will receive during his first full year of retirement. He uses a benefit estimator that he finds on the Social Security Administration's website at www.ssa.gov/benefits/retirement/estimator.html, and he verifies the amount of pension payments that he earned during his past employment as a public school teacher. He concludes that the combined annual amount that he'll receive from these sources will be $45,000.

Neville subtracts the estimated annual institutional income from his estimated annual expenses, and realizes that his first full year shortfall is $35,000.

$80,000	-	$45,000	=	$35,000

He completes the step by entering the annual retirement budget shortfall ($35,000), number of years in retirement (20), and annual inflation rate (3%) in a compound interest formula. The result is a cumulative gap of $940,500. He thinks "That's still a lot, but at least it's not over two million dollars."

Personal Sources

On the other side of the coin is money that'll be withdrawn from personal sources, including funds in both workplace and privately-held assets. Unfortunately, this is frustrating to many employees that I meet because it can get confusing. In an attempt to help them understand and manage their options, I explain their resources based on how they'll be taxed.

Taxable assets like bank depository accounts, Certificates of Deposit, and brokerage accounts don't offer tax breaks. The principal is subjected to ordin-

154

ary income taxes before being contributed. And the earnings are exposed to ordinary income taxes when they're on assets that are held less than a year, or to capital gains taxes when they're on assets that are held a year or longer.

Tax-preferred assets potentially offer investors valuable tax advantages. For most of the *DIY financial planners* that I help, these comprise the bulk of their personal sources of future retirement income.

The most common type of tax-preferred assets are referred to as *tax-deferred*. Contributions, including extra amounts that older individuals can defer (or *catch-up contributions*), can be made on a pre-tax basis provided that they comply with IRS rules, and the earnings grow tax-free until distribution. This reduces peoples' current taxable income and allows their nest eggs to grow faster. But withdrawals will be taxed as ordinary income at the recipients' future rates, and might be penalized if they're taken prior to reaching IRS minimum ages or after exceeding IRS maximum ages. Examples include:

➢ *Traditional 401(k) Plans* allow employees to defer current compensation into retirement-related accounts, and they're offered by many for-profit and some non-profit employers.
➢ *Profit Sharing Plans* are used by some for-profit organizations to disperse portions of their profits as assets that are meant to help employees during retirement.
➢ *Traditional 403(b) Plans* (or *Tax-Sheltered Annuities*) are similar to traditional 401(k) plans, and they're offered by many non-profit employers.
➢ *Individual Retirement Accounts* (*IRAs*) allow people to defer their current income in personal accounts, and some employers use them in *Simplified Employee Pensions* (*SEPs*) for the benefit of their employees.

Another type of tax-preferred assets are known as *tax-exempt.* These are funded with money that was previously taxed, but future earnings and distributions are or might be tax-free at federal and state levels. Examples include:

➢ *Roth 401(k) Plans* are traditional 401(k)s that allow participants to make after-tax contributions that grow and are withdrawn tax-free, and they're offered by some for-profit and non-profit employers.
➢ *Roth IRAs* are personal accounts used by individuals to address various needs, such as retirement savings and wealth transfers to beneficiaries.

➢ *Home Equity* is the value of homeowners' interests in dwellings that they inhabit, and some or all of the capital gains earned on the sale of qualified properties might be tax-free if applicable IRS rules and tests are satisfied.

A third type are *partially tax-exempt*. These assets possess features that have the potential to create unique tax-advantages. Examples include:

➢ *Municipal Bonds* are debt securities issued by state or local governments, and public agencies, and the interest is usually free from federal taxation.
➢ *Permanent* (or *Whole*) *Life Insurance* accumulates money (or *cash value*) that policyholders can access via tax-free loans.
➢ *Annuities* are insurance products that are designed to pay annuitants fixed and guaranteed monthly income for certain time periods or their entire lives, and they often provide benefits to survivors and beneficiaries.

Finally, some assets have the potential to be completely *tax-free*, such as:

➢ *Health Savings Accounts* allow funds to be contributed on a pre-tax basis, earnings to grow tax-free, and withdrawals that are used for qualified expenses to avoid ordinary income taxes.
➢ *Reverse Mortgages* are loans that allow homeowners that are Age 62 or older to convert accumulated home equity into tax-free income streams that they'll receive while they're living in the dwellings.

Generally, actions that don't comply with laws and regulations governing tax-preferred assets expose investors to taxes and penalties. But there are instances when rules are relaxed. For example, guidelines for early withdrawals from 401(k)s, 403(b)s, and IRAs were altered in 2016 and 2017 to help hurricane victims, and in 2020 to help citizens cope with the financial hardships associated with the Coronavirus pandemic.

Finally, workplace plans that satisfy applicable qualification rules often provide enhancements that individual assets don't, like employer contributions, higher deferral limits, reduced expenses, fiduciary oversight, and bankruptcy protection. And they might offer features that make it easier for employees to participate (or *auto-enroll*), boost their ongoing deferrals (or *auto-escalate*), and maintain desired asset allocation mixes (or *auto-rebalance*).

As Neville assesses his retirement budget shortfall, he realizes that much of what he needs to fund his fresh start is or can be in his reach. For example, he: has been participating in workplace tax-preferred accounts since his late 20s; is eligible to open an HSA if he enrolls in his employer's High Deductible Health Plan; and is somewhat familiar with Roth IRAs. But he knows that he needs to learn a lot more about these assets.

NOW IT'S YOUR TURN
Estimate your retirement income shortfall

Spend 15 minutes estimating the total amount of annual payments that you'll receive during retirement from institutional sources. Then subtract that sum from your estimated annual expenses to find the annual budget shortfall that you'll need to overcome via personal income sources.

Accumulate Your Personal Sources

The third question is "How will I accumulate enough money to achieve my retirement goals?" Since this answer combines many facets of personal finance (e.g., earning, spending, saving) that are addressed elsewhere, I tend to focus on four essential parts during my conversations with employees.

The first part requires them to define "enough money." At a minimum, they should aim for amounts that are adequate to address their estimated shortfalls and get them through retirement. But for those that want to be prepared for best and worst case scenarios, it can be ranges of figures.

The next part involves setting aside (or *deferring*) current income and existing assets for future use.

Employees regularly ask me about popular deferral rate rules of thumb. They hear that they should set certain portions of their annual incomes aside, like 10%, 15%, or 20%, and want to know which one they should choose. It's tempting for me to choose the highest of the percentages and say "it's better to be safe than sorry," but that doesn't necessarily serve them well; it might be too much for some, and too little for others.

As such, I recommend that they use online tools offered by trusted financial partners to identify optimum personalized deferral rates. In exchange for entering their information, like the value of their current retirement assets, years to retirement, and rates of return, they'll receive specific suggestions or can infer suitable amounts to set aside.

Another part of the answer compels them to invest. Given the long term nature of retirement planning and the accelerating effects of compounding on wealth accumulation, people should periodically ensure that:

✓ Their investment objectives and assets align.
✓ Their assets are rewarding them appropriately (delivering competitive long-term rates of return) for the risks that they're taking.
✓ The expenses and fees that they're paying are reasonable.

Additionally, they should progressively reduce the risk in their portfolios as they get closer to withdrawing the funds. However, this doesn't mean that they should immediately or completely eliminate risk. In fact, investing some money in assets that offer potentially higher rates of return in exchange for taking reasonable risk can protect against the eroding effects of inflation.

Here, an understanding of age-based asset allocation (or *glide path*) rules of thumb can help investors manage their retirement assets and visualize the basic premise of *target date funds* (*TDFs*).

The *Rule of 100* suggests that their exposure to equity investments should equal the percentage produced by the following equation:

$$100 \quad - \quad \text{Current Age} \quad = \quad \text{Equity Exposure}$$
$$\text{(as \% of Securities Portfolio)}$$

Put differently, the percentage of investors' cash and fixed income assets should equal their ages. Theoretically, this means that their portfolios will not have any cash or fixed income assets when they're born, and the portions of those assets in relation to their overall portfolios will increase 1% each year until they reach Age 100.

The *Rule of 120* is almost identical to the Rule of 100. It's used by people that believe that it's desirable to maintain larger portions of equities in their investment portfolios later in life. Here's the formula.

120   -   Current Age   =   Equity Exposure
                                        (as % of Securities Portfolio)

The final part is tax planning. It receives scant attention in the places that many employees get their financial insights, but it's as important to answering this question as defining, deferring, and investing.

I regularly meet employees that boast about deferring large sums or the maximum amounts allowable to their 401(k)s. While that might sound smart, too many of them admit that these plans (and the homes that they own) are their only personal sources of retirement income, and too few understand the lurking nature of future taxation on these assets.

✓ *Reality Check.* Some types of investments are more or less tax-effective when they're combined with certain types of tax-preferred accounts. For example, mutual funds that feature a lot of buying and selling of underlying assets produce higher net returns in 401(k)s, 403(b)s, and IRAs than in taxable brokerage accounts because investors can avoid capital gains taxes. Conversely, municipal bonds will lose their unique tax advantages when they're held in those types of tax-deferred accounts.

✓ *Reality Check.* People that rely heavily or entirely on tax-deferred assets might unknowingly position themselves to pay higher income tax rates to withdraw their funds during retirement than they avoid when they defer them. This becomes more likely as their assets reach 6 and 7 figure sums.

✓ *Reality Check.* Contrary to what some employees believe, 50% to 85% of their Social Security retirement, disability, or survivor payments will be taxable as ordinary income if earnings from other income sources such as wages, interest, dividends, and pensions exceed statutory thresholds.

✓ *Reality Check.* People that claim Social Security prior to their FRAs might have portions of their already-reduced benefits withheld if they continue working and the related income exceeds statutory earnings limits. This can feel like a tax, but the reductions will cease when the recipients reach their FRAs and the payments will permanently increase to compensate them for previously withheld money. Visit the Social Security Administration's earnings test calculator at www.ssa.gov/oact/cola/rteffect.html to learn more.

✓ *Reality Check.* Since federal and state tax policies aren't set in stone, future retirees should strive to monitor relevant changes and understand any tax-related assumptions that form the basis of proposed retirement products (e.g., permanent life insurance, annuities). I find that top notch financial advisors and partners can be sources of useful insights and reliable information.

DIY financial planners that overlook or dismiss the taxation of their future retirement income sources might be jeopardizing years of spending potential. If they're concerned or confused, they should proactively seek guidance from reputable tax and wealth planning professionals.

Let's return to Neville. During the past decade, he's consistently deferred 10% to his 401(k) and has accumulated a total of $125,000. And in the course of evaluating his tax-preferred options, he remembers that future retirement withdrawals from this asset will be taxed as ordinary income, and he realizes that a significant portion of his Social Security payments might also be taxed.

Given his goals, he plans for two scenarios. He says "Worst case, I'll need $940,500 to keep the life that I have. But $1,200,000 might allow me to teach abroad without worrying about money. So, I'll aim for the higher figure and do my best to avoid retiring until I at least hit the lower one."

Before making any changes, Neville talks to a tax professional. The person confirms that he's going to lose some of his future spending power if he fails to make some changes, and recommends that he allocate a portion of his future retirement contributions to other tax-preferred assets.

Neville takes the advice. First, he lowers his 401(k) deferral to $3,500 per year, or 5% of his $70,000 annual salary. This qualifies him for another $2,800 a year from his employer's 4% match. Next, he initiates an automatic investment plan that'll transfer $400 per month, or $4,800 per year, from his checking account to a Roth IRA. And, when allowed, he enrolls in a health insurance plan at work that'll let him save in an HSA. Given the combined contribution limit of $3,600 for self-only coverage in 2021, his employer will deposit *$500* during the year and he'll fund the remaining $3,100 via payroll deduction. In total, he'll add $14,700 to his tax-preferred assets each year that he does this.

Neville also analyzes his investments. In the past, he kept his retirement dollars in conservative investment options in his company's 401(k). But after learning the Rule of 120, he adjusts his overall investment strategy to include more equity. This boosts his confidence in his ability to earn an average annual rate of return of 5% (net of expenses) on these nest egg assets during the 20 years that he expects to continue working.

He concludes by entering the following information in a future value calculator that he finds online: existing assets of $125,000; total annual additions of $14,700; 5% annual rate of return (net of expenses); and 20 years to continue working. After clicking the submit button, the site informs him that the future value of his tax-preferred assets will be nearly $817,700 by Age 65.

At first blush, the output implies that Neville will fall short of his fresh start goal. But he quickly realizes that the figure doesn't account for other important sources of personal income. Specifically: future increases in his contributions to his workplace plans due to pay raises and catch-up provisions; other pre-retirement investments; any post-retirement income earned as a result of teaching, growth of accumulated nest egg assets, and home equity accessed via the sale of his home or a reverse mortgage.

Neville takes a deep and relaxed breath, and says "I can't rest on my laurels, but I think I'm gonna be alright."

NOW IT'S YOUR TURN
Review your efforts to overcome your retirement income shortfall

Take 30 minutes to review your efforts to overcome your retirement income shortfall. This includes defining (or redefining) enough money, and addressing your deferring, investing, and tax-planning activities. And, if needed, talk to a reputable tax or wealth planner (see **Section VI**). Finally, schedule future reviews to ensure that you periodically re-examine and modify your plan.

Plan Your Withdrawals

"How will I withdraw funds from my nest egg so that it lasts as long as I need it to?" is the last question, and it's potentially the most crucial to people that accumulate hundreds of thousands or millions of dollars in tax-preferred assets. For this reason, *DIY financial planners* should begin formulating their retirement spending (or *draw down*) strategies many years in advance.

First, they need to decide the order in which they'll withdraw money from their institutional and personal sources of future retirement income. This is because the liquidation of these assets can cause tax problems when people can least afford them; after their regular workplace paychecks cease.

Unfortunately, sequencing distributions to achieve tax efficiencies can be challenging because there's a lot to consider. Internal factors include peoples' goals and circumstances, like marital status, existing assets, early retirement, and post-retirement employment. And external ones vary by income source, and potentially expose retirees and beneficiaries to a myriad of rules, timetables, and penalties.

Perhaps one of the more difficult obstacles for some people to navigate are rules mandating partial payments from their tax-deferred assets. Known as *required minimum distributions* (*RMDs*), they're compelled to start withdrawing specific portions from these types of accounts each year based on their ages. It's important to understand that RMDs can supplant draw down strategies because failing to comply can lead to severe penalties.

Generally, retirees must begin taking RMDs not later than April 1st of the year after the calendar years in which they reach Age 70½ (if they were born before July 1st, 1949) or Age 72 (if they were born July 1st, 1949 or later). But there are exceptions. For example, people who work beyond their respective RMD ages don't need to take RMDs from workplace 401(k)s, 403(b)s, or profit sharing or other defined contribution plans until April 1st of the year after they retire, provided that the plans allow them to do so. Rules are also different for IRAs inherited from deceased account owners, and for those that own 5% or more of the businesses sponsoring the 401(k)s, profit sharing or other defined contribution plans in which they participate.

As a general rule, retirees should strive to withdraw tax-deferred assets when their ordinary income tax rates are at their lowest levels and their tax-exempt assets when their rates are at their highest levels. They should also be mindful that the sale of certain types of assets might impact income that they expect to receive from Social Security.

Second, they need to decide the amounts that they can safely withdraw from their personal sources of retirement income. This is to ensure that they don't inadvertently take too much or too little in any given year.

Some retirees prefer straightforward draw down techniques. At retirement, they commit to withdrawing fixed amounts each year. They might take the same flat dollar amounts (e.g., $20,000, $50,000), the same fixed percentages of their initial principal (e.g., 3%, 5%), or only the money that they earn on their principal (e.g., interest, dividends, gains).

Others choose elaborate alternatives. One requires retirees to withdraw amounts in their first years of retirement that are equal to fixed portions of their total nest eggs. However, the amounts are altered in subsequent years to account for the effects of inflation. Here, a person starting retirement with $1,000,000 might take $50,000 (or 5%) in their first year, and $50,000 plus extra amounts thereafter to address cost of living increases.

Another technique compels retirees to set minimum and maximum withdrawal percentages that correlate with annual changes in the values of their nest eggs that are due to investment performance. So, a retiree might start with the assumption that they'll take $50,000 per year, but adjust the amount down to $47,500 if their portfolio's rate of return falls short of pre-set targets or up to $55,000 if it exceeds them.

Third, they need to decide how they will manage the ongoing investment of their nest eggs during retirement. This is because they need assets that are not required for immediate or short-term consumption to continue growing.

In addition to applying investing concepts mentioned previously, retirees might consider using a technique, originally proposed by Harold Evensky, referred to as a *bucket approach*.[32] It calls them to spread their personal sources of future retirement income into multiple buckets that are characterized by different investment characteristics, and to adhere to a process whereby they gradually shift assets in a cascading manner from buckets that involve some risk of loss to others that have virtually no risk.

---

[32] Jeff Benjamin, "Bucket strategies provide a pot of 'safe money'" (March 27, 2011, www.investmentnews.com, Web, March, 10, 2020).

For example, a person who believes that they'll live for 30 years after retiring might create three buckets. In the first, they'll set enough money aside in assets like cash or CDs to address short-term and emergency (e.g., 0 to 2 years) spending. Next, they fund a bucket for intermediate (e.g., 2 to 10 years) spending, and it's invested in low-risk fixed income or high-quality equity securities. Then they will fund a bucket for long-term spending (e.g., 10 to 30 years) that invests in higher-risk assets that offer opportunities for growth. As time passes and the short-term bucket is depleted, it's replenished with funds generated by the sale of assets from the other buckets.

And fourth, while draw down strategies should be sufficiently flexible to address extraordinary hardships that can disrupt their plans, such as financial shocks and long-term care needs, people must decide how they'll ensure that they'll stick to their plans throughout retirement. Examples of scenarios that derail some retirees include:

➢ *A soft spot.* She had a foolproof strategy to draw down her nest egg, but lacked discipline when it came to family. In the first 5 years of retirement, she paid for big ticket items that were never budgeted: two all-inclusive vacation cruises for her kids and grandkids, and a personal loan to help a spendthrift son avoid bankruptcy.

➢ *Cognitive decline.* He made a lot of sacrifices during his career to create a sizeable nest egg, but 6 years into retirement he began forgetting things and making bad financial decisions. He was eventually diagnosed with dementia, but not before misusing most of his money.

➢ *Fear of scarcity.* Early in retirement, she began to worry excessively about running out of money. There wasn't a rational basis for her fear, but she abandoned the plan that she'd put in place earlier in her life. Instead of chasing her dreams, she curtailed her spending and began hoarding cash.

➢ *Snake charmers.* Several years into retirement, he attended a free wealth planning seminar and was smooth-talked into giving an advisor half of his nest egg. Sadly, the decision wasn't in his best interests and he didn't realize the pitfalls until it was too late to cancel the contract.

➢ *The weaker link.* The couple worked hard to build their nest egg. She was financially savvy and engineered a brilliant draw down strategy, but died 6 months after retiring. He was terrible with money, never understood the plan, and quickly bungled things after her passing.

There are many techniques and resources that *DIY financial planners* can use to develop their own draw down strategies, but the degree of success or failure that they experience depends on numerous factors. Given the magnitude of these decisions and the heavy price that's paid for poor planning, they can't afford to bury their heads in the sand. At a minimum, they should consider either engaging good retirement advisors who'll design sustainable strategies for them, or purchasing annuities from high-quality insurers that'll do most or all of this work for them.

Let's visit Neville one more time. As his retirement approaches, he becomes increasingly certain that he'll have enough to do everything that he hopes to during his fresh start. This makes him happy, but he's worried about going-it-alone the rest of the way. So he conducts a formal search and hires an advisor who's compatible with his goals and needs.

The advisor recommends and, with Neville's blessing, implements a draw down strategy that: activates each retirement income source in the most tax-efficient manner; administers withdrawal amounts from his personal income sources that increase the likelihood that his nest egg will last as long as intended; establishes three distinct retirement income buckets that'll hold a diverse mix of assets and be rebalanced regularly; and assures that all aspects of the ongoing process will be overseen by a reliable professional.

NOW IT'S YOUR TURN
Contemplate and test your retirement income draw down strategy

If you've never considered your draw down strategy, take 15 minutes now to ask your financial partners about any expertise and resources that they offer to help you in this task, so that you can begin implementing a sound plan. If you've already adopted a draw down strategy, spend 15 minutes asking your financial partners to help you test and improve it.

SECTION V

A PROTECTING MINDSET

CHAPTER 14

WHEN LIFE BREAKS OUR HEARTS

The world is constantly changing, and so is risk. Imagine the futility that the following mid-20th Century super hero might feel upon being instantly and permanently teleported to the present day...

The Masked Owl was a 1960s crusader who protected the citizens of Capital City from all manner of mayhem. She had night vision, an inescapable grip, and the ability to sneak up on people without being detected; premium attributes in her profession. Thanks to her tireless efforts, the metropolis was crime-free, accident-free, and ranked as the country's safest place to live five years in a row.

Sadly, tragedy struck in 1968 when Masked Owl vanished during a battle with a time-traveling criminal named Clock Face. During the melee, the two became entangled as she bore down and he attempted to escape using his teleportation device. Witnesses reported seeing a small explosion. The police couldn't find any evidence that she'd survived. And the community eventually grieved. But she was alive.

Just as Clock Face stepped into a time portal, Masked Owl got a firm hold of him, and the two combatants made a 50-year tandem-leap into the future. When the jump was complete, she was victorious but the one-of-a-kind contraption was destroyed. Both the hero and the villain were stuck in a new era.

With the passage of time, the Masked Owl accepted that life had changed. While some threats were the same, many had evolved and new ones had emerged. She yearned to press on, but realized that her talents and techniques were outdated. The do-gooder knew that she needed an upgrade.

The moral of the story is that it's going to be difficult for 21st Century *DIY financial planners* to build wealth if they rely on 20th Century approaches to protecting it.

You Must Choose

Most days, people are oblivious to the threats that are in their midst. It's only when they do harm that their omnipresence is truly felt.

The surest way to avoid risk is to never take it, but this strategy is rarely practical. Plus, it stifles opportunities and can't guarantee that calamity won't strike anyway. Other methods include ignoring risks, minimizing them, or insuring against them. Each of these approaches has its place, but only the last one offers peace of mind when the others fail.

Insurance is a legal agreement between two parties whereby *insureds* are assured by *insurers* that they will be financially shielded (or *covered*) against losses that occur under certain conditions. The concept is based on the premise that people would prefer to pay small amounts for protection than large amounts should they be unlucky. Because it's essential to preserving wealth, they must answer the question "What will I do to make it happen?"

Let's reprise the role of professional financial advisors and imagine that we're trying to guide two new clients, Clock Face and Masked Owl, that are making up for lost time. Based on the following statements, which protecting mindset seems more likely to ensure success?

Clock Face	*"Buying insurance is like playing poker against a dealer who's using a rigged deck; total sucker's game! Some chumps do ok, but everyone knows that insurance companies make their money when they don't pay claims. And with my luck, I'd lose that bet. To be honest, I'm only gonna have it if: 'A,' I know I'll use it; 'B', I'm forced to buy it; or 'C', someone else is paying for it. Otherwise, I'm not interested."*

"As a super hero, I always knew that I was taking risks, but I never really considered that everything I had could disappear in a flash. If lightning strikes again, I don't want to start over. So, I'm OK paying something to protect the things that I've worked hard to accumulate or would struggle to replace. Worst case, it'll help me feel better."

Clock Face's anti-insurance sentiment is understandable: nobody relishes paying for products that may never be used or might not perform as needed when called upon. But it's also dicey to forego the protection that insurance can provide. Conversely, Masked Owl's beliefs and attitudes give her a better shot at preserving the things that matter to her.

Most of the *DIY financial planners* that I encounter don't enjoy discussing insurance; they frequently detest it. I find that those that possess weak mindsets generally prefer to avoid the topic or take it for granted, except in cases where the focus is on applying for benefits or reducing costs. Ironically, their unconscious approaches undercut their efforts to get ahead and contribute to preventable mistakes like:

✓ Forgetting to disclose key information

✓ Failing to list people, property, or liabilities

✓ Misinterpreting policy features

✓ Neglecting to pay premiums on time

✓ Ignoring key dates

✓ Purchasing shoddy coverage

This isn't to suggest that people with strong mindsets like to talk about it; they don't either. But I find that they're more likely to acknowledge it's value and to try to understand its ins-and-outs. To shed light on how some of them put this aspect of personal finance into perspective, following is a glimpse at an exchange that occurred in one memorable benefits enrollment meeting.

A group of employees was grumbling about insurance when an older employee interjected. She said "Bad things happen to other people all the time, and one of these days it'll be my turn. Hopefully I'm wrong, but I want the right coverage in case I'm right."

Her coworker asked "So, what's your advice?" She replied "Well, I'm no expert, but I'll tell you what our old chief financial officer told me. He said 'Each year, decide what you want to insure. Then ask our benefits manager and your insurance agent to confirm that your policies have you appropriately covered. Be sure they focus on benefits, services, and costs, and ask for help fixing things that aren't right."

She finished by saying "He was smart. He knew I'd pay a bit more, but said 'you're more likely to be ok when life breaks your heart'."

Mindset Concept: Public Safety Nets

Public safety nets ensure that people have basic protection against specific losses. They might be designed to cover the vast majority of citizens or narrowly defined groups, and serve as the footing for many private insurance solutions.

Some public safety nets are strictly governmental. Federally, *Social Security Disability Insurance* (*SSDI*) provides covered individuals with reliable income after they're diagnosed with medical conditions that result in their permanent or long-term inabilities to work. Similarly, the *Supplemental Security Income* (*SSI*) program offers payments to adults and children that are disabled, blind, or have limited income. However, where SSDI is generally available to people that have worked 5 of the past 10 years and paid taxes under the *Federal Insurance Contribution Act* (*FICA*), or to applicants that are under Age 22,[33] SSI is granted to applicants that can prove financial need.

At the state-level, several safety nets exist. *Unemployment Insurance* is a state-administered program that's mandated by federal law and it restores portions of qualified employees' lost earnings. *Workers' Compensation* is a state-governed program that pays for approved health care services and replaces lost earnings for qualified disabilities relating to work-related injuries

---

[33] Social Security Administration, "Disability Benefits: How You Qualify" (2020, www.ssa.gov, Web, June 27, 2020).

or illnesses. And some states offer their own supplemental income programs when residents become disabled.

Other safety nets are collaborative efforts between government and private sector insurers. For example, the 1965 *Medicare Amendment to the Social Security Act* created: *Medicaid* to help low-income individuals of any age pay for health care; and *Medicare* to help retired people Age 65 or older that aren't insured at work, those under Age 65 with specific disabilities, and anyone that suffers permanent kidney failure. While both are administered and funded by the government, they're bolstered by insurers that offer eligible individuals financial protection for services that aren't adequately addressed by the public coverage.

And the *National Flood Insurance Program* (*NFIP*) provides designated homeowners with protection that would be difficult or impossible to secure, especially for those residing in areas that are at high risk of flooding. It's managed by the Federal Emergency Management Agency and covered by private insurers.

NOW IT'S YOUR TURN
Learn about your public safety nets

Take 15 minutes now to ask your financial partners to explain the benefits that public safety nets might provide you (or your spouse or dependents, if applicable), and seek to understand the manner in which they complement, supplement, or conflict with your existing resources.

Mindset Concept: Private Insurance

Private insurance exists to fill the gaps between public safety nets and personal resources. It's not government-run, but civil servants pass and enforce a myriad of laws that regulate and enforce it. For many types of coverage, each state and U.S. Territory is responsible for overseeing the organizations and people that engage in these agreements and the markets in which they operate. However, there are other types of coverage that fall, in part or whole, under federal or local jurisdictions.

Insurers are organizations that establish risk-sharing pools in which individuals and groups enroll. They collect fees, communicate rights, assume risk, and pay benefits, and can be for-profit or non-profit companies, associations, or large employers that self-insure their own risks. *Intermediaries* are *agents* that market and sell insurance on behalf of insurers, or *brokers* that shop the market for their insured clients. And *plan sponsors* are employers that maintain group insurance plans for the benefit of their employees and employees' dependents.

It's easy to forgive *DIY financial planners* for dismissing the relationships between government oversight and insurance products, but it's nonetheless important. First, it affects their rights, benefits, and obligations, and it guides their insurers' operations (e.g., rules, requirements, processes). Second, it accounts for some of the complexity that infuriates them. And third, it dictates where they'll go to report grievances, request interventions, or file lawsuits.

Surprisingly, governmental efforts to inform consumers about insurer financial strength often aren't useful to insureds. Luckily, third-party industry rating agencies, such as Weiss Ratings, Standard & Poor's, and A.M. Best, offer free and user friendly grading systems that help consumers distinguish between weak, average, and strong insurers. However, it's also important for current and perspective buyers to realize: that these watchdogs might have conflicts of interest if they're paid by the insurers that are being evaluated; and that weak and average insurers will go to great lengths to seek and promote favorable ratings that are produced by less reputable firms.

NOW IT'S YOUR TURN
Verify the strength of your insurers

Take 15 minutes now to verify the strength of your insurers using the free resources in your reach. If you find any that are weak, you might consider moving to others that are more viable.

Mindset Concept: Application and Acceptance

Insurers are obligated to preserve the long term viability of their risk-sharing pools. Sometimes they will guarantee coverage up to specified limits without requiring insurance applicants to provide proof that they're insurable risks (or *evidence of insurability*). However, they typically adhere to a formal process known as *underwriting* to determine whether they'll accept or deny coverage, or request additional information. They might also impose *waiting periods* before allowing people to apply or enroll.

Once coverage is approved, insureds receive *policy certificates* that outline their benefits and rights, explain the parameters in which funds will be disbursed, and assign policy numbers to identify covered individuals. And, for some workplace plans, they receive *Summary Plan Descriptions* (*SPDs*) that disclose legally-required information that isn't included in policy certificates, and group numbers that might be in addition to or in lieu of policy numbers.

There are two general types of insurance agreements. In the first, known as *indemnity policies*, insurers pay insureds lump sum amounts for covered losses regardless of the actual costs to provide the promised benefits. An example is the death benefit found in a life insurance policy. The second, called *reimbursement policies*, reimburses insureds for out-of-pocket costs that relate to covered events or services. An example is a homeowner's policy that covers the full cost to replace a covered structure in the event of a total loss.

From the first date that policies are effective (or *effective dates*), insureds can request benefit payments for qualified events or expenses (or *claims*). But that doesn't necessarily mean that they'll be approved. Insurers will review the facts and circumstances of the claims, and decide whether to pay them, deny them, or request additional information.

In most policies, specific events, conditions, and expenses are limited or excluded. Some claims are only covered up to specific amounts (or *limitations*), like a $5,000 cap on basement water damage in a standard homeowner's policy. Some aren't covered during pre-determined waiting periods (or *elimination periods*), such as a root canal performed in the first 6 months of a new dental policy. And some aren't covered at all (or *exclusions*), like the costs related to an injury sustained by an insured who is involved in the commission of a crime.

Some insureds incorrectly assume that all insurers are legally prohibited from excluding coverage for physical or mental health conditions that existed prior to the policy effective dates (or *pre-existing conditions*). It's important for them to understand that such rules only apply to certain health plans. In fact, many types of policies, like accident, disability, and pet insurance, continue to include and enforce these types of provisions.

Finally, there are occasions that claimants feel that insurers improperly deny their claims. In these disputes, it's wise for them to review the appeals procedures communicated in their policy certificates or SPDs, and to talk to their insurers, intermediaries, attorneys, or state insurance commissioners.

Mindset Concept: Cost Sharing

After insurers and insureds agree on what's insured, they need to decide how they'll share the costs associated with insurance and claims. In some policies, these amounts are based largely on individual risk factors. In others, they're driven by group characteristics, such as cell phone protection plans, workplace health insurance options, and Medicare Part B plans.

Since cost-sharing can be difficult to monitor, it helps to realize that there are two general instances where insureds might pay. The first is at the *point-of-coverage*. Similar to member fees that people pay to belong to buyers' clubs like Sam's Club or Amazon Prime, insureds must agree to periodically pay fixed amounts (or *premiums*) for insurers to begin or continue insuring them during specified timeframes (or *policy periods*).

On rare occasions, insureds don't pay point-of-coverage costs, like when employers provide fully paid life insurance or when others own the policies. But typically, they'll pay some or all of the costs, and must do so in accordance with prearranged due dates. If they fail to do so on time, their policies typically provide extra time (or *grace periods*). If their grace periods elapse without payment being received by the insurers, then the policies are deemed to be expired (or *lapsed*) and the insureds might not be permitted to reinstate their coverage.

Point-of-coverage costs tend to be straightforward, but there are times that they can become a bit muddled. For example, insurers might award discounts to insureds that purchase multiple types of coverage from them (or *bundling*). And in certain workplace group policies, employers might pay portions of the total costs, apply credits and surcharges, or allow employees to pay their shares of the premiums on a pre-tax basis.

The second instance is at the *point-of-claim*. While some policies provide immediate and full benefits for approved claims, like a life insurance death benefit, most require insureds to pay extra amounts toward the costs of covered charges before the insurers will begin paying.

For example, sometimes insureds must pay small, fixed amounts (or *copays*) toward specific claims, like a $50 copay for a windshield replacement under an auto policy or a $10 copay for a 30-day supply of a prescribed medication in a health insurance policy. These are convenience features included in certain types of coverage that may or may not count toward policy out-of-pocket maximums.

Other times, insureds are responsible for initial amounts associated with covered claims (or *deductibles*) before insurers will pay anything. These prevent insurers from being bombarded by higher-frequency claims, and reduce point-of-coverage costs paid by insureds. The size and function of deductibles varies significantly between policies. They can be per year, per event, or per person, and can be reset in new policy years, or carried forward into the new policy year.

Deductibles can represent the full extent of insureds' exposure, or be part of multi-layered point-of-claim cost-sharing arrangements between insureds and insurers. In the former, the insurers cover all of the costs for approved claims up to maximum limits after insureds reach their deductibles. In the latter, the insurers split the costs that exceed the deductibles with the insureds (or *coinsurance*) up to a limit (or *out-of-pocket maximums*), and thereafter cover approved expenses at 100%.

It's helpful for *DIY financial planners* to understand that there's an inverse relationship between point-of-coverage and point-of-claim costs. Generally, one goes up when the other goes down.

CHAPTER 15

THE MOST VALUABLE ASSET

My first encounter with most *DIY financial planners* occurs during their annual benefits sign-up. Not surprising, it's usually a lousy backdrop for teaching employees enduring concepts because they don't have a lot of time and their focus is on changes that'll affect their bottom lines.

For many of them, health insurance is the hardest pill to swallow. They reveal their misgivings with questions like "Is this really better than government run health care?", making remarks such as "I'm sick of health insurance companies getting rich at our expense!", and shaking their heads in silent protest. At best, they see it as a necessary evil, and there's nothing that I can say that'll change their minds.

But others view it as good medicine. Citing personal or family experiences, they credit health insurance for giving them access to cures that saved or improved the quality of life for someone that they cherished; treatments that would've otherwise been out of reach. They extoll the freedom and power it entitles them to when they can't afford to go it alone.

Understand Your Care

As with the following example, employees might be divided about health insurance, but they seem unified when they're asked "What's your most valuable asset?"

"Good health!" a veteran Emergency Medical Technician replied during a memorable workplace exchange. He added "After every dispatch, I thank God for mine because everything stops when it's gone."

Sadly, nobody's immune to physical and mental afflictions. Some, like the flu, broken bones, or chipped teeth, strike quickly and are known as *acute*. Others, such as heart disease, diabetes, or depression, progress gradually and are referred to as *chronic*. Fortunately, a large and diverse group of skilled professionals and institutions (or *providers*) stand ready to help.

Obviously, different conditions require different levels of care from different types of providers. Some, like licensed practical nurses, general internists, and dentists, dispense preventive, routine, and diagnostic services, and are engaged in *primary care*. Others, such as oncologists and therapists develop deep expertise in specialized fields and offer *secondary care*. And those administering highly coordinated services deliver either *tertiary care* like local hospitals and nursing homes, or *quaternary care* like regional trauma centers and research hospitals.

Instinctively, these practitioners push their craft toward better outcomes for people that are suffering. Their dedication produces extraordinary results and recent news headlines suggest they're on the verge of discovering safe remedies for countless diseases. But there are some frustrating side effects.

For example, I regularly witness insureds that are overwhelmed by the entire process. They forfeit control of numerous aspects of their lives because they don't know what to ask or how to decode what they're told, and they don't want to upset their caregivers. Conversely, their insurers are constantly second-guessing providers, and demanding mountains of evidence to prove that proposed treatments are necessary and effective before they'll agree to pay the bills. This leads to additional strain on physicians and higher costs. It's a vicious and expensive circle.

The one certainty about health care is that patients and their guardians must live with the outcomes of their decisions. As such, a key step is for them to learn to proactively ask their providers crucial questions about prescribed care.[34]

---

[34] American Board of Internal Medicine and Consumer Reports, *"Choosing Wisely"* campaign (Philadelphia, Pennsylvania, ABIM Foundation, 2012).

Optimize Your Health Insurance

Health insurance helps people solve problems that they might face when their need for care exceeds their desire or ability to fund it themselves. It pays for approved services dispensed by qualified providers to treat covered conditions, and can reduce costs, eliminate administrative hassles, and improve access to information.

It's so vital that employers frequently subsidize the cost of coverage for employees, and federal and state governments grant generous tax breaks to help both. And, as evidenced by the passage of the *Patient Protection & Affordable Care Act (ACA)* and similar state laws, some policymakers will go to great lengths to compel the former to offer it and the later to have it.

Unfortunately, health insurance continues to be a burden, and it changes from year-to-year, place-to-place, and plan-to-plan. New tools make it easier to personalize, and many would-be critics are subdued by employer, government, and non-profit subsidies. But it continues to be a source of frustration for many employees. For this reason, I teach those that want to optimize their coverage to focus on five enduring concepts that never seem to change.

About Coverage: Take Nothing For Granted

The main purpose of health insurance is to reimburse insureds for money that they spend on covered services, medications, and equipment, especially in serious and catastrophic situations. Since insurers aren't in the business of writing blank checks, it's wise to ask "Who's covered?" and "What's covered?" before receiving care.

On the surface, "Who's covered?" seems clear. It's people identified by policies as *primary insureds* or *dependents*. But there are times that it's not that simple. For example, some spouses are common law, separated, or non-citizens, and some children are adopted, children-of-children, or disabled adults that are legally dependent. Ultimately, the law, legal contracts, and insurance policies define eligibility, and sometimes verification with insurers, employers, tax advisors, and state insurance commissioners is required.

Occasionally, primary insureds will cover beneficiaries that are no longer or never were eligible. Accidental or deliberate, this is perilous because insurers will likely expose the truth with tools known as *dependent eligibility audits*. In best-case scenarios, ineligible people will lose their coverage and their insurers will attempt to recoup improperly paid benefits. Worst case, primary insureds will lose their coverage, and might lose their jobs and face criminal prosecution for fraud.

Given that "Who's covered?" can be complicated, it shouldn't come as a surprise that "What's covered?" is equally so. It's shaped to some degree by government laws that impose coverage baselines, and a host of other factors at the insurer and insured level. For example, workplace health insurance can be driven by employers' needs, insurer practices, group demographics, and union agreements, and personal policies can be affected by insurer practices and individuals' specific needs, attributes, and limitations.

Medical insurance generally pays for a broad scope of care including preventive, ambulatory, emergency, outpatient, inpatient, hospitalization, laboratory, imaging, maternity, newborn, mental health and substance abuse, and prescription drugs. Most plans don't impose annual or lifetime benefit maximums, or require insureds to satisfy waiting periods, but they will limit or deny coverage for unnecessary or experimental procedures, and services rendered by unqualified providers.

Dental insurance addresses oral health and it's different from medical insurance in several ways. First, it classifies procedures as preventive (e.g., routine check-ups, fluoride treatments), basic (e.g., fillings, sealants), major (e.g., crowns, bridges) and orthodontia (e.g., braces, retainers), and it layers coverage in ways that reduce benefits for pricier services. Second, it imposes waiting periods on non-preventive dental services. Third, it limits annual and lifetime payments. And fourth, some insurers apply portions of amounts that insureds paid under their previous policies to new policy maximums.

And *vision insurance* pays for common ophthalmology products and procedures that aren't covered by medical insurance, such as exams, glasses, and contacts. But it caps benefits in perplexing ways. For example, an insured may be limited to either a single new pair of glasses or resupply of contact lenses during a fixed period, like 24 months; they aren't typically entitled to both.

While insurers are legally required to provide written descriptions of coverage, the overtly legal and technical nature of the documents is confusing. Fortunately, those insuring medical and prescription drug services must provide primary insureds with user-friendly four-page *Summaries of Benefits and Coverage* (*SBCs*) during enrollments, in conjunction with policy renewals, and anytime copies are requested. These documents must satisfy legally required criteria. For example, they must avoid jargon and small print, and they must include glossaries of basic terms and definitions.

NOW IT'S YOUR TURN
Review your current and proposed policy benefits, terms and conditions

Take 15 minutes now to secure your SBC, certificates, and documents, and schedule a conversation with your HR or benefits colleague, advisor, or insurer. The purpose of this task is to determine the degree to which your current health insurance coverage fits your needs and to identify the next opportunity to consider alternatives.

About Managed Care: Get the Most from Membership

Health insurers often boast about the exclusive savings and special perks that they offer. They do this to attract the types of insureds that'll buy their coverage, let them manage their care, and contain related costs. Similar to the previously mentioned buyers' clubs, it's ultimately up to the members to get maximum value from these programs.

The most commonly used managed care tools are *health care networks* in which patients presumably pay substantially less by receiving services from providers that have contractually agreed to discount their standard prices (or *reimbursement rates*). Typically, other tools like telemedicine, 24-hour nurse helplines, and pharmacy management, are integrated in the networks to create one-stop-shop customer experiences.

The least restrictive managed care options are *Preferred Provider Organizations* (*PPOs*) for medical services and prescription drugs, and *Dental Provider Organizations* (*DPOs*) for dental services. These plans pay for network and non-network services, but offer richer benefits for care received from contracted providers. *Point of Service Plans* (*POSs*) are PPOs that require *primary care physicians* (*PCPs*) to coordinate non-emergency care. Insureds are permitted to act without PCP referrals, but will pay considerably more out-of-pocket at the points of claim. Typically, people that want greater flexibility and can afford to pay more will enroll in these types of programs.

Occasionally, PPO, DPO, or POS insureds learn that they're responsible for additional costs after receiving non-emergency care from non-network providers. They're surprised because they feel that their out-of-pocket exposure should be limited to the non-network level, but their policies allow insurers to deny amounts that exceed *Usual, Customary, or Reasonable* (*UCR*) amounts for performed procedures. When insurers don't pay the invoices in full, providers charge insureds for the unpaid amounts (or *balance bill*).

And the most restrictive plans are *Health Maintenance Organizations* (*HMOs*) and *Dental Maintenance Organizations* (*DMOs*). Both offer comprehensive coordinated care, and cover unexpected emergencies wherever they occur, but they'll only pay for non-emergency services received from or directed by member PCPs. *Exclusive Provider Organizations* (*EPOs*) are similar to HMOs, but don't mandate that insureds obtain PCP referrals for non-emergency care received from other network providers. Often, enrollees in these plans don't have provider preferences, don't travel far from their homes, or aren't concerned about making their own care decisions, or they value lower costs, less paperwork, and convenient copays.

Sometimes, modified versions of PPO, POS, EPO, and HMO plans are created and sold on the premise that some of the existing network providers do better jobs at delivering both low cost and high quality services. One example are *narrow networks*. Here, insurers use small subsets of providers from their larger networks to deliver care. Another example are *tiered networks* where providers are ranked on cost and quality metrics, and are then separated into tiers (e.g., 1st, 2nd, 3rd). Insureds are rewarded by the insurers with lower out-of-pocket costs for using the higher-tier providers.

Unfortunately, there are scenarios in some of these plans that cause balance billing nightmares. For example, non-network physicians occasionally treat patients in network facilities. Referred to as *hidden providers*, they do not have managed care agreements, their fees aren't discounted, and insureds that are treated by them incur unexpectedly higher point-of-claim costs. Another is care received when insureds are determined to be out-of-area and aren't able to access network services. After the deductibles are satisfied, insureds and insurers split the costs up to the coinsurance limits, but any amounts that exceed the UCR will be billed to the insureds. Other examples involve providers that terminate their participation in networks mid-year or mid-treatment, or insureds that reside in areas with low numbers of network providers.

NOW IT'S YOUR TURN
Understand managed care features, benefits, and restrictions

Take 15 minutes to ask your HR or benefits colleague, insurance advisor, or insurer, for an overview of your managed care plan and insights that will help you make better use of it.

About Wellness: It's Cheaper to Stay Healthy than to Treat Illness

From national studies to standalone employer plans, data suggests that the vast majority of health care dollars are used to treat chronic conditions.

Afflictions range from genetic to lifestyle related, and they affect numerous aspects of people's lives. In response, insurers and employers tend to combine preventive care and wellness initiatives with medical and prescription drug plans, and it's often in the best interests of insureds to embrace them since they're frequently responsible for paying large portions of their bills.

Preventive care focuses on the detection and treatment of illnesses and injuries before they escalate into crises. Services like annual physicals, routine exams, screenings, and immunizations are often the first line of defense in health care and insurance, and employees should make concerted efforts to incorporate it into their efforts to build and preserve wealth.

Wellness initiatives are used by insurers and plan sponsors to promote and reward behaviors that they believe will reduce the likelihood, frequency, and severity of large health claims. These programs typically commence with communication campaigns that include: upbeat endorsements from their organizational leaders; themes that highlight healthier lifestyles; and events to build enthusiasm among the insured population.

Next, insurers and employers often ask insured employees to complete surveys known as *Health Risk Assessments* (*HRAs*) so that the general health of the workforce can be assessed and future health care needs can be anticipated. The degrees to which gathered information is meaningful or impactful to individual insureds depends on the ways in which plan managers apply it.

Simultaneously, insurers and employers might conduct abbreviated medical exams (or *biometric screenings*) at worksites or offsite facilities to identify latent diseases and illnesses among their employee populations. Health care professionals will typically: record employees' heights, weights, and blood pressures; draw blood; and calculate *Body Mass Index* (*BMI*).

From there, insurers and plan sponsors use the insights to refine their wellness efforts, initiate early interventions, and offer personalized feedback and support. They might target their communications to specific high risk audiences, schedule educational seminars, offer individual coaching, or conduct organization-wide contests. To the extent that they're legally permitted, they might reward those that achieve specific goals with perks like extra vacation days, retail gift cards, health insurance premium reductions, or contributions to Health Savings Accounts (HSAs).

About Cost Sharing: It's A Constant Tug-Of-War

Annual growth in average health care costs usually outpaces general inflation and workplace earnings. There are valid reasons for this phenomenon, but they're typically not useful to employees that are principally concerned about anticipating their costs for the coming year and minimizing the impact of increases on their household budgets. They prefer practical insights.

The first place that insureds should look for insights into the cost-sharing tug-of-war is at *point-of-coverage costs*. At work, these are driven by broader factors such as group health characteristics, expected inflation rates for available plans (or *trend*), and premium contributions. They're also shaped by the coverage selections of those with dependents, like self-and-spouse, self-and-child(ren), and family.

Insureds should also look at incentives that help them reduce their health care costs because they offer glimpses into future plan design and costs. For example, many workplace plans grant cost reductions (or *wellness credits*) to insureds that comply with wellness initiatives. Similarly, insurers and employers that offer insureds multiple plan options frequently: reduce (or *discount*) employee contributions to insurance options that plan managers believe will be better at containing costs; and raise (or *load*) rates on alternatives that are likely to result in higher claims costs.

Finally, employers usually deduct employee contributions to point-of-coverage costs on a pre-tax basis. This reduces the net impact on take home pay because the payments aren't subject to payroll or income taxes. And for some insureds, their portion of the costs might be eligible for various tax deductions or credits.

The next place to look is at *point-of-claim costs*. First, nearly all plans cover certain preventive care services at 100%. This is valuable, but it can create confusion. Some insureds overestimate the scope of services that are covered. Others incur unexpected bills because their providers fail to bill the visits as preventive or dispense unrelated services during their appointments.

Second, some plans use copays to provide convenience or reward desired behaviors. They tend to be applied to network providers (e.g., doctors, urgent care clinics, emergency rooms) and prescriptions. The amounts that insureds pay might count toward point-of-claim maximums, like their annual out-of-pocket, or they might not; plans vary.

Third, health insurance deductibles differ greatly among plans and can be gimmicky. Unfortunately, some insureds pay a big price for incorrectly assuming that they're all the same. Following are features that they should assess when they change plans or expect to incur claims.

➢ *Family Deductible Multiples.* Insureds that cover their dependents have additional financial liability that's expressed as multiples of the self-only deductibles. Most policies cap the extra potential point-of-claim costs at twice the self-only amounts, regardless how many dependents are covered. For example, if a self-only deductible is $1,500 and the family multiple is 2-times, then the total family deductible will be $3,000.

➢ *Embedded and Aggregate Deductibles.* Insurers use one of two methods to decide when they'll start splitting point-of-claim costs with insureds in family plans. Most use *individual* (or *embedded*) deductibles where each covered family member has their own deductible, and will begin paying benefits for each individual that reaches their limit (regardless what other family members incur toward their own deductible limits). But a small number of insurers use *shared* (or *aggregate*) deductibles in which all of the claims incurred by family members are combined, and the insurers will only begin paying benefits when the full family deductible is satisfied.

➢ *Network and Non-Network Deductibles.* Managed care plans typically include separate network and non-network deductibles to discourage the use of non-network providers and simplify claims administration. But this creates higher point-of-claim costs for insureds that are treated by both network and non-network providers, or by hidden providers. Some states have attempted to legislatively fix the issue of both deductibles applying, and other states leave it to insureds to confront.

➢ *Deductible Carry-Forward.* It's possible that some or all of the deductibles paid by insureds during the final three months of their current plan year will be applied to their deductibles in the subsequent plan year. It's a valuable benefit to investigate with current and new insurers.

Fourth, the annual *out-of-pocket maximums* are limits on point-of-claim costs that insureds will pay during fixed policy periods. Similar to deductibles, these can be confusing because: there are different techniques that insurers use to classify payments; some out-of-pocket expenses might be excluded; and network and non-network payments accrue toward separate limits.

Finally, employers might use special accounts to help employees pay for qualified health care expenses.

➢ *Flexible Spending Accounts* (*FSAs*) allow employees to defer money on a pre-tax basis up to limits set by the IRS and their employers, and employers can contribute money on behalf of their employees as well.

➢ *Health Reimbursement Accounts* (*HRAs*) are used by employers to help employees pay portions of their out-of-pocket expenses. Both FSAs and HRAs have use-it-or-lose-it rules that account owners must understand.

➢ *Health Savings Accounts* (*HSAs*) can be funded with employer and employee money, and be used to pay for qualified health care expenses. But they're only allowed when the money is used in conjunction with *High Deductible Health Plans* (*HDHPs*) that meet deductible, out-of-pocket, and other requirements that are established by the IRS.

NOW IT'S YOUR TURN
Understand point-of-claim costs liability

Take 15 minutes now to ask your HR or benefits colleague, insurer, or advisor to explain the point-of-claim cost liability in your health insurance policy.

About Continuation: Understand the Rights, the Rules, & the Risks

Planned or unplanned, major life events like layoffs, divorces, and early retirements can result in the loss of employment based medical, pharmacy, dental, and vision coverage. Given the high cost of care and insurance, these scenarios can amplify peoples' problems when they're already vulnerable.

Fortunately, the federal law known as the *Consolidated Omnibus Reconciliation Relief Act* (*COBRA*) and similar state laws (or *mini-COBRA*) allow some transitioning employees to continue participating in their workplace health care plans on a short term basis. To be considered eligible, they must satisfy three criteria prior to termination. First, they were enrolled in plans that were offered by qualified employers. Second, they experienced qualifying events. And third, they were qualified beneficiaries. Insights into these requirements can be found on the Employee Benefits Security Administration and state insurance commissioners websites.

When these situations arise, someone must notify plan administrators so that they can initiate the enrollment process. For some qualifying events, like job terminations, Medicare eligibility, employee deaths, and employer bankruptcies, employers are responsible for this step and must act within 30 days. For others, such as martial separations and divorces, or children losing their dependent status, the onus falls on employees or their beneficiaries.

Within 14 days of notification, plan administrators must furnish qualified beneficiaries with written summaries of their COBRA rights, enrollment instructions, and coverage options and costs. They must treat these individuals the same as active employees in similar situations and tell them how they can get more information. Similarly, the plan must give formal explanations (or a *notice of unavailability of continuous coverage*) of their decisions to deny continuation in situations where they deem individuals to be ineligible.

People that have never been eligible for COBRA (or failed to pay attention to new hire disclosures about the price to continue in their employers' health insurance plans) are frequently shocked when they learn the cost of coverage in their COBRA notification materials. It's financially prohibitive because most employers remove their subsidies when employees leave their organizations and, as permitted under COBRA law, charge enrollees an additional 2% (or up to 50% for special circumstances) for plan administration.

The employers establish the time limits for COBRA sign-up, but it can't be fewer than 60 days from the later of the date the notification is provided or the date that the coverage ends due to the qualifying event. During this time, those that aren't eligible to join other workplace plans should evaluate all of their options including COBRA, their working spouses' plans, or individual policies purchased via government-run public exchanges or insurance agents. They should also investigate their eligibility for federal and state tax credits.

People that enroll can continue in the plans for up to 18 months, or for extended periods (up to 29 or 36 months) if they have subsequent qualifying events during their initial periods, provided that they pay their premiums. Federal law allows plan administrators to cancel coverage for enrollees that fail to pay on time, but it also forces them to retroactively reinstate coverage (to the beginning of the periods) when premiums are fully paid within established grace periods.

Unfortunately, some of the people that intend to enroll make disastrous mistakes. For example, they take too long to evaluate their options and miss their chances to enroll, or they fail to fully pay their COBRA premiums before their grace periods end. Others incorrectly assume that they'll find coverage elsewhere, and allow their rights to expire without actually having it in place.

NOW IT'S YOUR TURN
Confirm eligibility for federal or state health insurance continuation

Prior to experiencing a break in health insurance coverage, spend 15 minutes confirming your continuation rights. If you're eligible to do so, study the rules, seek further input, compare your options, and act promptly. If you determine that you aren't eligible, investigate your ability to enroll in your spouse's plan or parent's plan (if you're eligible to do so), or in plans found via insurance intermediaries or public health insurance exchanges.

Remember Your Pet

People that seek care for pets realize that it's generally different from doing so for themselves or someone they cherish. The animals are unable to describe their ailments, their average life spans are shorter, and the conditions and prognoses vary by breed. However, there's at least one big similarity: the cost to prevent, diagnose, and treat their afflictions can be expensive. This can lead to potentially difficult decisions for owners confronted by unaffordable veterinary bills.

Pet health insurance gives those that own certain domestic dogs and cats an alternative. It pays benefits for services like routine exams, vaccinations, and surgeries, and for common illnesses and injuries. It's underwritten and sold by insurers in the individual market and in workplaces, and it's frequently designed to look like traditional health insurance.

But there are differences. First, policyholders have fewer statutory rights and protections. Second, insurers are allowed to deny coverage for any reason (e.g., breeds, pre-existing conditions), and they can gradually raise rates and reduce benefits as animals age. Third, policies can limit or exclude benefits for treatments and conditions that might seem reasonable to consumers, like pregnancies or DNA testing, and impose annual and lifetime caps on benefits. And finally, it can take several months before approved claims are reimbursed.

NOW IT'S YOUR TURN
Investigate pet insurance benefits, terms, and conditions

Before purchasing pet insurance, spend 15 minutes investigating policy exclusions and limitations, read online reviews, and search for complaints that have been filed against insurers with state insurance commissioners, the Better Business Bureau, and other consumer watchdogs.

CHAPTER 16

IT'S NEARLY IRREPLACABLE

I believe that employees that apply their skills, talents, and energy are able to move mountains. When they are fully engaged at work, at home, or in their families and communities, they become powerful engines that inspire others to do the same.

Sadly, some of them are destined to endure afflictions that'll suppress or extinguish their unique gifts. As healthy as they are today, roughly 1-in-4 20-year-olds will be unable to work for a period of at least a year due to injuries or illnesses by the time they reach Age 67,[35] and nearly half of those turning Age 65 will require prolonged care in the future.[36] It's not "If?", but "Who?", "When?", "What?", "How severe?", and "How will it change their lives?"

Disability and long-term care insurance are valuable protection tools, but they're frequently overshadowed by other priorities. Similar to the following family, I find that the employees that express interest in them have previously confronted the heavy burdens, anxious moments, and unimaginable choices associated with worst-case scenarios that can often seem as tragic as death...

The fraternal twins were polar opposites, but as close as sisters could be. Angie married Roy, had a son she named Sean, and earned her living as a bookkeeper. Gretchen chose to be single and worked part-time jobs so that she could play guitar in rock cover bands on the weekends. The sisters' connection grew after their mom died of cancer, and they became inseparable when Gretchen was diagnosed with Multiple Sclerosis at Age 38.

---

[35] Social Security Administration, "Fact Sheet: Social Security" (2020, www.ssa.gov, Web, June 26, 2020).
[36] Vivian Nguyen, "AARP Public Policy Institute Fact Sheet: Long-Term Support and Services" (Washington, DC: AARP Public Policy Institute, 2017).

Other than government and non-profit programs, Gretchen didn't have many financial resources to help her as the disease progressed; she'd focused so intensely on being a musician earlier in life that she hadn't prepared for such a downfall. Worse, her friendships quickly dissolved as she withdrew from social interactions. Not long after her prognosis, she openly discussed suicide, but her sister talked her out of it.

It didn't take long for Angie and Roy to understand that Gretchen would need their support. Since he had a steady job with good benefits, she got permission from her employer to change her schedule and cut down to 30 hours a week. This allowed her to transport Gretchen to doctors' visits and therapy, assist with homemaking tasks, and pay the bills on time.

As Angie and Roy witnessed the terrible effects of Gretchen's illness, they began to discuss their own preparedness for similar fates.

"Roy, what'll we do if this happens to one of us? Or both of us?" Angie asked. "I can't imagine. And what would it do to Sean?"

Roy replied "I don't know, but we need to figure it out..."

Let's look at some of the basics that Angie and Roy need to learn as they try to understand this nearly irreplaceable aspect of their financial wellbeing.

Protect Your Workplace Earnings

In my conversations with employees at all levels, I often find that many have narrow views of the term *disability*. They frequently equate it to health conditions or associate it with DMV-issued Disabled Person parking permits. Although it's not entirely inaccurate, it overlooks the serious economic fallout that occurs when physical or mental impairments prevent individuals from performing their normal job duties and earning the incomes to which they're accustomed.

For people affected by work-related (or *occupational*) disabilities, Workers' Compensation might pay related health care bills and replace some lost income while they're incapacitated. But if their conditions are *non-occupational*, disabled individuals and their families will have to look elsewhere for the money they'll need to survive, at least until they return to work, qualify for government benefits, or die. Fortunately, there are better alternatives.

At work, employees are often covered by multiple programs. First, they usually have *salary continuation*, like *paid sick days* and *paid time-off*, to replace income that's lost due to conditions that last from a day to many weeks. Their benefits accrue in accordance with rules that are set by their employers, are tied to eligibility requirements such as years of service or full-time status, and are usually disbursed on their next paychecks.

Next, they have *Short Term Disability* (*STD*), which provides weekly benefits that can last up to 90 or 180 days for approved illness or injury related absences. They're likely to be managed by employers or insurers, and usually require continuous leaves of one to four weeks (or *elimination period*) before payments commence. While some plans offer slim benefits of 40% or 50% of employees' pre-disability earnings and others generously replace 100%, most deliver something in the middle to meet the needs of covered participants.

Prior to receiving STD payments, eligible employees must rely on their accumulated salary continuation benefits or other income streams to replace whatever's lost, or they must live without it. Similarly, after the payouts end, they must find ways to fill the financial gaps in their household budgets until they're eligible for government programs. Unfortunately, that can take many months or several years, and still not cover the lost income.

Finally, they have *Long Term Disability* (*LTD*), which offers monthly benefits for disabilities that extend beyond elimination periods that are established by their plans (usually 90 or 180 days of continuous leave). Once approved, individuals that submit claims (or *claimants*) are eligible for monthly payments equal to portions of their pre-disability workplace earnings until they return to work, qualify for Social Security Disability, or insurers' payment obligations end.

Too often, the prevailing attitudes that I find among employees are akin to "I'll worry about LTD when I become disabled," but that's too late. While many employees dismiss its importance, I find that the resourceful ones take steps to understand and adjust to key features. Seven key provisions include:

1st *Definition of disability*. This is the most important provision. It decides whether claimants are entitled to benefits. Many plans start by narrowly defining it as inabilities to perform one or more of the core functions of peoples' own occupations (*OwnOcc*). They eventually shift to broader definitions that include core functions of any occupation (*AnyOcc*). As such, claimants might be declared disabled during OwnOcc periods, but fail thereafter because they don't meet the looser AnyOcc definitions.

2nd *Type of disability*. This identifies the varying degrees of functioning that occur once insureds are deemed to be disabled. *Total disabilities* refer to insureds that are unable to perform all of the duties of their jobs, and *partial disabilities* occur when they are unable to do at least one of the duties. *Recurring disabilities* are continuations of previous disabilities, and *residual disabilities* are those that impede the claimants' abilities to function at 100% after they return to work.

3rd *Benefit duration*. This is the timeframe in which payments will be made for approved claims. Plans might reference Normal Social Security Retirement Age, but this feature is affected by other policy provisions like the definition of disability, and accommodations that employers make for claimants' rehabilitations and returns to work.

4th *Definition of earnings*. This is the amounts of covered income that insureds received prior to being deemed disabled, and that insurers use to calculate benefits. Some plans only cover fixed compensation, and others include variable compensation.

5th *Minimum and maximum monthly benefits*. This is the range of monthly payments that insurers will disperse for approved claims.

6th *Benefit reductions* (or *offsets*). These are dollar-for-dollar benefit reductions that insurers apply to claimants' benefits, and it accounts for income received from sources like Workers Compensation, state plans, or early pension payouts.

7th *Benefits taxation.* Portions of LTD payments that are paid by employers are taxable. So, if an employer pays 100% of the insurance premium, then 100% of the benefit payments will be taxed. Some employers add the premiums that they pay as taxable income to employees' paychecks (or *gross up*), thereby creating the effect of a 100% employee paid, non-taxable benefit for those that might eventually become disabled.

Outside work, an array of personal policies are available for people that lack or aren't sufficiently insured by disability coverage. Unlike group plans, these products require applicants to complete individual underwriting and provide detailed health information, and they impose limits on benefits for pre-existing conditions. But once approved, insureds can keep their policies as long as premiums are paid; their insurers can't modify or cancel them.

Non-Occupational Disability Claims

The disability claims application process is critical to those seeking benefits. Since decisions are based on legal and clinical interpretations of wording conveyed in the policies, or by claimants, physicians, or employers, it's necessary to be accurate and timely. Glitches that can delay or derail payments include: failure to provide information and records; statements that create doubts about abilities to work; and missing key appointments and deadlines.

Claimants and their representatives must take it seriously. They shouldn't lie, exaggerate, or misrepresent facts, or definitively respond to questions if they're uncomfortable with or uncertain about the answers. They should understand their coverage and rights, and monitor statements made by those involved. And, they should seek clarifications for anything they don't understand or agree with, demand opportunities to review medical records before physicians submit them to insurers, and maintain copies of all documents. Finally, they should investigate the merits of retaining attorneys that specialize in disability claims if they're worried that theirs' will be denied.

NOW IT'S YOUR TURN
Solidify your personal disability safety net

Take time now, or anytime your disability coverage changes, to ask your financial partners to explain your benefits, identify gaps that might arise in the event of a claim, and assess options to enhance your protection.

Protect Your Nest Egg

As lifespans increase, growing numbers of people will experience long term impairments that'll make it difficult or impossible to take basic care of themselves. Since professional services are expensive and not covered by health insurance, many that face these scenarios will quickly deplete their accumulated wealth. Here are recent national averages for general services:

Long Term Health Care Services	2019 National Average Annual Cost[37]
Homemaker Services	$53,772
Home Health Aide	$54,912
Adult Day Health Care	$19,236
Assisted Living Facility	$51,600
Nursing Home, Semi-Private Room	$93,072
Nursing Home, Private Room	$105,852

For perspective, Fidelity Investments, one of the nation's largest workplace retirement plan administrators, reported that average 401(k) balances in late 2019 were $182, 000 for account owners Age 60 to 69 and $38,000 for those Age 30 to 39.[38] This suggests that people that are relying on their nest eggs to pay future long term care bills won't get far, particularly if they live in places where prices are drastically higher than elsewhere in the country.

In response to the shortfall, many employees that I help admit that their plans are to do what others do: lean on family, friends, and volunteers for unpaid and untrained care. But this strategy shifts uncertain costs and incalc-

---

[37] Genworth Financial, "Cost of Care Survey" (2020, www.genworth.com, Web, December 14, 2020).
[38] Tim Parker, "What's the Average 401(k) Balance by Age" (October 30, 2020, Investopedia, www.investopedia.com, Web, December 14, 2020).

ulable stress to people that they cherish, and it's less doable for those that have smaller families, or remain single, divorced, or childless.

Fortunately, a better solution is in some people's reach. *Long Term Care insurance* (*LTCi*) is a highly regulated form of protection that helps insureds preserve their capital, remain independent, and avoid burdening others. It insures against expenses for professional in-home care, assisted living, and nursing homes, and sometimes includes benefits for services rendered by non-professional caregivers, such as house cleaning and meal preparation.

There are two types of LTCi policies. *Reimbursement* contracts provide benefits when insureds submit receipts for qualified expenses that they pay out of their pockets. And *indemnity* contracts pay fixed daily amounts regardless of the costs. The former tends to be less expensive, but is a hassle because claimants are only paid after producing receipts. The latter is typically more expensive because it's more convenient and reliable.

An important element of LTCi policies are benefit *triggers* that determine if and when claims will be paid. The first are *waiting periods* that insureds must satisfy before insurers will begin paying benefits. The average is 90 or 180 days, but it depends on the type of services received. The second are *Activities of Daily Living* (*ADL*) provisions. These require proof that insureds are unable to complete specified numbers of self-care activities like eating, bathing, dressing, and toileting, without substantial assistance.

Another important element is the *maximum benefit duration*. Since the average length of stay in nursing homes is roughly two years (2.5 years for women, 1.5 years for men),[39] it's crucial to avoid policies that prematurely terminate benefits. Typically, insurers make payments for finite periods ranging from 2 to 6 years. But some pay amounts based on benefits that accumulate over time and cease paying when the accrued amounts are gone.

Similarly, LTCi policies impose benefit caps. *Daily maximums* limit the amounts that insurers will pay for each day of covered and approved services, and *lifetime maximums* are equal to the daily maximums multiplied by the maximum benefit duration periods. A cost-saving option for married couples is to purchase *shared care* (or *pooling*) riders that allow the spouses to draw payments from single lifetime maximum benefits.

---

[39] Vivian Nguyen, "AARP Public Policy Institute Fact Sheet: Long-Term Support and Services" (Washington, DC, AARP Public Policy Institute, 2017).

Since this protection is potentially purchased decades in advance of potential claims, insureds should consider common enhancements. The first are *cost of living adjustment* (*COLA*) riders to ensure that policy maximums will rise with inflation. The second are *waiver of premium* features that eliminate claimants' needs to continue paying premium while they're drawing benefits.

Fearing the financial exposure associated with high-risk insureds, insurers scrutinize applicants' health characteristics, such as conditions, impairments, therapies, medications, and family history. They also use *exclusion and limitation* clauses to avoid potential large claims related to high risk factors such as pre-existing conditions, mental or nervous disorders, and alcohol and drug addictions.

The people that I meet that haven't built or aren't likely to build sizeable nest eggs probably won't want LTCi since the cost can be exorbitant and they would likely qualify for Medicaid in a long-term care event. Conversely, those that have accumulated a lot of wealth probably aren't concerned about such situations causing hardships for them or loved ones, so they wouldn't bother with it either. Ultimately, it seems ideally suited for households that have net worth ranging from $750,000 to $3,000,000, or that own assets that can't be easily liquidated (e.g., collectibles, family farms, business partnerships).

Given common and long-standing obstacles in the LTCi marketplace, like high costs and stringent underwriting, alternative products exist that offer similar, albeit narrower and potentially less reliable protection. For example, *Short-Term Care insurance* (*STCi*) is similar to LTCi, except that it only provides benefits for a year or less. Also, some *variable annuities* and *permanent life insurance* products offer riders that create pools of money that can be used to pay long term care expenses.

NOW IT'S YOUR TURN
Review your long term care insurance options

Spend 5 minutes asking an HR or benefits teammate if your organization offers LTCi. It's rare, but you might be able to secure coverage during the next enrollment. If not, ask your financial partners to suggest licensed LTCi agents and begin a formal process to investigate your coverage options.

Think Twice About Buying Cheap Alternatives

Limited protection plans pay benefits to insureds that experience narrowly defined conditions or require specific treatments. They're inexpensive policies that mimic certain aspects of other products, like disability and LTCi, and are increasingly common at work. Some employers offer them to help employees fill wealth protection gaps via payroll deduction. Others use them to improve perceptions of their total rewards programs, to receive extra services (e.g., enrollment, communication, administration), or to gain cost concessions elsewhere in their total rewards programs.

Accidental death and dismemberment (*AD&D*) *insurance* is typically bundled with workplace basic and supplemental term life coverage, and it provides two types of benefits. The first is known as double indemnity protection and it pays beneficiaries amounts that match their workplace benefits if insureds' deaths are accidental. The second is crudely referred to as bits-and-pieces coverage and it pays insureds pre-determined amounts for events like the loss of their limbs, sight, and hearing.

Accident, *critical illness*, and *cancer insurance* supplement medical and disability benefits with payments intended to reduce the burdens of unexpected out-of-pocket costs, lost income, and suffering linked to dreaded events and diagnoses. Accident addresses costs associated with acute injuries requiring emergency rooms, urgent care, or therapy. Critical Illness relates to conditions like heart disease, kidney disease, and other non-cancer illnesses. And cancer insurance covers breast cancer, lung cancer, leukemia, and other similar diseases.

Although some of the employees that I help are content with these types of coverage, I'm not a raving fan. Too many of them overestimate their value and reliability, erroneously liken them to comprehensive products, and incorrectly assume that their employers thoroughly vet the coverage before offering it to them. All that I'll add here is "Buyer, beware!"

NOW IT'S YOUR TURN
Evaluate your limited protection plan options

If you're considering or have already enrolled in a limited protection plan, spend 15 minutes now reviewing the policy benefits and exclusions to ensure that it's something that you can trust and want to continue.

CHAPTER 17

THE SPICE OF LIFE

There's an industry that uses every form of media to remind consumers of dangers that could, at any moment, destroy everything that they've built. Happily, they dish their doom and gloom with funny stories, catchy jingles, and promises to save customers hundreds of dollars a year.

I'm talking about property and casualty insurers, and it's difficult to name other advertisers that spend more or work harder to feed the public a steady diet of memorable spokespeople. From fictitious characters such as Flo and a talking gecko to famous celebrities like Peyton Manning and Shaquille O'Neill, they all insist that their companies are the best.

There are 3 practical reasons for *DIY financial planners* to listen to these emissaries: the risk of damage to or loss of their worldly possessions is always present; the financial exposure related to harming others is nearly unlimited; and this coverage is a major household expense for many of them. While the gambling types might roll the dice and forgo it, the employees that I help realize that it's invaluable because they could be ruined without it.

Ironically, many people ignore the incessant calls to action. In some of my seminars, I ask "By show of hands, how many of you have talked to your home or auto insurance agent in the last three years?" Fewer than half raise a hand. Then I ask those that admit they haven't to share their reasons. The explanations typically include "I call when I have a claim," "I assume that she's gonna be there if I need her," "I hate talking to him," and "It's all handled online."

Light-hearted portrayals of calamity are effective staples in property and casualty advertising, but they eclipse one of this industry's strengths: deep insight into the ingredients that give individuals and households their unique flavors. The stuff that these insurers protect represents a lot of the spice in people's lives, and the policies that they underwrite are essential to replacing most or all of whatever could be lost.

The *property* sections of these policies insure people against threats of damage, destruction, or loss of possessions like homes, automobiles, jewelry, and electronics. They tend to be easier to follow because they identify tangible items to be covered, describe the conditions in which submitted claims will be approved, and specify the amounts to be paid.

First, the property that people want to insure must be clearly identified in their policies, either explicitly or implicitly, and insurers will demand proof of ownership and value before agreeing to cover them. These items are also subject to maximum limits. In situations where items are valued at amounts exceeding the limits, amendments known as *endorsements* can be purchased to overrule standard policy features. For example, an insured who owns a lot of fine jewelry should pay extra to override a $2500 standard sub-limit in their homeowners policy by adding a separate list (or *schedule*) of the items with valid appraisals.

Second, damages and losses must be due to covered events known as *perils* in homeowner's policies and *occurrences* in auto policies. It's important to understand that claims related to some events and activities, like floods, earthquakes, and home businesses, aren't covered by typical policies. For that reason, riders or separate policies are sometimes necessary to guarantee proper protection.

Third, insurers use one of two methods to determine the amounts that they'll pay insureds for damaged or lost property (or *replacement costs*). The more common is known as *actual cash value*, and it pays to repair or replace covered items after reducing the replacement costs by depreciation and their conditions at point-of-claim. The alternative is referred to as *full replacement value*, and it restores or replaces covered items at present costs. Both formulas rely on public tools and expert appraisals in their calculations, but the latter provides better protection at higher prices.

The *casualty* (or *liability*) portions are less tangible, but might be more important because they help insureds preserve their wealth in situations where they're held legally liable for harm caused to others. They cover losses associated with ownership and use of named properties, and actions that may or may not have anything to do with them. Examples of common claims include the repairs to another driver's car after being damaged in a collision caused by an insured, or medical bills incurred by a guest who's seriously injured after a fall in a policyholder's home.

DIY financial planners should review their property and casualty policies at least bi-annually to ensure that all aspects satisfy their needs. They can begin by reviewing their policies' *declaration pages* (or *face pages*) which summarize the covered items and various dollar limits. They can also talk to their licensed agents about any life changes that have occurred, will occur, or might occur. And, just as important, they should decide if it's time to shop their coverage.

NOW IT'S YOUR TURN
Review your property and casualty policies (at least annually)

Take 15 minutes now to find and review your property and casualty policy declaration pages, and schedule a conversation with your insurance agent or insurer. You should talk to them at least annually, and when you do, be sure to disclose relevant changes (e.g., family, property, vehicles) so that they can ensure your coverage properly addresses your ongoing needs.

Protect Your Dwelling (And Related Liability)

People frequently invest fortunes in the places they reside and the contents they keep in them, so it makes sense that they should possess reliable and comprehensive protection. While there are different types of policies designed to protect different types of dwellings, all address contents, temporary housing, and liabilities, and can be upgraded to provide full protection.

Homeowners Insurance

The majority of American households are headed by people that own their homes,[40] either outright or with the aid of mortgages. Since their dwellings, related structures, and contents, represent substantial portions of their wealth and liabilities, this is essential coverage.

Four types of homeowners' policies are used to insure their property. Two are referred to as *named peril*, and they require insureds to prove that damages and losses are caused by specifically named perils. The *basic* version covers the most common perils, like fire, smoke, lightening, and theft. The *broad* version expands the basic list to include others, such as burglary, accidental water damage, falling objects, weight of ice or snow, and frozen pipes.

The other two are known as *open perils*. They require insurers to prove that damages or losses are caused by excluded perils. *Special form* versions give insureds peace-of-mind that they're protected against perils that insurers haven't specifically excluded, and *comprehensive form* versions overcome shortcomings in special form policies, such as the exclusion of perils like damage from mold and pets, by reducing the number of excluded perils. Open peril policies are more favorable to insureds than named peril options, but they're more expensive.

Regardless whether people buy named peril or open peril homeowner policies, each addresses four general needs. The first is the need to potentially repair or replace dwellings or attached structures due to damage caused by covered perils. To achieve their goal, insurers will estimate the cost to fully replace the structures if they're completely destroyed.

Next is the need to cover the costs to repair or replace other fixed and detached structures on the covered properties, like carports, sheds, fences, or gazebos. Here, insurers standardly assume that smaller percentages of the primary structures' replacement costs, like 10%, will provide adequate protection. Some insureds might find that acceptable, but others will want to upgrade their protection using applicable riders.

---

[40] Anthony Cilluffo, A.W. Geiger, and Richard Fry, "More U.S. households are renting than at any point in 50 years" (July 19, 2017, www.pewresearch.org, Web, June 26, 2020).

Additionally, insureds need to cover the costs associated with repairing or replacing contents in their properties, like furniture, clothes, electronics, kitchenware, and toys. Again, insurers base standard coverage on predefined percentages of dwelling replacement costs, such as 40% or 50%. More, policies standardly include lower sub-limits for specified items like money, gold, gift cards, and silverware. These limitations might be sufficient to replace everything that some insureds own, but not for those that have nicer things or many possessions.

It also addresses a need to cover expenses, such as hotel bills, rental fees, and incidental living costs that stem from insureds' inabilities to use their dwellings while they're being repaired or rebuilt. These features reduce financial and emotional burdens associated with the costs to reside elsewhere or occupy unsafe dwellings.

Finally, it protects insureds against the legal and financial liabilities that courts might assign to them or covered individuals for harm caused to third parties. Typically, these policies allot fixed amounts of money, like $250,000 or $500,000, to cover costs related to resolving liability lawsuits, and small amounts to quickly pay medical bills incurred by people that are physically injured by insureds' property or actions.

Renters Insurance

As the average American family shrinks, and the rate of single, divorced, and never-married adults rises, the portion of households that rent grows.[41] Although some tenants are forced to have renters insurance, most don't because they underestimate their vulnerability to common perils or incorrectly assume their landlords are responsible for damages and losses. Based on my firsthand experience, the uninsured are potentially making a costly mistake...

Years ago, my wife and I accepted a job transfer with my employer. Our house in Wisconsin sold fast, but we couldn't find a place in the Twin Cities and opted to rent an apartment for 6 months. It was

---

[41] Anthony Cilluffo, A.W. Geiger, and Richard Fry, "More U.S. households are renting than at any point in 50 years" (July 19, 2017, www.pewresearch.org, Web, June 26, 2020).

a hectic time and we operated on many assumptions; one being that renters insurance wasn't an option for us. I remember thinking "It's OK. We'll be fine."

One day, midway through our lease, my wife removed her wedding ring, set it by a sink, and left the apartment to run errands. When she returned, it was gone. She called me at work and asked "Tony, did you take my ring?" As soon as I said "No," panic ensued. We retraced her steps, turned the place upside down, and had a plumber check the drains, but it never turned up. It was gone.

The ring's fate will forever remain a mystery, but not the second-guessing. Had I talked to an agent, I could've secured a renter's policy and jewelry endorsement for almost nothing, and we could've avoided spending thousands out of pocket to replace it.

I do my best to help renters understand the reasons that they should insure themselves and those that live with them. First, they need to cover costs to repair or replace their personal property. Since replacement costs can't be based on the occupied dwellings, insurers frequently offer minimum amounts of coverage that can be increased in increments of $10,000 or $25,000. These policies also feature sub-limits and exclusions for certain items, like jewelry and home business items, that can be addressed via endorsements.

Next, they need to cover lodging expenses, like short term hotel stays or long term apartment rentals, and offsite storage, which they'll incur if they're forced from their dwellings due to damage to or destruction of the property. This allows insureds to live elsewhere for reasonable amounts of time without draining their savings and nest eggs, or borrowing money.

Finally, landlords are responsible for shared living spaces like sidewalks, pools, and garages, but tenants are responsible for harm that they, their dependents, or their pets cause to others. As such, they need protection against expenses associated with liabilities. Typical policies provide fixed amounts like $50,000 or $100,000 to cover related costs and legal fees, and smaller amounts to quickly pay for guests' medical bills if they're injured in insureds' dwellings.

Perhaps the biggest incentive for renters insurance is its cost. While average monthly premiums are low ($15 in 2017),[42] insureds that bundle it with other policies might not pay anything due to multi-policy discounts offered by insurers. For example, a couple paying $1800 a year for an auto policy on two vehicles might qualify for a 10% discount on their total premium; the entire cost of some renters' policies.

Condominium Insurance

Driving in cities or near tourist destinations, people are likely to see condominium complexes being built. They're popular with adults of all ages because they combine the perks of owning and renting. But behind the beautiful facades, gorgeous views, and privacy walls, owners will find some of the biggest headaches in residential insurance.

The complexity starts with their physical design. Condo owners share property like garages, walkways, and pools with others in their enclaves, and ceilings, floors, and walls with their adjacent neighbors. It continues with patchworks of related laws. In some states, condo associations are responsible for anything viewed as studs-out, such as roofing, siding, and plumbing, and unit owners are liable for everything walls-in, like lighting, flooring, and cabinets. In other states, duties aren't as clearly defined. Next, the associations themselves have bylaws governing the conditions and commitments that residents must obey, and they must secure insurance that reflects an array of needs. The complexity ends with each resident's personal circumstances.

Since any losses that aren't covered by associations' master policies or condo owners' policies become condo owners' responsibilities, personal policies need to be rock solid. First, they must protect against the perils that affect the units or spread into neighboring units, and large claims that are incurred by condo associations but are spread proportionately among all of the members (known as a *loss assessment*). This includes repairs required by condo associations' bylaws and personal modifications.

---

[42] National Association of Insurance Commissioners, "NAIC Releases Report on Homeowners Insurance" (November 25, 2019, www.content.naic.org, Web, June 26, 2020).

Next, they must insure condo owners' personal possessions and small modifications that they make to their units. Insurers will base the coverage limits on portions of dwelling replacement costs, like 40% or 50%, and include sub-limits for special items like jewelry. If the limits aren't adequate to protect the insureds' possessions, or exclude perils or activities like earthquakes, floods, and home-based businesses, then appropriate endorsements or separate policies should be purchased. They should also cover costs associated with the insureds' inabilities to use their dwellings due to related repairs and construction.

Finally, they must cover condo owners against broad legal and financial liabilities that might be assigned to them or covered individuals for harm caused to third parties. Unlike single-family homes, the communal nature of these dwellings exposes insureds to liabilities for harm to guests that might happen outside the units, but while on association property. In addition, owners that allow guests to occupy their property for extended periods, especially if they're charging rent, must design their coverage to protect against those people's actions as well.

Since condominium ownership and liability can be complex, condo owners should retain intermediaries that possess the experience and insights necessary to properly design their policies. They'll need copies of their condo association bylaws and master insurance policies, detailed knowledge of how their property will be used (e.g., modifications, rentals, homebased business), and the willingness to spend enough to secure protection that's free of gaps.

NOW IT'S YOUR TURN
Create a video inventory of your personal property

Take time now to use your smartphone or tablet to create a video inventory of your household possessions. Remember to record all of the items in your closets, drawers, cupboards, attic, and any attached or unattached structures and storage spaces. Once complete, transfer the video to your cloud, email, or other long-term storage device for safekeeping.

Protect Your Auto (And Related Liability)

Most of the people that I help own at least one vehicle. Given the financial and legal risks associated with getting behind the wheel, it's wise for them to insure themselves and the licensed drivers in their households.

Auto insurance is governed and regulated by the states, so variations in coverage are common. Major differences stem from the legal processes that are used to settle disputes between parties involved in accidents. Nearly 4-in-5 are known as *at-fault states* because they deem drivers that cause incidents to be responsible for any harm that befalls those that aren't to blame. The rest are *no-fault states* because they presume that involved drivers are accountable for their own property damage and bodily injuries irrespective of who's at fault.

Regardless, auto insurance addresses three protection needs. First, it covers the cost to repair or replace vehicles when they're involved in collisions with other vehicles or objects, or in rollover accidents. Known as *collision coverage*, payments are typically limited to the fair market values of the insured vehicles prior to the accidents, but riders can be added to cover the full replacement costs. Second, it pays expenses related to damages or losses due to unusual non-collision events like theft, hail, vandalism, or falling trees. This is referred to as *comprehensive coverage*, and it also pays for other related services, like roadside assistance and car rentals. These features aren't mandatory, but consumers that finance their vehicle purchases through lenders are often required to have them.

Third, it covers liabilities that are associated with bodily injuries and property damage. Some policies do so by splitting coverage into three separate limits: one for expenses related to bodily injuries sustained by one individual; one for the total amount that'll be paid for bodily injuries to multiple people; and one to repair or replace property. It's expressed using three amounts like $100,000/$300,000/$100,000. Other policies combine all related claims under single dollar limits. Both policy types also pay insureds' legal expenses.

Casualty also addresses other costs. For example, some policies include coverage for medical and non-medical expenses incurred by injured at-fault drivers and their passengers. The more common approach, known as *personal injury protection*, pays expenses related to health care, dependent care, lost income, funeral expenses, and survivor benefits. The less typical, referred to as *medical payment protection*, only pays medical and funeral expenses. Others cover expenses that arise from accidents caused by *uninsured or underinsured motorists*, so insureds that aren't to blame don't have to pay the bills. Irrespective of whether these features are required by state law, they're good to have.

NOW IT'S YOUR TURN
Start conversations about your auto insurance needs

For what you pay for auto insurance, it's reckless to be underinsured or to overpay. Here are 3 rules to consider.

✓ *The 2-Year Rule.* If you haven't reviewed your coverage with your intermediary or insurer in the past 2 years, take time now to schedule a conversation about your current policies and areas for improvement.

✓ *The 3-Year Rule.* If you haven't shopped your coverage in the past 3 years, ask your intermediary to ensure that you're still getting quality protection at a fair price, and consider allowing other intermediaries or insurers to provide competitive quotes.

✓ *The Anytime Rule.* If you're unhappy with your coverage, intermediary, or insurer, take 15 minutes now to seek the names of others that might want you as a customer.

Boost Your Protection

Sadly, the predominance of ambulance-chaser ads and headline-grabbing lawsuits causes some of the people that I help to exhibit exaggerated fears of being sued. It's not always obvious, but I frequently see it in comments such as "I don't allow guests in my condo when I'm not around because I worry they'll get hurt and sue me" and "I won't let my teenagers babysit because I don't wanna be held responsible for anything bad that happens to somebody else's kid."

While property ownership and personal actions create obvious risks, liability disputes seldom involve awards that exceed insureds' dwelling or auto policy limits. As difficult as it is for some people to accept:

➢ Only 1.9% of all homeowner claims in 2018 were for liabilities, and the average losses for bodily injuries and property damage were $26,872 and $3,707 for medical payments;[43]

➢ Only 1.1% of auto policyholders filed liability claims for bodily injuries to others in 2018, and the average payments were $15,785.[44]

That's not to say that multi-million dollar claims and excluded perils don't exist; they clearly do. When they occur, unlucky people might take desperate measures, like liquidating their assets, filing for bankruptcy, or running from their troubles. But insureds that own *excess liability* (or *umbrella*) insurance have a little more breathing room.

People that choose to buy umbrella policies will have extra protection for claims that exceed the maximum limits on their home or auto policies. They are ideal for those that have significant wealth, high earning potential, or exposure to uncommon risks, and have underlying policies that meet minimum coverage rules. This insurance is also relatively inexpensive.

Some of the employees that I help want to know how much excess liability coverage they need. One guideline tells them to buy amounts that are

---

[43] Insurance Information Institute, "Facts + Statistics: Homeowners and renters insurance" (2020, www.iii.org, Web, June 26, 2020).
[44] Insurance Information Institute, "Facts + Statistics: Auto insurance" (2020, www.iii.org, Web, June 26, 2020).

equal to the greater of either their household net worth or their projected net future earnings, but rounded to the next higher million dollars. Notable exceptions to this rule of thumb include those that are landlords, own vacant property, or are public figures and can be sued for libel or slander; they might want extra protection.

Business

Sometimes, I help *DIY financial planners* that use their homes, vehicles, or other possessions to generate income, but fail to realize that their personal policies exclude claims related to side gigs, property rentals, or homebased businesses. Worse, they're unaware that those activities can result in the reduction or denial of payments for legitimate losses that aren't related in any way to their business activities.

The solution is for them to ask their property and casualty agents to identify exclusions that might apply, and to help them purchase the policies (e.g., professional liability, general liability, errors and omissions coverage) that are necessary to ensure that their personal assets and their money making endeavors are properly covered. Failing to take these simple steps leaves them exposed to risks that probably dwarf whatever income that they might earn.

CHAPTER 18

OLD VILLAINS, NEW TRICKS

How can anyone place a value on personal identities? Plaintiffs' lawyers try to quantify it when arguing that their clients' good names have been tarnished, and cyber protection companies do it when they advertise "We'll pay up to $10,000 to restore your good name." But it's hard to monetize because it's enmeshed in nearly every crucial aspect of peoples' lives...

➤ Drive to work	➤ Secure a job	➤ Apply for a loan
➤ Rent an apartment	➤ Buy a home	➤ Pay a utility bill
➤ See a doctor	➤ Get married	➤ Open a bank account
➤ Coach youth sports	➤ Register to vote	➤ Take a newborn home

Unfortunately, criminals that aren't satisfied with or want to protect their identities find that it's easy to use those belonging to other people. The issue is so pervasive that it ensnared 14.2 million consumer credit card accounts and 158 million social security numbers in 2017,[45] and nobody's immune.

For example, a Hollywood beautician stole the identities of A-list clients like Jennifer Aniston and Anne Hathaway,[46] so she could spend hundreds of thousands of dollars that wasn't hers. A teenager in Minnesota hacked Paris Hilton's phone and illegally posted her personal information online; it was subsequently used by other con artists that ran a different scam on her.[47] And

---

[45] Identity Theft Resource Center (ITRC) and CyberScout, *2017 Annual Data Breach Year-End Review* (San Diego: ITRC, 2017, pg. 5).

[46] Jill Serjeant, "Jennifer Aniston named as victim in salon fraud" (August 18, 2010, www.reuters.com, Web, June 26, 2020).

[47] The Associated Press, "Paris Hilton Hacker Gets 11 Months" (September 14, 2005, www.cbsnews.com, Web, June 26, 2020).

hundreds of the richest people in America had theirs pilfered by a restaurant busboy.[48]

In my workplace seminars, I see the problem spreading. 10 to 15 years ago, maybe 1-in-10 of the people that I met admitted that they were victimized by identity thieves, and they were usually pitied by their colleagues. In recent years, 1-in-2 confess to it, and nobody seems surprised.

➤ A senior business executive discovered that someone in another state had stolen his credit card information and was using it to make very large purchases. He was irritated when he learned that neither his credit card company nor the local police would pursue the case.

➤ A 60-year-old office administrator received an amusing email from a good friend and thought her grandkids would enjoy it. Unfortunately, a link to an infected website was embedded in the message. When her recipients opened the email, their devices were infected by a virus that transferred bank and credit card information to faceless thugs in another country. She felt terrible that she'd inadvertently caused so much pain.

➤ A group of U.S. employees was told that a coworker had improperly stored their data on a flash drive that was subsequently stolen. The HR staff assembled the affected individuals so a cyber security expert could talk about spotting signs of identity theft and offer a free year of identity protection, but everyone knew the gesture was insufficient and lame.

The old villains haven't gone away. They found new tricks and are more dangerous than ever.

---

[48] The Associated Press, "Man Held on Identity-Theft Charges" (March 21, 2001, www.latimes.com, Web, June 26, 2020).

Know Your Enemy

Identity thieves use victims' information to commit theft or fraud. Most want *Personally Identifiable Information* (*PII*) like names, dates of birth, Social Security numbers, and places of birth so they can steal money, evade arrest, or avoid prosecution. But some want *Protected Health Information* (*PHI*) like family health histories, biometric identifiers, and device identifiers to engage in blackmail, insurance fraud, and human trafficking.

When the people that I help share their stories, their attackers seem to fit in one of two categories. Classic crooks employ techniques that have existed for decades. *Burglars* snag purses, mail, tax returns, or workplace personnel files, or engage accomplices that have access to victims' PII or PHI. *Dumpster divers* rummage through victims' trash. *Impersonators* convince third parties like public utilities, mobile phone providers, or banks that they are the victims, represent their victims, or are their victims' employers or landlords. And *squatters* use post office change of address forms to divert mail containing their victims' information.

The contemporary crowd is technologically sophisticated. *Skimmers* use special data capturing devices to copy account numbers when processing credit card payments. *Spammers* use junk emails and texts that appear legitimate, but are gateways to scams. *Internet spies* use websites, mobile apps, or downloadable programs to infect victims' devices with malicious software that secretly monitors activities and grabs data. *Phishers* use legit-sounding websites, emails, or texts to convince victims to provide their PII or PHI, and *spoofers* manipulate phone networks and caller ID features to do the same. *Hackers* penetrate smartphones, PCs, and cloud-based networks and applications, and *breachers* hack systems used by organizations so that they can sell sensitive data and information on the digital black market (or *Dark Web*).

NOW IT'S YOUR TURN
Determine if your data is on the dark web

Spend 15 minutes learning if your PII or PHI is circulating on the Dark Web by visiting www.haveibeenpwned.com. If it is, ask your financial partners to help you assess and minimize the threat.

Limit Your Exposure

Most of the people that I meet aren't prepared for the costs, stress, and complexities, associated with attacks on their PII and PHI, and I doubt that any of them want to waste their time and energy restoring their identities. For this reason, they should take steps to limit their exposure to fraud and theft.

Physical Space and Surroundings

Identity thieves gather a lot of PII and PHI by getting close to victims and perusing the physical spaces they inhabit. People that want to defend against these attacks can start by purging their domains (e.g., purses, vehicles, households) of unneeded or improperly guarded items, and destroying unessential materials with crosscut shredders. They should also be wary of eavesdropping whenever they're disclosing their PII and PHI in public spaces.

Bank Checks and Debit Cards

Most identity thieves are primarily interested in stealing money. People that want to prevent attacks on their bank accounts should curtail their use of checks because each one includes bank names, routing numbers, account numbers, and signatures. They should also arrange to collect supplies of new checks at local bank branches rather than via the mail, and use credit cards instead of debit cards for financial transactions because it shifts the burdens of dealing with fraudulent activities to their financial partners.

Electronic Devices and Applications

Smart devices, laptops, and cloud accounts are powerful tools in consumers' hands, but are equally useful gateways to their PII and PHI. Those that want to protect themselves should regularly install updates and security patches on their devices, and never transmit sensitive data on public computers or over unsecure Wi-Fi networks. And, as difficult as it is for some to do, they should never post messages like "Just arrived in Vegas!" or images embedded with descriptive locational references on their social media sites.

Security Alerts

People trust their financial partners with their life savings, lending agreements, and insurance protection, but often ignore their security alerts. Those that want to reduce their odds of being victimized when vendors notify them of corporate data breaches should monitor their credit reports and take precautionary steps prescribed by these organizations. They might also consider going paperless because it makes it harder for others to steal their PII or PHI.

Passcode Protection and Authentication

Crooks can do a lot of damage with a little PII or PHI, Internet access, and trial-and-error guesswork. For that reason, people that want to decrease the likelihood of being hacked should adopt strategies to protect their passcodes.

A high-tech option involves the purchase of 256-bit encryption software. This allows users to password-protect their data and documents in ways that virtually guarantee that protected items can never be hacked. Many of these products also generate, remember, and assess the strength of passcodes.

A low-tech alternative entails the manual management of self-generated passcodes. Here, people establish multiple levels of passcode security based on the types of material being transmitted or stored in their online accounts.

- ✓ *Low security* accounts that don't include PII or PHI, such as job sites and news feeds, share one simple passcode that's changed at least annually.
- ✓ *Moderate security* accounts that store some PII or PHI, like social network and retailers' sites, share a moderately complex passcode that's changed at least semi-annually.
- ✓ *High security* accounts that require and retain substantial amounts of PII or PHI, like financial partners and mobile phone companies, use complex and sometimes unique passcodes that are changed every 90 days.

Where possible, people should also consider using a site access verification process known as *two-factor* (or *multi-factor*) *authentication*. This forces them to key-in additional codes that are digitally transmitted to them when they want to gain entry to sensitive accounts. Those that want to determine if their financial partners offer it can visit www.twofactorauth.org.

Protect Your Identity

In response to the threat, a growing field of workplace and public-domain vendors are offering consumers protection. While they can help, there are significant variations in features and benefits, and discerning between them can be challenging. Generally, there are two degrees of support.

For less handholding, there are basic solutions designed to monitor people's PII and PHI, and alert them to potentially unauthorized, unusual, or harmful activities. These services tend to be free or inexpensive, but require customers to handle most of the clean-up work once they've been notified.

For more handholding, there are comprehensive options. When attacks occur, vendors offer services that might include: expert counselling to educate and help victims undo the damage; case managers that intervene and work with lenders, collectors, etc., for the victims; identity restoration that addresses related legal issues; and monetary reimbursement to replace out-of-pocket expenses or lost wages related to the crimes.

Restore Your Identity

Occasionally, I meet employees that have had their identities completely stripped from them. It's truly breathtaking and difficult to believe that situations like the following can occur...

> *During a workplace seminar, a middle-aged administrator shared her personal insight into an extreme case of identity theft with her colleagues and me. She said that thieves used her PII to create a fake identity and embarked on a multi-state crime spree that led to multiple warrants for her arrest. The damage to her name and reputation was so severe that she'd spent over $10,000 on legal fees. She also needed to secure "identity validation" letters signed by Judges anytime she applied for jobs, insurance, or credit, or opened financial accounts. When a colleague asked how she realized she had a problem, she said "When a half-dozen police were surrounding my house."*

Thankfully, the vast majority of identity crimes aren't life shattering, and the first sign of trouble doesn't involve police knocking at the door. The people that I help typically realize they've been victimized when they:

- ➢ Stop receiving residential postal service for no apparent reason
- ➢ Start receiving grossly inaccurate account statements from current financial partners
- ➢ Start receiving calls from debt collectors seeking payment for unfamiliar bills
- ➢ Stop receiving statements for their financial accounts
- ➢ Start receiving confusing calls from current financial partners regarding existing services
- ➢ Lose the ability to make outbound calls or receive texts on their smartphone

Sadly, damage to PII or PHI isn't the only hardship that victims face. They will spend considerable time and effort, and sometimes money, restoring it; minor events might take hours to resolve, and severe ones may never disappear. There's also psychological effects; the worse the crime, the longer the sense of vulnerability and distrust might linger. Regardless, it's important for victims to take quick steps to stop the bleeding and repair the damage.

1st *Scrutinize The Messenger.* Before reacting to notifications that identity crimes might have occurred, people must assess the authenticity of the messages. Some scams start when villains convince victims that thefts or fraud were already perpetrated, and they're attempting to help.

2nd *Assess The Damage.* The best place for potential victims to begin their assessments is by reviewing their credit reports. They should examine at least one and determine the extent to which criminals compromised existing accounts, opened new ones, or altered information to avoid detection.

3rd *Change Passcodes.* Everyone should regularly change their passcodes. But it's especially important for those that suspect or know that they've been victimized. In those situations, people might need their financial partners' help to reset and restore accounts if they've been hijacked in ways that impede their ability to close the breaches.

4th *Notify Financial Partners.* People that suspect or know crimes occurred should contact their financial partners' fraud departments and explain the circumstances, request that accounts be frozen or closed, and seek insights into unauthorized activities. For accounts that are fraudulently created, they should demand that they be frozen immediately. If additional proof is required, subsequent calls might be necessary.

5th *Initiate A Fraud Alert.* Victims should work with their financial partners to place free fraud alerts on their credit reports. *Initial alerts* last a year and are used when crimes are suspected. *Extended alerts* last 7 years and are used when crimes are confirmed.

6th *File An Identity Theft Report.* Victims should report crimes to the Federal Trade Commission by filing reports at www.identitytheft.gov or calling 877.ID.THEFT. Once completed, victims receive affidavits that they can present to institutions as proof their identities were fraudulently used.

7th *File A Police Report.* For severe or ongoing cases, or situations where victims know the suspects, they should file reports with local police. Once submitted, copies of the reports should be retained since they might be needed to file applicable insurance claims.

8th *File Agency Reports.* For crimes involving social security numbers, victims should call the Social Security Administration at 800.269.0271 or visit a local office. For fraud related to tax returns, the IRS should be contacted at 800.908.4490.

In severe cases, it might be wise to engage lawyers that have experience with identity crimes and can help manage the recovery process. This includes working with financial partners, employers, and government agencies, and dealing with the civil and criminal aspects of these situations.

NOW IT'S YOUR TURN
Review your credit history reports for unauthorized or unfamiliar activity

Spend 15 minutes reviewing your credit history reports. If you find information that you suspect relates to identity crime, take the prescribed steps and contact each credit agency's fraud department:

Equifax	www.equifax.com	800.525.6285
Experian	www.experian.com	888.397.3742
Transunion	www.transunion.com	800.680.7289

Help Your Family

I meet a lot of employees that have been compelled to help their children or parents unravel identity crimes. Here's a good example:

A grocery store manager was stunned when her 18-year-old was barred entry in the U.S. Army because of unpaid bills and disqualifying credit. She was thoroughly upset and he was adamant that he'd never done anything to establish a credit history, much less do what the recruiter was claiming. She was advised to call the credit agencies.

It took a few phone calls for the mother and son to discover the depth of the problem. Unbeknownst to them, a person they'd never met had stolen the soldier-to-be's PII and used the ill-gotten information to engage in bank and credit card fraud. As they investigated further, they learned the crime had been occurring for many years.

The sickening experience tested their faith and patience in the nation he was volunteering to serve, but they found help through her employer's benefits program and ultimately prevailed. One year and thousands of dollars later, his name was cleared and he was allowed to enlist.

Similar to the soldier-to-be, a million minors are targeted annually[49] because abuses often remain undetected for years. Parents and guardians can protect their kids by adding their phone numbers to the national do-not-call registry, opting them out of credit card solicitations, monitoring their credit reports, and placing security freezes on their credit reports.

More, they should teach them to never: share their PII or PHI with strangers; keep Social Security cards with them; open emails, texts, or other mess-

---

[49] Herb Weisbaum, "More than 1 million children were victims of ID theft last year" (June 21, 2018, www.nbcnews.com, Web, June 26, 2020).

ages from strangers; and post geocoded pictures taken with smart phones on social media sites.

And, although the problem is pervasive among the elderly, reliable crime figures don't exist. Criminals prey on these individuals because they tend to have substantial assets, are easily deceived, and are unlikely to engage police. People can help them by monitoring their bank accounts, accessing and reviewing their credit reports, creating durable powers of attorney for finance, adding their residential phone numbers to the national do-not-call registry, and opting them out of credit card solicitations at www.optoutprescreen.com and direct mail solicitations at www.dmachoice.org.

NOW IT'S YOUR TURN
Help those you cherish preserve their identities

Once you've taken steps to preserve and protect your PII and PHI, take 15 minutes to help those that you cherish do the same.

CHAPTER 19

MAKE THINGS RIGHT

Throughout their lives, people create legacies that reflect their best and worst attributes and achievements. From highlights that they hope will be etched in stone to lowlights that they pray will be swept away, they leave their marks. They just don't know when their time will end.

Many of the *DIY financial planners* that I meet aren't financially or legally ready for their final chapters. By the show-of-hands questions that I ask during my workplace seminars, I find that roughly 3-in-10 have a Last Will & Testament, but less than 2-in-10 have documents that have been updated in the past 3 to 5 years. The ratios get worse when I ask audiences about other legacy planning tools.

Then, when I ask "What prevents you from acting?" some share logical reasons like "It triggers bad memories" or "It reminds me that I'm going to die alone." Others volunteer indefensible excuses such as "I don't have anything that anyone will want" or "I'll let my kids deal with it." But the most common justification is simply "I'm too busy to think about it."

Whatever their rationale, their failure to proactively plan for their inevitable passing sets the stage for unnecessary messes for themselves and those they cherish. In an effort to shake them from their zombie-like approaches, I invite them to imagine scenarios where their doctors inform them that they have a month or two to live, and then I ask "What will you do to ensure that you're remembered the way that you want to be remembered?"

Your Legacy Planning Toolbox

Legacy planning gives people extraordinary power when they have none. It's a chance to have their voices heard and desired actions taken when they are silenced by loss-of-capacity or death. It's a process that helps them dismantle personal and institutional barriers so that they can maintain control, care for loved ones, safeguard property, and keep their promises. Luckily, it's never been cheaper or easier to put it to good use and to make things right.

Powers of Attorney (POAs)

These documents allow people (or *grantors*) to appoint others to legally act on their behalf as *attorneys-in-fact* in situations where they either don't want to make decisions, or aren't able to do so because they're unavailable or incapacitated.

Although there are many types of POAs, two are commonly used in legacy planning. *POAs for Health Care* (or *health care proxies*) allow grantors to legally authorize their preferred attorneys-in-fact to make health-related decisions for them if they're incapacitated, and *POAs for Finance and Property* basically do the same thing for financial and real estate matters. Both documents can be written in ways that make them effective at all times (or *durable POAs*) or only when activated by specific events (or *springing POAs*).

Given the rights that grantors transfer via POAs, they should ensure that their attorneys-in-fact are reliable individuals that understand their wishes. They should also name *alternate attorneys-in-fact* in case their first choices for the role are incapacitated or deceased when they're called upon. And it should be clear that the grantors are mentally competent when they enact these documents.

Living Wills

There was a time when many of the people that I helped knew the tragic story of a woman who unwillingly became the face of a national debate over the right to life and death. And the unprecedented legal tug-of-war over her survival was a continuous news headline...

Terri Schindler was born in 1963 to Robert and Mary. She met Michael Schiavo in 1982 and married him in 1984.

Although she was young, healthy, and attractive, she was uncomfortable with her weight and tried some extreme diets. One led her to replace solid foods with excessive amounts of fluids, and it caused her to suffer a terrible brain injury in February 1990 that left her in a permanent vegetative state.[50] She was 26.

Terri didn't have a Living Will to communicate her preferences, so Michael was appointed her legal guardian. He sought treatment for her for several years, but none was effective. Then, in May 1998, he legally petitioned to have her feeding tube removed because he felt she wouldn't have wanted to live in that manner. Her family and friends felt otherwise, and fought to deny the request. In the absence of her own testimony, others were compelled to decide her fate.

In late-March, 2005, Michael prevailed. Terri survived for a week after being removed from the machines that kept her alive for nearly 15 years. She succumbed on March 31. She was 41.

Terri Schiavo's ordeal reminds *DIY financial planners* to create Living Wills (or *advanced health care directives*). These are legal tools that allow people to convey their preferences for life-sustaining medical care and organ donation in cases where they become incapacitated, might not recover, and can't express themselves. Similar to POAs, these documents are enforceable when it's clear that people were mentally competent when they created them.

NOW IT'S YOUR TURN
Secure your Powers of Attorney and Living Will

Take time to create or update your POAs and Living Wills. You might find that your financial partners and state governments offer basic documents for free, or you can pay an online provider or local attorney to create personalized versions that might be more reliable. And while you're at it, help those that you cherish take the same steps.

---

[50] Unattributed, "Terri Schiavo's Story" (www.terrischiavo.org, June 26, 2020).

Funeral and Burial Pre-Plans

Funeral and burial pre-planning creates opportunities for people to share their preferences for these services and to control related decisions that'll otherwise fall to their survivors. Over the years, I've observed growing interest among those that I help, presumably because costs are rising, options are expanding, taboos are fading, and consumer protection is improving.

Some people favor informal approaches, like writing lists of their desires relating to their obituaries, wakes, services, and burials. This can be valuable to survivors because it reduces uncertainty, but it doesn't eliminate the need to coordinate and pay for services, and it doesn't guarantee that their wishes will be observed. Others prefer formal approaches to minimize the chaos of last minute planning, like recording their precise instructions and signing pre-payment agreements with service providers.

Regardless of the pre-planning approach, their first step is to identify and assess funeral homes, and to focus on those that are licensed, reputable, stable, and can accommodate their preferences. This can be completed by asking family, friends, or Employee Assistance Program counsellors, searching provider directories on the Funeral Consumer Alliance at www.funerals.org or National Funeral Directors Association at www.nfda.org, and investigating complaints registered with state governmental agencies.

Next, they should verify that the agreements that they're considering include provisions that will protect them, those they cherish, and their estates. This means confirming that the contracts are *transferable* in cases where they move out of the area, *cancelable* if the providers make major changes without their prior approval, and *revocable* by the customers at any time. It also means that all services, prices, and future requests for changes made by customers or their representatives need to be clearly articulated.

Since a lot of money is tied up in pre-pay plans, it's wise to make three demands before signing these contracts. First, pre-paid amounts should be fully refundable without penalty, particularly if funeral homes file for bankruptcy. Second, interest earned on the principal payments must be paid to the customers' accounts. Third, any unspent funds must be returned to the contract holders' estates. If these requests aren't acceptable to the service providers, consumers should look elsewhere or create their own pre-pay plan by saving the necessary funds in personal bank accounts that are *payable on death* (*POD*) to the funeral home.

Life Insurance

These are policies in which insurers agree to pay named individuals or entities (or *beneficiaries*) pre-determined amounts if insureds die while they're covered. Some people hate it, but most embrace the idea that they can create instant windfalls upon death that'll help those they cherish pay final expenses, debts, and taxes, and replace lost income and fulfill shared dreams.

Term life insurance is the most common. It pays benefits when insureds die during the policy periods, and it ceases to have value if premiums aren't paid within given grace periods or the insureds are alive when the contract terms expire. *Permanent* life insurance isn't as common. Like term, it pays specified amounts at the time of insureds' deaths, but it's designed to continue as long as they're alive and their premiums are paid. Both types of coverage pay proceeds to insureds' named beneficiaries or their estates, provided that the deaths aren't the results of excluded events.

Since term life tends to be inexpensive and easy to administer, employers often offer it (instead of permanent life) as a two-tiered workplace perk. The first tier is employer-paid *basic* term life. Benefit amounts might be fixed, like $25,000 or $50,000, or they're based on employees' earnings, such as 100% or 150% of wages. The second tier is employee-paid *supplemental* term life. Similar to basic term life, the cash benefits are predetermined by employers to be either fixed amounts or multiples of employees' earnings.

Basic and supplemental term life offer employees many advantages. Both are guaranteed up to specific amounts without *evidence of insurability* (*EOI*) and can often be kept on a self-paid basis when employment terminates. The costs tend to be affordable, employee premiums are paid via payroll deduction, and death benefits might double for accidental deaths.

But there are disadvantages to workplace plans. First, the group coverage generally ceases 30 days after employment ends. Second, supplemental life rates are age-banded in 5-year increments and increase anytime participants cross new age-thresholds. Third, healthier individuals can usually find better policies in private markets. And finally, employees have minimal control over the policy features because they're procured by their employers.

231

Let's pause here. A common rule of thumb for working-aged adults is to have life insurance that's equal to 3 to 10 times their gross annual incomes. This guidance means that many employees can secure most or all of the coverage that they need in the workplace. Here's an example:

> Jasmin's never had life insurance, but she recently began working for an employer that'll help her fill this gap. It offers her a fully paid basic life benefit of 100% of her annual salary, and it guarantees that she can buy extra term life coverage up to 2-times her annual earnings without providing evidence of insurability.
>
> She uses an online calculator provided by her employer's term life insurer to estimate the money that her husband Len and her 10-year-old daughter Mia will need if she dies prematurely. It projects $15,000 to pay her final health, funeral, and burial expenses, and $100,000 to settle the mortgage, credit cards, and car loans. It also notes that they will need to replace the after-tax benefits of her $60,000 annual gross earnings, and the $100,000 of disposable income that they'd otherwise save in the coming years to fund Mia's college education.
>
> In minutes, Jasmin realizes the need for life insurance and is relieved to learn that she can secure up to $180,000 of coverage at work for a reasonable price and without a lot of hassle.

Workplace term life gives *DIY financial planners* opportunities to secure valuable protection, but they need to take extra steps to ensure that it's adequate to meet their needs. First, they should identify any workplace income, like overtime pay, commissions, and bonuses, which might be excluded from (or not covered by) their group policies' *definition of earnings*. Failing to notice omitted compensation can result in less coverage than is desired.

Next, they should compare the features and benefits of their work-based supplemental term life versus individual term life policies that they can find in the personal marketplace. After all, they might discover that they can get better coverage elsewhere, or that they can maximize the advantages that both types of coverage provide. They might also consider buying some permanent life insurance because value that accumulates in the policy can be used to pay future policy premiums, provide retirement income, or serve as emergency savings vehicles.

Jasmin doubts that she needs life insurance equal to 10-times her income, but realizes that her workplace coverage isn't enough to satisfy all of her family's needs if she dies. She determines that another $200,000 will cover the shortfall, and happily discovers that the coverage that she needs (a 20-year individual term life policy found on a popular website) costs less than $20 per month.

And employees should secure coverage for their spouses. Although some employers provide fully-paid basic term life to cover the death of spouses and children, it's usually only sufficient to pay for funeral and burial expenses. As such, a separate needs-assessment is necessary. For employed spouses, the rule of thumb or workplace calculators can be useful. But for self-employed spouses and unpaid homemakers, it may be better to use estimates that are between 50% and 100% of the employees' coverage, or to precisely quantify the potential financial loss associated with their deaths.

Since workplace supplemental term life typically doesn't permit employees to purchase amounts equal to their own for their spouses, coverage must be found elsewhere.

Len's income has been unpredictable since he lost his full-time job a year ago. He receives unemployment, works cash-only side gigs, and spends time caring for Mia.

Jasmin assumes that Len nets $30,000 of annual income. The rule of thumb suggests that the family needs $90,000 to $300,000 of life insurance to fill the gap if he dies. She finds that she can secure $60,000 of coverage for him via her supplemental term life policy at work (if she buys $120,000 for herself), and $100,000 via a 20-year individual term life policy that she finds online for $15 per month.

She talks to Len, and he agrees that they should purchase it. After completing the application process, he's approved and the couple has enough protection to ensure that Jasmin and Mia will be ok if he dies.

When presented with opportunities to secure life insurance for their minor children (where parents are the beneficiaries), many employees that I help prefer to decline the coverage because they're superstitious; they worry that buying these policies might curse their kids. But others do it to proactively address financial gaps that accompany these devastating scenarios. For those that are interested, workplace supplemental term life plans typically offer opportunities to secure small $5,000 or $10,000 policies for as little as $1.00 or $2.00 per month.

NOW IT'S YOUR TURN
Secure adequate life insurance protection

Take 15 minutes now to conduct a life insurance needs assessment using online calculators offered by your financial partners or reputable service providers. Once complete, compare your needs with your current coverage. If a gap exists, ask them how they can help, or determine how a reputable life insurance agent can help you secure adequate protection.

Last Will & Testament

The United States uses a legal process called *probate* to ensure that deceased citizens' (or *decedents'*) affairs are settled in proper and orderly fashions, and to protect their survivors and honor their final wishes where practical. It's initiated when government institutions issue death certificates and local courts are notified of peoples' passing.

Since municipal courts aren't adequately staffed to unravel estates, they need community members to step forward and act on behalf of decedents. In cases where people die without having legally appointed someone to manage probate for them, state-specific *intestate* (or *dying without a will*) rules are followed and reliable administrators are judicially selected to handle related tasks.

While many people ultimately opt for this approach, including famous public figures like Aretha Franklin, Sonny Bono, and Kurt Cobain,[51] it can create unnecessary hardships and frustration for survivors. Fortunately, there's a better alternative.

---

[51] Andrea Mandell, "7 legendary stars who died without wills: Aretha Franklin, Prince, and more" (August 22, 2018, www.usatoday.com, Web, June 26, 2020).

Last Will & Testaments (*Wills*) are written expressions of decedents' (or *testator's*) wishes and instructions for settling their affairs. They are presented to the appropriate courts by appointed representatives (or *executors*), and are allowed to guide the unwinding of the estates if presiding judges or magistrates are satisfied that the documents meet statutory requirements and the decedents were competent when they signed them.

A key function of Wills is to identify individuals that are pertinent to the estate. First, the documents name decedents' dependents, in particular minor and adult-dependent children. Second, they name executors that'll handle the decedents' affairs. Given that probate can be complex, time consuming, and thankless, and that disputed decisions can result in lawsuits, it's wise to choose the right representatives. Specific responsibilities can include:

➢ Releasing public obituaries
➢ Safeguarding and insuring property
➢ Paying debts, expenses, and taxes

➢ Inventorying assets and liabilities
➢ Temporarily managing the estate
➢ Making distributions of the net estate

Since managing this entire process is a big job, executors are entitled to compensation for their time and to retain separate attorneys to protect their personal interests in related matters (if needed). And in some situations, testators might hire professional executors or assign multiple co-executors to minimize the headaches and liabilities for the designated executors.

Third, Wills name *guardians* to care for minor and dependent-adult children, and individuals or entities (or *trustees*) to manage funds bequeathed to the kids (if there are concerns about guardians' ability to do so). In cases involving divorce, the birth parents are usually appointed for the role unless courts rule otherwise, and some states allow children over Age 13 to nominate their preferred guardians.

Fourth, Wills name beneficiaries that are to receive property that's to be disbursed upon decedents' passing. They're often spouses, children, parents, siblings, friends, charities, estates, or business partners.

Given that Wills are affected by significant changes that occur in testators' lives, it's essential to regularly review and update them. People should confirm their previous decisions about executors, guardians, and beneficiaries (including those named as alternates that'll replace primary appointees that might not be willing or able to act) and provide revised copies to their executors and guardians.

Living Trusts

The purpose of these planning tools is to allow people to maintain control of and use their assets in the event they become incapacitated, and to efficiently transfer ownership of held assets to their heirs soon after their deaths.

Although they frequently function in conjunction with Wills, properly designed and managed living trusts offer benefits that stand-alone Wills can't. First, they can accelerate the transfers of decedents' property. Second, they can shield specific details, like naming specific valuables, from public disclosure requirements. Third, they can make it harder for disgruntled parties to legally challenge decedents' intentions. And fourth, they can potentially reduce the legal costs associated with excessive probate hearings.

Living trusts name three parties. *Trustors* are individuals or couples that create and own the trusts. *Beneficiaries* are those that inherit the property held in the trusts following the deaths of the trustors. And *trustees* are people or entities that are appointed to: manage the trusts for the trustors' benefit if the trustors become incapacitated; or gather assets, settle debts, pay taxes, notify beneficiaries, distribute assets, and terminate the trusts.

After trusts are established, assets like bank accounts, real estate, collectibles, and small business interests can be placed in them. Whatever's transferred becomes their property, provided that it's retitled in the trusts' names and listed in the trust documents prior to trustors' deaths. If trustors are uneasy about transferring certain assets to the trusts, they can list themselves as trustees and name *successor trustees* in case they become incapacitated.

Upon death, court officials scrutinize the living trust documents to verify that the trustors properly transferred their property prior to death and were mentally competent at the time. Once they're satisfied, the trustees are likely to be permitted to distribute the property.

There are many times that living trusts merit special types of Wills that are known as *pour-overs*. These documents help trustors ensure that property that's either not placed in the trusts when they're established, or is acquired after distributions occur, are transferred to heirs in accordance with the trustors' wishes. There are also some assets that either shouldn't be held in them (e.g., retirement accounts, annuities, foreign property) or may not be worth the associated time, hassles, and costs (e.g., vehicles).

People that should consider establishing living trusts include parents of minor children, and those that: want to mitigate or avert the hassles of probate; own property outside of their home states; or have gross estates that exceed federal and state estate tax exemptions. Those that are less likely to benefit from these tools possess few assets or have no dependent children.

Unfortunately, the moment of truth arrives after the trustors are gone. But, at that point, it's usually too late for alterations. As such, it's essential for people to consult reputable and trustworthy estate planning attorneys before they design or modify these critical documents.

Beneficiary Designations

Beneficiary designations identify individuals or entities that owners of life insurance policies, annuities, pensions, retirement accounts, Wills, and living trusts, will transfer assets to upon their deaths. It's a powerful legacy planning tool that many people take for granted.

For some, it should be straightforward because their circumstances are uncomplicated, or their state laws provide specific directions. For others, like couples in blended families, parents that disinherit children, or families transferring businesses or protecting assets against third party legal challenges, it can be confusing. Regardless, *DIY financial planners* should periodically ask their financial partners to confirm that they've:

✓ Submitted completed forms	✓ Listed desired beneficiaries
✓ Provided accurate information	✓ Updated beneficiary information
✓ Calculated desired allocations	✓ Complied with laws, orders, and contracts

Many are also confused about the coordination between their Wills and beneficiary-controlled assets. They assume that their Wills automatically supersede beneficiary designations made elsewhere, but that's incorrect. Where discrepancies exist, proceeds might bypass probate and be disbursed directly to listed beneficiaries. In other words, the Wills won't have authority. For that reason, it's important for people to periodically confirm that their beneficiary designations reflect their specific wishes and intentions.

Instead of listing individuals by name, living trusts can be designated as beneficiaries. This removes hassles associated with managing multiple beneficiary designations, but can also delay the transfer of proceeds because it relies on custodians to act expeditiously. Since this can get highly technical, it's wise to engage reputable estate planning attorneys.

NOW IT'S YOUR TURN
Review, confirm, and update your beneficiary designations

It's essential that your beneficiary designations accurately reflect your intent. Take time to review all of your legacy planning documents to ensure that your choices match your vision. If you've never done this before or if it's been a while, consider asking your financial partners to help you complete this task. Also, once all of these documents are updated, be sure to attach or store copies with your current Will.

Other Tools

There are other tools that *DIY financial planners* might be able to use to avoid probate, or bypass Wills or living trusts, but rules and restrictions vary across the country because state laws govern the transfer of their property.

For depository accounts, they might be able to create *joint accounts* with other individuals, presumably their executors, guardians, or heirs, where the two parties are co-equal owners and have full and immediate access to the assets. When one dies, the survivor becomes the sole owner of the property regardless of what the decedents communicate in their Wills. It's an easy solution, but risky because it requires a lot of trust between the joint owners.

If joint ownership of accounts is impractical or undesirable, there are other options. One is to establish the accounts as *payable on death* (*POD*) so that custodians are required to disperse assets to named beneficiaries upon notification of the death of the account owners. Another is to create *in trust for* (*ITF*) accounts that permit account owners to designate trustees that will manage the assets for the benefit of the beneficiaries.

For property like real estate or vehicles, *joint tenancy* arrangements may be useful. These are forms of shared ownership whereby tenants have equal ownership of properties, and surviving owners receive the deceased owners' shares outside of probate regardless of what is communicated in the decedents' Wills. But it can also be problematic if owners want to sell their shares, become incapacitated, or change their minds. Another option is *transfer on death deeds* where ownership is transferred to designated beneficiaries after the owners die.

Finally, for securities, such as stocks, bonds, mutual funds, and brokerage accounts, *transfer on death* registrations allow investors to transfer ownership of the assets upon their deaths. Executors aren't involved in these transactions, but designated beneficiaries must provide copies of the decedents' death certificates to the legal entities holding the properties before they'll be permitted to re-register the securities or to liquidate them.

SECTION VI

AN UNRELENTING DEVOTION

CHAPTER 20

SEEK VALIDATION

Employees at all levels often ask "Once I begin, how will I know that I'm going in the right direction?" It's an important question since destinations aren't always clearly defined, life is continually changing, and decisions that made sense yesterday might not make sense tomorrow.

Early in the book, I depicted the orchestrated pre-flight ritual that people witness as they board a jet to highlight the similarities between airline pilots and *DIY financial planners*. For both to succeed, they need to take the right steps using the right tools at the right times.

The analogy works here too. While in the air, pilots use the time-tested techniques and tools in their reach to verify that they're on track and adjust the flight plans if necessary. Once on the ground, they take deliberate steps to verify that their approaches are effective and make necessary refinements. They know that their jobs aren't truly finished until the final landing, and that an unrelenting devotion is essential for continued success.

Schedule Your Review

After executing their plans, resourceful employees schedule times in the future to review their progress. It's their chance to update their records, reassess their situations, set new goals, and revise their plans. They might invite others, such as their spouses or financial advisors, and will set aside adequate time; maybe two hours for annual events if their needs are straightforward, or a half-day semi-annually or a full day annually if circumstances are more complicated.

Ideally, the reviews coincide with employees' annual benefit enrollment periods which usually occur within organizations around the same time each year, and 75 to 120 days from the dates that employers renew their group health insurance plans.

For example, if a business renews its coverage on January 1st, it might announce changes for the coming year on September 1st or October 1st. As such, employees should consider scheduling their reviews in mid-September or mid-October. In dual-income couples where both spouses have separate workplace benefits, they're wise to pick mid-summer dates to allow time to adjust their finances in tax-efficient ways.

In addition, employees that anticipate that significant life events might occur in the near-term should discuss their situations with their financial partners. Some events, like marriages, divorces, births, adoptions, losses of qualified insurance coverage, or long-term moves to new locations where different plans are offered, might entitle them to alter their benefit elections outside their normal enrollments. However, it's vital to act promptly since some changes must be made within narrow timeframes.

NOW IT'S YOUR TURN
Schedule an annual review of your financial progress

If you haven't done so already, take 5 minutes now to schedule your own personal annual review. If applicable, include your spouse or advisors.

Measure Your Progress

Before *DIY financial planners* begin their periodic reviews, I encourage them to ask personal and workplace financial partners to identify free or low-cost resources that might help them measure their progress, such as worksheets, personalized reports, and professional counsellors. If they're unsatisfied with those, they might find value in tools offered by government agencies like the Employee Benefits Security Administration, and non-profits like the American Institute of CPAs, American Association of Retired Persons, and Consumer Federation of America.

Quantitative Assessment

Estimating the total value of personal wealth (or *net worth*) helps people determine the degrees to which they're going forward or backward, or remaining in place. Some don't like it because precision is cumbersome, results can be disappointing, and the efforts might seem self-aggrandizing. Others realize that it's a valuable self-assessment tool that can position them for future opportunities.

These assessments require two steps. First, people must quantify the total value of everything that they own and owe. *Owned* consists of the estimated value of *tangible assets* like savings, real estate and investments, and *intangible assets* such as patents, trademarks, and copyrights. *Owed* includes the estimated value of all unpaid debts. Second, they must subtract the total value of everything that they owe from the total value of everything that they own. It's calculated using the following formula:

The Sum	-	The Sum	=	Net Worth
of Everything Owned		of Everything Owed		

Let's use an example. Cardale is a 29-year-old supervisor who's been serious about improving his personal finances for several years. In the past 12 months, he's increased his emergency savings, contributed to his company's 401(k), and made small after-tax investments. However, he also has college debt, a mortgage on his condo, and modest credit card debt. After estimating his net worth a year ago, he wants to know where he stands today. With a little effort, he estimates that the total value of the assets that he owns is $200,000 and that the sum of his unpaid debt is $175,000.

$200,000	-	$175,000	=	$25,000

Having positive net worth of $25,000 might not seem like a big deal to some people, but it's an improvement from where Cardale was one year ago; the last time that he assessed it. At that time, his assets were $180,000, his outstanding debt was $190,000, and his net worth was negative $10,000.

$$\$180,000 \quad - \quad \$190,000 \quad = \quad -\$10,000$$

So, in a relatively short time, Cardale has successfully repositioned himself to take advantage of wealth building opportunities and confront unforeseeable challenges. He's clearly heading in the right direction and should be proud of his results.

NOW IT'S YOUR TURN
Estimate your net worth

Take 15 minutes to ask your financial partners if they provide free or low-cost tools that'll help you estimate your net worth. If they do, request a demonstration and try it yourself. If they don't, visit the following sites:

➢ *Employee Benefits Security Administration's* Savings Fitness net worth tool at www.askebsa.dol.gov/savingsfitness/worksheets.
➢ *American Association of Retired Persons'* Saving & Investing net worth calculator at www.aarp.org/money/investing.
➢ *Consumer Federation of America's* America Saves personal wealth estimator at www.americasaves.org/for-savers.

This activity should become part of your ongoing annual review process.

Qualitative Assessment

Not everything that *DIY financial planners* do to build and preserve their wealth is measurable. In fact, some of the most important activities can't be monetized or quantified.

For that reason, over 70 activities that I teach during my workshops and that many resourceful employees complete are included in the *Now It's Your*

Turn boxes embedded throughout the book. These activities provide valuable starting points for important qualitative assessments and should be revisited regularly.

Affirm Your Devotion

In my interactions with *DIY financial planners*, I observe a wide spectrum of devotees. Some seem supremely confident in their abilities and are committed to going-it-alone. Others are barely holding on and are afraid that they are messing things up. Regardless, it's important for all of them to affirm their devotions to being their own advisors, or quickly take different paths.

Employees at all levels face many obstacles, so it's natural for them to feel uncertain. But results are and always will be the most important aspect of wealth creation efforts. Should they doubt their abilities or appetites for flying solo, either in part or whole, they should answer simple questions like those below. The more that their answers are "No" or "Unsure," the more urgent it probably is for them to begin searching for the right advisors.

Self-Reflective Questions for Continuing to Go-It-Alone	Answer		
	Yes	*No*	*Unsure*
➢ Do I know what I'm doing?	○	○	○
➢ Do I have time to do this well?	○	○	○
➢ Do I make the right decisions?	○	○	○
➢ Am I certain my analysis is reliable?	○	○	○
➢ Do I enjoy doing this on my own?	○	○	○
➢ Do I know what I need to do to get better?	○	○	○

CHAPTER 21

HIRED HANDS

Eventually, many *DIY financial planners* reach points where they lack the attention, interest, or time to continue self-navigating. When those moments arrive, it's typical for them to seek help from financial advisors, like insurance intermediaries, investment brokers, wealth planners, and lawyers. Unfortunately, hiring the right ones is seldom easy. In fact, it can be among the most difficult, and ultimately costly, decisions that they'll ever make.

I regularly survey the employees that attend my seminars about their use of these professionals and find that easily 4-in-5 don't work with them (when their property and casualty insurance advisors aren't included). Their reasons normally make sense, but deeper conversations reveal their Achilles' Heels. Here's a glimpse into a typical workplace conversation...

Midway through a seminar for 40 employees, I ask "By show-of-hands, how many of you work with someone that you consider to be a 'financial advisor'?" After a few seconds, 5 put a hand up. I mentally note who they are and say "Thanks. You can lower your hands."

I continue "So that means the rest of you are doing it all yourselves, right?" Some nod in agreement and others verbally answer "Yes." Then I ask "With another show-of-hands, how many of you current 'DIY types' worked with one in the past?" 7 attendees quickly raise a hand. From experience, I know that they have stories to tell.

I react with "Wow! That was quick. Please keep your hands up." I look to a man with his hand raised and ask "Why'd you stop working with your advisor?" He says "He was a crook." I retort "A 'real' one?" and he confirms "Yep. Stole money. Went to jail. It was bad."

I look to a young woman with her hand in the air. "What about you?" She says "He changed careers. He said he hated the constant

249

pressure to sell." I look to another and ask the same question. She responds "She was awesome and I loved working with her. But one day she called to 'apologize' and said that her colleague was taking over for her so that I'd get the attention that I deserved!" I ask "How did that go?" and she finishes with "Not good! It was a total step back."

Having led many of these types of discussions, it's time for me to make an important point. First, I ask "Alright, for those that have used one, how did you find them?" Some of their answers are "We met at Church," "She was a college friend," "My Dad introduced him," and "I heard her on the radio."

Then I ask "What did you like about them?" Now it gets uncomfortable because these people must justify their past decisions. Their responses include "He was nice," "She was sharp," "I felt that he'd do a good job," and "I wanted to help her succeed."

I close with "Got it. So, what process did you use to hire them?" This question is greeted by utter silence, but I know what many are thinking: "Process? What process?"

And voila! The truth about countless failed relationships is exposed. It's easy to blame the financial advisors, but the reality is that the clients that do the hiring don't know what they need, what questions to ask, or how to compare candidates. In lieu of a formal search process, they instinctively default to something that they do know: likeability.

Look Beyond Likeability

There are throngs of good financial professionals. They possess abilities to create measurable value that propels their clients forward, and their partnership and guidance can't be replicated by Google searches or Amazon's Alexa. But there are also horrible ones that engage in unethical and criminal acts, cloak themselves in misleading ornamental titles, abandon low-revenue clients, and conceal conflicts of interest and compensation. The impact of the bad eggs is reflected in consumer sentiment surveys, such as one showing a whopping 65% of respondents mistrust them to some degree and a paltry 2% trust them a lot.[52]

In response, many financial services firms use slick and dubious tactics to soften the public's perception. They use door-opener gimmicks like free consultations, reports, and events. They saturate the airwaves with altruistic clichés such as "It's all about you," "I never stop listening," or "Our firm doesn't have any products to sell." They finagle their way into garnering token or purchased accolades, and shamelessly self-promote their made-for-the-cameras philanthropy and volunteerism.

And most important, they employ the types of people that they believe their desired clientele will perceive as likeable. The vast majority of financial advisors are nice, polite, and friendly because those are the prerequisites to earning trust, building relationships, and acquiring new customers.

Genuine or not, the emphasis on likability reflects an old sales adage that goes like this:

"All things being equal, people buy from the people they like. And all things being unequal, people still buy from the people they like."

Focus On Compatibility

I don't trivialize likeability. Rather, I urge *DIY financial planners* to act with the purpose and discernment of shrewd hiring managers that are searching for the right talent. They should focus intensely on the compatibility between their personal needs and candidates' professional attributes.

---

[52] Maurie Backman, "Most Americans Don't Trust Their Financial Advisors. Should They?" (July 11, 2017, www.fool.com, Web, June 26, 2020).

Niche and Focus

Although most professional advisors specialize in one or two general areas within financial services, some try to be all things to all people. They might be reliable in a field like banking, investing, or estate planning, but it's unlikely that they're experts in all. Frustratingly, candidates might not admit that specific needs or problems exceed their skills. Before hiring them, it's important to understand their focus and confirm that they consistently work with similar types of clientele.

Knowledge, Experience, and Ethics

The thresholds to become financial advisors are shockingly low and attrition rates among people in the industry, especially those earlier in their careers, are high. For this reason, it's crucial to assess their knowledge, experience, and ethics by investigating academic backgrounds, ongoing education, work histories, industry affiliations, professional designations, and corrective or punitive actions levied against them or their organizations.

Capacity for Strategy and Planning

Regardless of the scope of their engagement, financial advisors should have a positive and lasting impact. As such, they must possess the abilities to formulate realistic strategies, implement effective solutions, and make proper adjustments. Solid candidates make it clear that: their clients' goals are taken seriously; their communications are timely, accurate, and candid; and their recommendations are always in the best interests of their clients.

Services and Resources

Many financial advisors can offer clients dizzying arrays of services and resources. Some are valuable and others aren't, but all can be used by crafty candidates as shiny objects to tilt the hiring process in their favor. It's therefore important to scrutinize proposed solutions, and to confirm that they're actually relevant to and compatible with stated goals and needs.

Measurement and Reporting Capabilities

While not essential in every aspect of personal finance, tools that provide insight into performance can be valuable, especially in areas that frequently change like investments and tax planning. Candidates should be able to explain their capabilities in plain language, demonstrate their value, provide samples, and commit to their timing and delivery.

Compensation and Fees

Financial advisors are paid in many ways. Compensation and fees vary by products, services, and specialties, and might include combinations of: direct payments; flat fees; salaries; commissions; reimbursements; bonuses; overrides; training; vacations; and sponsorships.

It's reasonable to request accurate and written estimates of the money that candidates expect to receive from their recommendations, services, and sales, and to require them to provide full and ongoing disclosure in case they are hired. Those that gripe about or refuse to answer questions should probably be disqualified from further consideration.

Conduct Your Search

It's ok for *DIY financial planners* to admit that they don't know something. It's not ok if they hire financial advisors that know or care less than they do. For that reason, I advise them to conduct thorough and formal searches when they're looking for the right professional help.

First, they must solidify their goals and decide what types of support that they'll need to achieve them. They might not have all of the answers, but clear vision can prevent ill-intentioned candidates from hijacking their efforts and leading them in other directions. (In my seminars, some employees experience epiphanies when they discover that their financial advisors are formally trained to overcome objections and redirect perspective clients' searches.)

Next, they need to compile lists of candidates and contact information. They should ask their personal and professional connections for referrals and suggestions, and use online search tools provided by industry organizations, like the Certified Financial Planner Board of Standards or the Chartered Financial Analyst Institute, or LinkedIn to find others.

Then, they should send short introductory emails or letters to the candidates that they want to interview. The correspondence needs to summarize their goals, needs, and circumstances, and invite brief written responses to 4 or 5 deal-breaker questions (see **Appendix G** for samples). Some recipients ignore or rebuff such efforts, and others attempt to sidestep them, but it's a good way to break the ice, facilitate follow-up discussions, and create paper trails for future use. It also exposes weak candidates that should be avoided.

As responses arrive and their searches narrow, they should strive to gain deeper understandings of the remaining candidates. This can include scheduling times to talk or meet, asking detailed questions, taking thorough notes, scrutinizing answers, and ranking financial advisors from the strongest to the weakest. Vetting advisors and firms can be cumbersome, but it's better to make the effort before entering into written agreements.

It's also reasonable and necessary for candidates to ask questions during this process. However, before disclosing private information, they should be screened for industry violations and complaints, and criminality. This means accessing public data maintained by government agencies such as the federal *Financial Industry Regulatory Authority* (or *FINRA*), state insurance commissioners, and state court systems, and non-governmental consumer watchdog groups.

Not surprising, most *DIY financial planners* don't feel that they have the time or energy for this. In these situations, some will discover that their employers offer access to counsellors, coaches, and online advice tools for little or no cost. And, at some point, all might consider engaging fee-based, online matchmakers that'll attempt to pair them with financial advisors that are presumably well-suited to satisfy their needs. These options are convenient, but should still be thoroughly investigated.

Hold Them Accountable

Once hired, financial advisors must be held accountable for achieving desired results. Luckily, assessing their performance isn't as time consuming as running formal searches, and it might be as easy as remembering four words: *accurate*, *available*, *partnership*, and *guidance*.

On a basic level, financial advisors must be consistently accurate and regularly available. These aren't negotiable attributes. Those that make repeated mistakes or are difficult to reach probably aren't satisfying clients' basic needs and shouldn't be trusted to address others. At minimum, unhappy customers should unambiguously express their dissatisfaction and revive their formal searches for replacements if their current (or incumbent) advisors fail to improve in preferred timeframes.

On a deeper level, these professionals should also demonstrate that they are proactive partners and are able to provide valuable guidance. Occasionally attendees in my seminars gush about their financial advisors. They say things like "She's always two steps ahead of me," "He proactively addresses my fears," "She leaves nothing to chance," "He acts like my goals are his," and "They always exceed my expectations." These are special characteristics that should be cherished and rewarded.

A key to building solid relationships with financial advisors is to require regular updates. This isn't always convenient, but it creates opportunities to reinforce expectations, restate goals, and derive additional value. For needs that don't change much, such as insurance, accounting, and estate planning, in-depth discussions should happen at least annually. For those that are more fluid, like investment portfolios and wealth management, they should occur semi-annually or quarterly.

NOW IT'S YOUR TURN
Hold your current advisors accountable

Your financial advisors are paid to help you build and preserve wealth, but you're ultimately responsible for holding them accountable. If you haven't heard from them lately, take 15 minutes now to schedule a conversation.

The Digital Frontier

Some of the employees that I help, particularly Gen Xers and Millennials, express interest in or preferences for digital alternatives to traditional financial advice that require little or no human interaction (or *robo-advice*). These advice platforms rely on data, algorithms, and online interfaces to perform functions that are typically handled by people, like assessments, recommendations, and product activation, and they include software, web portals, and applications for smart devices.

Similar to technology used elsewhere in e-commerce, robo-advice offers *DIY financial planners* a low-cost and ease-of-use experience, and proponents argue that it puts expertise and insights historically reserved for wealthier households in everyone's reach. Early signs suggest that it'll help more people automate better financial behaviors, eliminate barriers, and increase access to generally accepted wealth building principles. But it also has a dark side.

Given that people can't easily investigate robo-advisers' internal workings or assumptions, important details like methods, conflicts of interest, and fees, might be difficult to verify and trust. More, users are potentially exposed to the sub-optimal results inherent in generic guidance and cookie cutter interactions. As such, whether it's accessed via the workplace or public domain, robo-generated advice must be scrutinized as if human beings dispensed it: with regularity, vigor, and skepticism.

The human touch isn't on the verge of extinction. There will always be a place for the valuable partnership and guidance that quality financial professionals offer. But it's also certain that robo-advice will be integrated into their core services, and be used to sell products and services. For this reason, it is vital for consumers to demand that their financial partners disclose any bias in the black box digital tools that they'll use and the degrees to which those tools will influence their recommendations.

NOW IT'S YOUR TURN
Evaluate your digital financial advice options

As the shift toward robo-advice gains momentum, you should investigate free or low-cost options that are in your reach. Take 15 minutes now to ask your financial partners to explain the digital solutions that they offer and determine the degree to which they can help you.

CONCLUSION

YOU ARE THE BIGGEST DIFFERENCE

At the beginning of this journey, I asked you to picture yourself in the role of a financial advisor who was meeting with a perspective client for the first time. I did it to underscore the reality that you are the de facto financial advisor to the most important person: *you*.

In many ways, being a *DIY financial planner* is easy, especially if you're a traditional employee who works for an employer that does a lot of the heavy lifting for you. You don't need any formal training or qualifications. You won't have supervisors or regulators second-guessing your decisions. And you can't sue yourself if you screw up. But it's still perilous.

If you've been struggling to build and preserve wealth, then it's time for you to try a better path. Start by replacing your rosy assumptions and zombie-like tendencies with a conscious approach. Continue by regularly taking steps to strengthen your core financial mindsets. And make it sustainable by embracing an unrelenting devotion to achieving results that matter.

I'm confident that you can do this. Based on my experience helping hundreds of employers and tens of thousands of employees, many of the resources that you'll need are or can be in your reach. Perhaps the most valuable among them are your financial partners, resourceful peers, and role models, and your willingness to act.

And if you use this book like a financial stepladder, then I believe that you will see what I do: an extraordinary opportunity to do special and meaningful things for yourself, those you cherish, and the nation and world we share.

APPENDIX A

AT-A-GLANCE WORKSHEET

An important part of getting started is inventorying essential financial information.

I created this worksheet to help you combine your information in a single document, but I don't want you to record it here. Instead, **I urge you to print a copy that you'll find at inourreach.com/book**. Once you have it, be sure to: write in pencil; add extra pages if needed; update it periodically; store it in a secure location; and tell your spouse, executor, or attorney, where it's kept.

PERSONAL INFORMATION			
Self			
Full Name:	--- Don't write here ---	Date of Birth:	--- Don't write here ---
Personal Phone:	--- Don't write here ---	Personal Email:	--- Don't write here ---
Work Phone:	--- Don't write here ---	Work Email:	--- Don't write here ---
SSN:	--- Don't write here ---	Junk Email:	--- Don't write here ---
Spouse			
Full Name:	--- Don't write here ---	Date of Birth:	--- Don't write here ---
Personal Phone:	--- Don't write here ---	Personal Email:	--- Don't write here ---
Work Phone:	--- Don't write here ---	Work Email:	--- Don't write here ---
SSN:	--- Don't write here ---	Junk Email:	--- Don't write here ---
1st Dependent			
Full Name:	--- Don't write here ---	Date of Birth:	--- Don't write here ---
Personal Phone:	--- Don't write here ---	Personal Email:	--- Don't write here ---
Work Phone:	--- Don't write here ---	Work Email:	--- Don't write here ---
SSN:	--- Don't write here ---	Junk Email:	--- Don't write here ---

PERSONAL INFORMATION

2nd Dependent

Full Name:	-- Don't write here --	Date of Birth:	-- Don't write here --
Personal Phone:	-- Don't write here --	Personal Email:	-- Don't write here --
Work Phone:	-- Don't write here --	Work Email:	-- Don't write here --
SSN:	-- Don't write here --	Junk Email:	-- Don't write here --

3rd Dependent

Full Name:	-- Don't write here --	Date of Birth:	-- Don't write here --
Personal Phone:	-- Don't write here --	Personal Email:	-- Don't write here --
Work Phone:	-- Don't write here --	Work Email:	-- Don't write here --
SSN:	-- Don't write here --	Junk Email:	-- Don't write here --

4th Dependent

Full Name:	-- Don't write here --	Date of Birth:	-- Don't write here --
Personal Phone:	-- Don't write here --	Personal Email:	-- Don't write here --
Work Phone:	-- Don't write here --	Work Email:	-- Don't write here --
SSN:	-- Don't write here --	Junk Email:	-- Don't write here --

5th Dependent

Full Name:	-- Don't write here --	Date of Birth:	-- Don't write here --
Personal Phone:	-- Don't write here --	Personal Email:	-- Don't write here --
Work Phone:	-- Don't write here --	Work Email:	-- Don't write here --
SSN:	-- Don't write here --	Junk Email:	-- Don't write here --

EMERGENCY CONTACT INFORMATION

	1st Contact	2nd Contact
Relationship:	□ Parent □ Child □ Friend □ Other	□ Parent □ Child □ Friend □ Other
Name:	-- Don't write here --	-- Don't write here --
City, State, ZIP:	-- Don't write here --	-- Don't write here --
Phone:	-- Don't write here --	-- Don't write here --
Email:	-- Don't write here --	-- Don't write here --

ADVISOR INFORMATION

	Banking	Credit & Lending
Name:	-- Don't write here --	-- Don't write here --
Street Address:	-- Don't write here --	-- Don't write here --
City, State, ZIP:	-- Don't write here --	-- Don't write here --
Phone:	-- Don't write here --	-- Don't write here --
Email:	-- Don't write here --	-- Don't write here --

	Investment	Retirement
Name:	-- Don't write here --	-- Don't write here --
Street Address:	-- Don't write here --	-- Don't write here --
City, State, ZIP:	-- Don't write here --	-- Don't write here --
Phone:	-- Don't write here --	-- Don't write here --
Email:	-- Don't write here --	-- Don't write here --

	Life & Health Insurance	Property & Casualty Insurance
Name:	-- Don't write here --	-- Don't write here --
Street Address:	-- Don't write here --	-- Don't write here --
City, State, ZIP:	-- Don't write here --	-- Don't write here --
Phone:	-- Don't write here --	-- Don't write here --
Email:	-- Don't write here --	-- Don't write here --

	Taxes	Legal
Name:	-- Don't write here --	-- Don't write here --
Street Address:	-- Don't write here --	-- Don't write here --
City, State, ZIP:	-- Don't write here --	-- Don't write here --
Phone:	-- Don't write here --	-- Don't write here --
Email:	-- Don't write here --	-- Don't write here --

	Other: _____	Other: _____
Name:	-- Don't write here --	-- Don't write here --
Street Address:	-- Don't write here --	-- Don't write here --
City, State, ZIP:	-- Don't write here --	-- Don't write here --
Phone:	-- Don't write here --	-- Don't write here --
Email:	-- Don't write here --	-- Don't write here --

BANK ACCOUNTS

	Account No. 1	**Account No. 2**
Account Type:	□ Checking □ Savings □ CD □ Other: _____	□ Checking □ Savings □ CD □ Other: _____
Account No.:	-- Don't write here --	-- Don't write here --
Institution Name:	-- Don't write here --	-- Don't write here --
Phone:	-- Don't write here --	-- Don't write here --
Website:	-- Don't write here --	-- Don't write here --

	Account No. 3	**Account No. 4**
Account Type:	□ Checking □ Savings □ CD □ Other: _____	□ Checking □ Savings □ CD □ Other: _____
Account No.:	-- Don't write here --	-- Don't write here --
Institution Name:	-- Don't write here --	-- Don't write here --
Phone:	-- Don't write here --	-- Don't write here --
Website:	-- Don't write here --	-- Don't write here --

DEBT ACCOUNTS

	Account No. 1	**Account No. 2**
Account Type:	□ Credit □ Auto □ Mortgage □ Student □ Other: _____	□ Credit □ Auto □ Mortgage □ Student □ Other: _____
Account No.:	-- Don't write here --	-- Don't write here --
Institution Name:	-- Don't write here --	-- Don't write here --
Phone:	-- Don't write here --	-- Don't write here --
Website:	-- Don't write here --	-- Don't write here --

	Account No. 3	**Account No. 4**
Account Type:	□ Credit □ Auto □ Mortgage □ Student □ Other: _____	□ Credit □ Auto □ Mortgage □ Student □ Other: _____
Account No.:	-- Don't write here --	-- Don't write here --
Institution Name:	-- Don't write here --	-- Don't write here --
Phone:	-- Don't write here --	-- Don't write here --
Website:	-- Don't write here --	-- Don't write here --

RETIREMENT ACCOUNTS

	Account No. 1	Account No. 2
Account Type:	□ IRA □ 401(k) □ 403(b) □ Pension	□ IRA □ 401(k) □ 403(b) □ Pension
	□ Other: _____	□ Other: _____
Plan/Account No.:	-- Don't write here --	-- Don't write here --
Institution Name:	-- Don't write here --	-- Don't write here --
Phone:	-- Don't write here --	-- Don't write here --
Website:	-- Don't write here --	-- Don't write here --

	Account No. 3	Account No. 4
Account Type:	□ IRA □ 401(k) □ 403(b) □ Pension	□ IRA □ 401(k) □ 403(b) □ Pension
	□ Other: _____	□ Other: _____
Plan/Account No.:	-- Don't write here --	-- Don't write here --
Institution Name:	-- Don't write here --	-- Don't write here --
Phone:	-- Don't write here --	-- Don't write here --
Website:	-- Don't write here --	-- Don't write here --

COLLEGE ACCOUNTS

	Account No. 1	Account No. 2
Account Type:	□ 529 □ ESA □ Other: _____	□ 529 □ ESA □ Other: _____
Dependent:	-- Don't write here --	-- Don't write here --
Account No.:	-- Don't write here --	-- Don't write here --
Institution Name:	-- Don't write here --	-- Don't write here --
Phone:	-- Don't write here --	-- Don't write here --
Website:	-- Don't write here --	-- Don't write here --

	Account No. 3	Account No. 4
Account Type:	□ 529 □ ESA □ Other: _____	□ 529 □ ESA □ Other: _____
Dependent:	-- Don't write here --	-- Don't write here --
Account No.:	-- Don't write here --	-- Don't write here --
Institution Name:	-- Don't write here --	-- Don't write here --
Phone:	-- Don't write here --	-- Don't write here --
Website:	-- Don't write here --	-- Don't write here --

HEALTH INSURANCE

	Policy No. 1	Policy No. 2
Insured Names:	-- Don't write here --	-- Don't write here --
Policy Type:	□ Medical □ Dental □ Vision	□ Medical □ Dental □ Vision
Policy No.:	-- Don't write here --	-- Don't write here --
Insurer Name:	-- Don't write here --	-- Don't write here --
Phone:	-- Don't write here --	-- Don't write here --
Website:	-- Don't write here --	-- Don't write here --

	Policy No. 3	Policy No. 4
Insured Names:	-- Don't write here --	-- Don't write here --
Policy Type:	□ Medical □ Dental □ Vision	□ Medical □ Dental □ Vision
Policy No.:	-- Don't write here --	-- Don't write here --
Insurer Name:	-- Don't write here --	-- Don't write here --
Phone:	-- Don't write here --	-- Don't write here --
Website:	-- Don't write here --	-- Don't write here --

DISABILITY & LONG TERM CARE INSURANCE

	Policy No. 1	Policy No. 2
Insured Names:	-- Don't write here --	-- Don't write here --
Policy Type:	□ Disability □ Long Term Care	□ Disability □ Long Term Care
Policy No.:	-- Don't write here --	-- Don't write here --
Insurer Name:	-- Don't write here --	-- Don't write here --
Phone:	-- Don't write here --	-- Don't write here --
Website:	-- Don't write here --	-- Don't write here --

	Policy No. 3	Policy No. 4
Insured Names:	-- Don't write here --	-- Don't write here --
Policy Type:	□ Disability □ Long Term Care	□ Disability □ Long Term Care
Policy No.:	-- Don't write here --	-- Don't write here --
Insurer Name:	-- Don't write here --	-- Don't write here --
Phone:	-- Don't write here --	-- Don't write here --
Website:	-- Don't write here --	-- Don't write here --

PROPERTY & CASUALTY INSURANCE

	Policy No. 1	**Policy No. 2**
Policy Type:	□ Dwelling □ Auto □ Recreation □ Umbrella	□ Dwelling □ Auto □ Recreation □ Umbrella
Policy No.:	-- Don't write here --	-- Don't write here --
Insurer Name:	-- Don't write here --	-- Don't write here --
Phone:	-- Don't write here --	-- Don't write here --
Website:	-- Don't write here --	-- Don't write here --

	Policy No. 3	**Policy No. 4**
Policy Type:	□ Dwelling □ Auto □ Recreation □ Umbrella	□ Dwelling □ Auto □ Recreation □ Umbrella
Policy No.:	-- Don't write here --	-- Don't write here --
Insurer Name:	-- Don't write here --	-- Don't write here --
Phone:	-- Don't write here --	-- Don't write here --
Website:	-- Don't write here --	-- Don't write here --

PROFESSIONAL, BUSINESSS, & IDENTITY THEFT INSURANCE

	Policy No. 1	**Policy No. 2**
Policy Type:	□ Professional □ Business □ Identity	□ Professional □ Business □ Identity
Policy No.:	-- Don't write here --	-- Don't write here --
Insurer Name:	-- Don't write here --	-- Don't write here --
Phone:	-- Don't write here --	-- Don't write here --
Website:	-- Don't write here --	-- Don't write here --

	Policy No. 3	**Policy No. 4**
Policy Type:	□ Professional □ Business □ Identity	□ Professional □ Business □ Identity
Policy No.:	-- Don't write here --	-- Don't write here --
Insurer Name:	-- Don't write here --	-- Don't write here --
Phone:	-- Don't write here --	-- Don't write here --
Website:	-- Don't write here --	-- Don't write here --

LIFE INSURANCE

	Policy No. 1	Policy No. 2
Policy Type:	□ Term □ Whole □ Universal	□ Term □ Whole □ Universal
Policy No.:	-- Don't write here --	-- Don't write here --
Insurer Name:	-- Don't write here --	-- Don't write here --
Phone:	-- Don't write here --	-- Don't write here --
Website:	-- Don't write here --	-- Don't write here --

	Policy No. 3	Policy No. 4
Policy Type:	□ Term □ Whole □ Universal	□ Term □ Whole □ Universal
Policy No.:	-- Don't write here --	-- Don't write here --
Insurer Name:	-- Don't write here --	-- Don't write here --
Phone:	-- Don't write here --	-- Don't write here --
Website:	-- Don't write here --	-- Don't write here --

ESTATE PLAN

	Document No. 1	Document No. 2
Document Type:	□ POA □ Directive □ Will □ Trust □ Other: _____	□ POA □ Directive □ Will □ Trust □ Other: _____
Owner Name:	-- Don't write here --	-- Don't write here --
Executor Name:	-- Don't write here --	-- Don't write here --
Executor Phone:	-- Don't write here --	-- Don't write here --
Attorney Name:	-- Don't write here --	-- Don't write here --
Attorney Phone:	-- Don't write here --	-- Don't write here --

	Document No. 3	Document No. 4
Document Type:	□ POA □ Directive □ Will □ Trust □ Other: _____	□ POA □ Directive □ Will □ Trust □ Other: _____
Owner Name:	-- Don't write here --	-- Don't write here --
Executor Name:	-- Don't write here --	-- Don't write here --
Executor Phone:	-- Don't write here --	-- Don't write here --
Attorney Name:	-- Don't write here --	-- Don't write here --
Attorney Phone:	-- Don't write here --	-- Don't write here --

REAL ESTATE

	Property No. 1	Property No. 2
Physical Address:	-- Don't write here --	-- Don't write here --
Property Type:	□ Residential □ Rental □ Commercial □ Land	□ Residential □ Rental □ Commercial □ Land
Title Registered to:	-- Don't write here --	-- Don't write here --
Tittle insured by:	-- Don't write here --	-- Don't write here --
Mortgage Holder:	-- Don't write here --	-- Don't write here --

	Property No. 3	Property No. 4
Physical Address:	-- Don't write here --	-- Don't write here --
Property Type:	□ Residential □ Rental □ Commercial □ Land	□ Residential □ Rental □ Commercial □ Land
Title Registered to:	-- Don't write here --	-- Don't write here --
Tittle insured by:	-- Don't write here --	-- Don't write here --
Mortgage Holder:	-- Don't write here --	-- Don't write here --

VEHICLES

	Vehicle No. 1	Vehicle No. 2
Make & Model:	-- Don't write here --	-- Don't write here --
Vehicle ID No.:	-- Don't write here --	-- Don't write here --
Title Holder:	□ You □ Lender □ Other: _____	□ You □ Lender □ Other: _____
Lender Name:	-- Don't write here --	-- Don't write here --
Vehicle Location:	-- Don't write here --	-- Don't write here --

	Vehicle No. 3	Vehicle No. 4
Make & Model:	-- Don't write here --	-- Don't write here --
Vehicle ID No.:	-- Don't write here --	-- Don't write here --
Title Holder:	□ You □ Lender □ Other: _____	□ You □ Lender □ Other: _____
Lender Name:	-- Don't write here --	-- Don't write here --
Vehicle Location:	-- Don't write here --	-- Don't write here --

SAFE DEPOSIT BOX

	Box No. 1	Box No. 2
Institution Name:	-- Don't write here --	-- Don't write here --
Box No.:	-- Don't write here --	-- Don't write here --
Street Address:	-- Don't write here --	-- Don't write here --
City, State, ZIP:	-- Don't write here --	-- Don't write here --
Phone:	-- Don't write here --	-- Don't write here --
Key Location:	-- Don't write here --	-- Don't write here --

DOCUMENT CHECKLIST

Similar to changing the batteries in smoke detectors, *DIY financial planners* should periodically inventory their financial documents and information. The following tables can be used in this process to create unique dividers and organize retained items.

Completing this step typically demands substantial time during the initial effort, but less in subsequent efforts. It also requires: up to 20 manila folders; a pen or pencil to complete the checklist; a fine-point marker to identify each folder; and a dry and secure location to store all materials, like a lockable file drawer for paper copies, encrypted USB storage device for digital copies, or access to a highly-secure online storage platform (or cloud).

Folder 1: Identification				
Items or information to include in this folder might include or relate to:	Does this apply?		Do you have it?	
	Yes	No	Yes	No
• Birth certificates				
• Social Security cards				
• Drivers' licenses				
• Passports (or copy of 1st page of passports)				
• Naturalization papers (e.g., Visas, Green Cards)				
• Death certificates (for deceased family members)				
• Pet licenses				

Folder 2: Earnings

Items or information to include in this folder might include or relate to:	Does this apply?		Do you have it?	
	Yes	No	Yes	No
▪ Copy of IRS Form W-4 (tax withholding worksheet)				
▪ Copy of previous three (3) annual federal and state tax returns				
▪ Total Compensation Statement (if provided by employer)				
▪ Bankruptcy documents				
▪ 1099s for side gigs, small businesses, etc.				

Folder 3: Marriage

Items or information to include in this folder might include or relate to:	Does this apply?		Do you have it?	
	Yes	No	Yes	No
▪ Marriage license				
▪ Prenuptial or Postnuptial agreements				
▪ Divorce decrees				
▪ Court Orders (e.g., child support documents)				
▪ Qualified Domestic Relations Orders				
▪ Retirement plan separation as result of divorce				

Folder 4: Career

Items or information to include in this folder might include or relate to:	Does this apply?		Do you have it?	
	Yes	No	Yes	No
▪ Degrees and diplomas				
▪ Professional licenses				
▪ Union membership records				
▪ Training certificates				
▪ Awards, recognition, letters of recommendation				
▪ Military discharge records (Form DD 214)				
▪ Veteran's Administration Benefits records				

Folder 5: Banking

Items or information to include in this folder might include or relate to:	Does this apply?		Do you have it?	
	Yes	No	Yes	No
▪ Checking accounts				
▪ Savings accounts				
▪ Money market accounts				
▪ Certificates of deposit				
▪ Safe deposit box records and location of keys				

Folder 6: Credit

Items or information to include in this folder might include or relate to:	Does this apply?		Do you have it?	
	Yes	No	Yes	No
▪ Credit history reports				
▪ Credit score disclosure forms				
▪ Credit card agreements and contracts				

Folder 7: Consumer Debt

Items or information to include in this folder might include or relate to:	Does this apply?		Do you have it?	
	Yes	No	Yes	No
▪ Credit card agreements and contracts				
▪ Loan payoff statements (e.g., car loan)				

Folder 8: Student Debt

Items or information to include in this folder might include or relate to:	Does this apply?		Do you have it?	
	Yes	No	Yes	No
▪ Free Application for Federal Student Aid				
▪ College transcripts				

Folder 9: Real Estate Debt

Items or information to include in this folder might include or relate to:	Does this apply?		Do you have it?	
	Yes	No	Yes	No
▪ Loan documents (ex. closing statement)				
▪ Property deeds				
▪ Real estate tax bills				
▪ Title insurance				
▪ Home warranties				
▪ Homeowner/Condominium Association agreements				
▪ Rental or lease agreements				

Folder 10: College

Items or information to include in this folder might include or relate to:	Does this apply?		Do you have it?	
	Yes	No	Yes	No
▪ Student transcripts and standardized test scores				
▪ Education IRA accounts				
▪ 529 accounts				
▪ Uniform Gift to Minors Act (UGMA) accounts				
▪ Uniform Transfer to Minors Act (UTMA) accounts				
▪ Other savings plans (e.g., college savings credit plans, Upromise reports, financial aid, scholarships)				

Folder 11: Retirement

Items or information to include in this folder might include or relate to:	Does this apply?		Do you have it?	
	Yes	No	Yes	No
▪ Workplace plan Summary Plan Descriptions				
▪ Annual, quarterly, or monthly statements				
▪ Copies of retirement plan beneficiary forms				
▪ IRA statements (traditional and Roth accounts)				
▪ Fixed & Variable annuity statements				
▪ Summary of Cash Value Insurance policies				
▪ Annual Social Security Benefit statements				

Folder 12: Other Investments

Items or information to include in this folder might include or relate to:	Does this apply?		Do you have it?	
	Yes	No	Yes	No
▪ Brokerage account statements				
▪ Mutual fund account statements				
▪ Stock, Bond, and other transaction records				
▪ Stock purchase plan or stock option plan records				
▪ Patent or trademark applications or registrations				
▪ Any other investment statements				

Folder 13: Property & Casualty Insurance

Items or information to include in this folder might include or relate to:	Does this apply?		Do you have it?	
	Yes	No	Yes	No
▪ Home owner's insurance policies				
▪ Condo owner's insurance policies				
▪ Renter's insurance policies				
▪ Umbrella insurance policies				
▪ Flood insurance policies				
▪ Collectibles appraisals and policy riders				

Folder 14: Auto Insurance

Items or information to include in this folder might include or relate to:	Does this apply?		Do you have it?	
	Yes	No	Yes	No
▪ Vehicle titles and registrations				
▪ Auto insurance policies				
▪ Vehicle loan and lease documents				
▪ Vehicle warranties, guarantees, or service plans				

Folder 15: Health Insurance (including Pet)				
Items or information to include in this folder might include or relate to:	Does this apply?		Do you have it?	
	Yes	No	Yes	No
▪ Extra medical and prescription benefit ID cards				
▪ Summary Plan Descriptions for workplace medical, pharmacy, dental, and vision plans				
▪ Individual medical insurance policies				
▪ Health Savings Accounts (HSAs) statements				
▪ Health Reimbursement Account (HRAs) statements				
▪ List of regular prescriptions and maintenance medications				
▪ Annual flexible spending account election statements				
▪ Employee Assistance Program materials				
▪ Pet health records				

Folder 16: Disability Insurance				
Items or information to include in this folder might include or relate to:	Does this apply?		Do you have it?	
	Yes	No	Yes	No
▪ Workplace policies, certificates, or Summary Plan Descriptions				
▪ Individual disability insurance policies				
▪ Workers' Compensation documents (e.g., filings, payments, transactions)				
▪ Social Security Disability benefits (if applicable)				

Folder 17: Long Term Care Insurance				
Items or information to include in this folder might include or relate to:	Does this apply?		Do you have it?	
	Yes	No	Yes	No
▪ Workplace policies, certificates, or Summary Plan Descriptions				
▪ Individual long term care insurance policies				
▪ Other voluntary insurance (e.g., Cancer, Critical Illness, Additional Accident, Dread Disease)				

Folder 18: Life Insurance				
Items or information to include in this folder might include or relate to:	Does this apply?		Do you have it?	
	Yes	No	Yes	No
▪ Workplace policies, certificates, or Summary Plan Descriptions				
▪ Copies of life insurance beneficiary forms				
▪ Individual term, whole, or universal life insurance policies				

Folder 19: Estate Planning				
Items or information to include in this folder might include or relate to:	Does this apply?		Do you have it?	
	Yes	No	Yes	No
▪ Workplace legal plan policy, certificate or Summary Plan Description				
▪ Durable Power of Attorney for Health Care documents				
▪ Living Will or Advanced Directive documents				
▪ Organ donation and funeral preferences				
▪ Funeral home preplanning contracts				
▪ Burial-related deeds (e.g., cemetery, cremation)				
▪ Last Will & Testament (including Codicil or changes made to Will) documents				
▪ Revocable or Living Trust agreements				
▪ Other Estate Plan documents and notes				

NOW IT'S YOUR TURN
Retaining and discarding your old tax returns

For most taxpayers, the IRS recommends keeping copies of old tax returns and related documents for 3 years. Following are basic guidelines to help you decide if it's time to discard them.

- ✓ If you owe additional taxes, the period of limitations on old returns is 3 years.
- ✓ If you file a claim for a credit or refund after the return is filed, the period of limitations is the later of 3 years or 2 years after taxes were paid.
- ✓ If you fail to report income and it is more than 25% of the gross income reported, the period of limitations is 6 years.
- ✓ If you file the claim for a loss from worthless securities, the period of limitations is 7 years.
- ✓ If you file a fraudulent return, there is no period of limitations.

Copies of your previously filed returns can be requested by mailing a completed Form 4506 to the IRS with a required fee for each tax year requested. To download the Form 4506, visit www.irs.gov.

Finally, be sure to shred tax returns once you decide to discard them.

WORKPLACE PERKS CHECKLIST

Most employers that I help view their workplace perks in the context of overall total rewards strategies that include compensation, training, benefits, and potential ownership. They invest their time, money, and energy balancing organizational and employee needs, and their decisions often revolve around four objectives:

➢ Improve workforce behavior to achieve desired outcomes
➢ Compete against other employers for preferred talent
➢ Create positive perception of values, fairness and goodwill
➢ Maximize cost, administrative, and tax advantages

Since *DIY financial planners* occasionally move to new employers and organizations are continually modifying these resources, it's important for employees to periodically review them.

General Planning and Counselling Resources		Availability		
		Yes	*No*	*Unsure*
	Benefits concierge service (phone or internet based)	O	O	O
	Comprehensive wellness coaching	O	O	O
	Employee Assistance Program	O	O	O
	Financial planning education	O	O	O
	Financial planning tools (online or print)	O	O	O
	Net worth planning tools (online or print)	O	O	O
	Pre-paid/Discounted legal service	O	O	O
	Wealth planning advice	O	O	O

Work-Life Balance Resources	Availability		
	Yes	No	Unsure
Compressed workweek	O	O	O
Flex time	O	O	O
Remote working arrangement	O	O	O
Telecommuting	O	O	O
Paid-Time Off, Vacation, or sick time benefits	O	O	O
Work/Life balance counselling	O	O	O

Earning Management Resources	Availability		
	Yes	No	Unsure
Career counselling	O	O	O
Professional development training	O	O	O
Leadership training	O	O	O
Professional certificates support	O	O	O
Professional designations support	O	O	O

Spending Management Resources	Availability		
	Yes	No	Unsure
Adoption assistance service or subsidy	O	O	O
Charitable donation matching program	O	O	O
Child care pre-tax spending account	O	O	O
Child care expenses subsidy	O	O	O
Child onsite daycare service	O	O	O
Commuter/Public Transit pre-tax spending account	O	O	O
Commuter/Public Transit subsidy	O	O	O
Discount membership program (e.g., Sam's Club)	O	O	O
Discount purchasing program (e.g., technology)	O	O	O
Elder care assistance	O	O	O
Entertainment/Event discount program	O	O	O
Onsite food and cafeteria subsidy	O	O	O
Onsite dry cleaning service	O	O	O
Uniform subsidy	O	O	O
Vacation/Travel discount or stipend	O	O	O

Savings Management Resources	Availability		
	Yes	No	Unsure
Automatic emergency savings plan (ref. "Side Car")	○	○	○
Advance payday benefit	○	○	○
Service anniversary cash award	○	○	○
Spot bonuses and rewards	○	○	○
Vacation buy-back program	○	○	○

Credit Management Resources	Availability		
	Yes	No	Unsure
Credit score	○	○	○
Credit history report	○	○	○
Credit monitoring	○	○	○
Credit education	○	○	○
Credit counseling	○	○	○

Debt Management Resources	Availability		
	Yes	No	Unsure
Consumer debt consolidation	○	○	○
Consumer debt counselling	○	○	○
Personal debt education	○	○	○
Personal debt counselling	○	○	○
Payday advance	○	○	○
Retirement plan loans and hardship withdrawal	○	○	○
Student loan debt consolidation	○	○	○
Student loan debt counselling	○	○	○
Student loan debt subsidy	○	○	○

College Planning Resources	Availability		
	Yes	No	Unsure
529 College Savings Account	○	○	○
College planning counselling	○	○	○
Scholarships for Employees or Dependents	○	○	○
Tuition reimbursement	○	○	○

Health Expense Management Resources	Availability		
	Yes	No	Unsure
Employer contributions to Health Savings Account	○	○	○
Health Savings Account	○	○	○
Retirement savings optimization tool	○	○	○

Retirement Planning Resources	Availability		
	Yes	No	Unsure
Pre-tax retirement plans [401(k), 403(b), 457, SEP IRA, SIMPLE IRA]	○	○	○
After-Tax Roth 401(k) or IRA	○	○	○
Profit sharing retirement plan	○	○	○
Employee stock ownership plan	○	○	○
Employee stock purchase plan	○	○	○
Retirement advice	○	○	○
Retirement calculator	○	○	○
Retirement counselling	○	○	○
Retirement education	○	○	○
Traditional defined benefit pension plan	○	○	○

Health Care Protection Resources	Availability		
	Yes	No	Unsure
Accident expenses	○	○	○
Bariatric surgery expenses	○	○	○
Cancer expenses	○	○	○
Cancer screenings	○	○	○
Chiropractic care	○	○	○
Dental expenses	○	○	○
Fertility expenses	○	○	○
Fitness clubs	○	○	○
Flu shots	○	○	○
Hearing screenings	○	○	○
Hearing aids and protection	○	○	○
Health care provider cost and quality comparisons	○	○	○

	Yes	No	Unsure
Health coaching	○	○	○
Health insurance premium reduction for wellness	○	○	○
Medical expenses	○	○	○
Mental health	○	○	○
Onsite healthcare clinics	○	○	○
Pet-related health care expenses	○	○	○
Prescription drugs	○	○	○
Preventive health screenings	○	○	○
Stress management	○	○	○
Stress reduction	○	○	○
Telemedicine	○	○	○
Tobacco cessation	○	○	○
Vision expenses	○	○	○
Weight loss	○	○	○
Well baby care	○	○	○

Income Protection Resources	Availability		
	Yes	No	Unsure
Short-term illness or injury	○	○	○
Short-term disabilities	○	○	○
Long-term disabilities	○	○	○
Leave of absence for adoption	○	○	○
Leave of absence for organ donation	○	○	○
Leave of absence for maternity or paternity	○	○	○
Leave of absence for sickness	○	○	○
Leave of absence for sabbatical	○	○	○
Long term care health care expenses	○	○	○

Property & Casualty Protection	Availability		
	Yes	No	Unsure
Auto insurance	○	○	○
Dwelling insurance	○	○	○
Identity theft monitoring	○	○	○
Identity theft insurance	○	○	○
Liability insurance	○	○	○

Legacy Planning Protection	Availability		
	Yes	No	Unsure
Legacy planning education	○	○	○
Life insurance for you	○	○	○
Life insurance for your spouse	○	○	○
Life insurance for your child(ren)	○	○	○
Living Will preparation	○	○	○
Pre-paid and discounted legal services	○	○	○
Trust preparation	○	○	○
Will preparation	○	○	○

APPENDIX D

PERSONAL PAYCHECK AUDIT

O ver the past two decades, the shift to automatic payroll deposit has become nearly universal. While most of the employees that I help have grown to appreciate the convenience, few review their paystubs using their online self-service portals. Given the importance of workplace earnings and the likelihood of experiencing significant paycheck errors at least once during their career, I urge them to schedule regular paystub audits.

For most, this should be quick, but it might require tutorials on using the payroll tools. Once usernames and passcodes are in-hand, employees should log into their sites, locate recent electronic paystubs, and confirm that the reported information is accurate.

✓ *Wages and Earnings.* The paystub should include compensation for the pay period before withholdings (or *gross pay*), year-to-date gross compensation, and paid amounts after withholdings are subtracted from gross earnings (or *net pay*).
✓ *Withholdings.* There are many withholdings, including the FICA Social Security tax (6.2% of gross earnings up to $142,800 in 2021), FICA Medicare tax (1.45% of gross earnings), federal income tax (established by the most recent completed W-4 Form), state and local income tax, retirement plan deferrals, insurance premiums, dependent care contributions, transit related contributions, etc.
✓ *Personal Information.* Additional information included on the paystub includes the employee's name, address, and state residence.

Employees that identify potential payroll errors should contact their supervisors, human resource colleagues, or payroll administrators, and request help to resolve the issue. For those that have multiple jobs or spouses that work, this should be repeated accordingly.

In addition to identifying mistakes, there are other benefits to this activity. First, it reminds employees of the amounts that they actually earn and might lead to spending restraints. Second, it inspires them to ask their tax preparers if their tax withholding elections are appropriate. Third, it invites them to modify their benefit elections when permissible. And finally, it helps them identify personal and dependent information that requires updating.

GOAL SETTING WORKSHEET

The challenge for many *DIY financial planners* is to convert wishful thinking into results. This worksheet offers a basic starting point.

Planning Worksheet	
What's the goal?	
What type of goal is it? (pgs. 147-148)	□ Continuation □ Transformative
Is there an *In Our Reach* activity associated with the goal?	□ Yes □ Not Sure □ No If "yes," what page is it found on? _____
Who will benefit if the goal is achieved?	□ You □ Your Employer □ Your Spouse □ Your Community □ Your Child(ren) □ Your Cause □ Your Grandchild(ren) □ Others: _____ □ Your Parents
When does the goal need to be achieved?	□ Immediate (Within 90 days) □ Short-Term (90 days to 2 years) □ Mid-Term (2 years to 10 years) □ Long-Term (10 years or longer)
Where will resources be found?	□ Personal Vendors: _____ □ Government or Non-Profits: _____ □ Employers: _____ □ Workplace Vendors: _____

Who will help complete tasks?	□ Spouse or Partner	□ Financial Partner(s)
	□ Parent(s)	□ Advisor(s)
	□ Child(ren)	□ Mentor(s)

What steps are involved?

Step
#___:_____

Step
#___:_____

Step
#___:_____

Step
#___:_____

Step
#___:_____

Step
#___:_____

Plan Timeline: Insert and label "Xs" on the plan timeline to signify steps identified above.

Start Date : _____   _____ : **End Date**

APPENDIX F

CASH FLOW WORKSHEET

Periodically evaluating household cash flow helps *DIY financial planners* examine their earning and spending, and reveals opportunities for them to increase their savings.

There are countless digital budget management tools, but I believe that valuable insight can be gained simply by tracking income and expense transactions for 30 days using 3 manila folders and the cash flow worksheets that I created. (Note: I don't want you to enter amounts in the book. Rather, **I urge you to print a copy that you'll find at inourreach.com/book**).

First Manila Folder

The first manila folder is labelled *Household Income*. It's used to compile copies of paystubs and handwritten summaries of the gross income earned during the tracking period.

For households whose earnings are mostly or entirely derived from fixed wages or salaries, this is straightforward. But for others that receive variable income, tracking it for a month can lead to inaccurate conclusions. As such, those in the latter category should estimate their average monthly incomes by adding their reported annual gross incomes from the past two federal tax returns, and dividing the sum of their returns by 24 months.

At the end of the 30-day period, all gross income should be tallied based on income source and entered in the following table.

Income Source	Monthly Amount	Income Source	Monthly Amount
Primary Workplace Earnings (Self)		*Primary Workplace Earnings (Spouse)*	
Gross Wages/Salary	Don't write	Gross Wages/Salary	Don't write
Gross Tips	Don't write	Gross Tips	Don't write
Gross Commission	Don't write	Gross Commission	Don't write
Gross Bonus	Don't write	Gross Bonus	Don't write
_____ : Other	Don't write	_____ : Other	Don't write
Subtotal	Don't write	**Subtotal**	Don't write
Secondary Workplace Earnings (Self)		*Secondary Workplace Earnings (Spouse)*	
Gross Wages/Salary	Don't write	Gross Wages/Salary	Don't write
Gross Tips	Don't write	Gross Tips	Don't write
Gross Commission	Don't write	Gross Commission	Don't write
Gross Bonus	Don't write	Gross Bonus	Don't write
_____ : Other	Don't write	_____ : Other	Don't write
Subtotal	Don't write	**Subtotal**	Don't write
Regular Interest And Dividends		*Small Business/Side Gigs Earnings*	
Interest on Savings	Don't write	Net Income/Profit	Don't write
Dividends on Investments	Don't write	Royalties	Don't write
Net Rental Income	Don't write	Net Farm Income	Don't write
_____ : Other	Don't write	_____ : Other	Don't write
Subtotal	Don't write	**Subtotal**	Don't write
Retirement Income		*Other Income*	
Pension Payments	Don't write	Alimony Payments	Don't write
Annuity Payments	Don't write	Child Support/Fostering Aid	Don't write
Social Security Payments	Don't write	Public Assistance	Don't write
_____ : Other	Don't write	_____ : Other	Don't write
Subtotal	Don't write	**Subtotal**	Don't write

Second Manila Folder

The second manila folder is labelled *Household Fixed Expenses*. It's used to compile copies of receipts and handwritten notes for payments (e.g., cash, check, debit, credit, PayPal) that remain the same for extended periods (often a year or longer), such as mortgage payments, insurance premiums, or online subscriptions, and are made during the 30-day tracking period.

In addition to inserting billing statements and handwritten summaries of expenses paid, bank and credit card statements should be reviewed to ensure that auto payments and recurring fixed expenses paid on a non-monthly basis (e.g., semi-annual auto insurance premium, annual homeowner's insurance premium) are included.

After 30 days, all of these items should be tallied by fixed expense category and the sums should be entered on the following table.

Fixed Expense Category	Monthly Amount	Fixed Expense Category	Monthly Amount
Fixed Housing Expenses		*Fixed Utility Expenses*	
Mortgage/Rent	Don't write	Water/Water-Softener	Don't write
Association/Condo Fees	Don't write	Trash Pick-Up	Don't write
Offsite Storage	Don't write	Cable/Satellite/Internet	Don't write
_____ : Other	Don't write	_____ : Other	Don't write
Subtotal	Don't write	**Subtotal**	Don't write
Fixed Transportation Expenses		*Fixed Banking and Finance Expenses*	
Loan (Personal Auto)	Don't write	Loan (Student, Other)	Don't write
Mass Transit (Bus/Train)	Don't write	Annual Fees (Credit/Bank)	Don't write
Parking	Don't write	Credit Monitoring	Don't write
Government Fees	Don't write	Safe Deposit Box	Don't write
_____ : Other	Don't write	_____ : Other	Don't write
Subtotal	Don't write	**Subtotal**	Don't write
Fixed Tax Withholdings and Payments		*Fixed Household Expenses*	
Tax Withholdings	Don't write	Security Service	Don't write
Property Tax (Escrow)	Don't write	Pest Control Service	Don't write
Tax Garnishments	Don't write	Housekeeping Service	Don't write
_____ : Other	Don't write	_____ : Other	Don't write
Subtotal	Don't write	**Subtotal**	Don't write

Fixed Technology Expenses		Fixed Kid-Related Expenses	
Licenses (Software/Apps)	Don't write	Day Care	Don't write
Virus/Malware Protection	Don't write	Alimony/Palimony	Don't write
_____ : Other	Don't write	_____ : Other	Don't write
Subtotal	Don't write	**Subtotal**	Don't write
Fixed Education Expenses		**Fixed Healthcare Expenses**	
School Tuition	Don't write	Gym/Club Membership	Don't write
_____ : Other	Don't write	_____ : Other	Don't write
Subtotal	Don't write	**Subtotal**	Don't write
Fixed Unreimbursed Work Expenses		**Fixed Insurance Expenses**	
Licenses/Union Dues	Don't write	Auto/Motorcycle	Don't write
_____ : Other	Don't write	Home/Renter/Umbrella	Don't write
Subtotal	Don't write	Medical/Dental/Vision	Don't write
Fixed Entertainment Expenses		Life/Disability/LTCi	Don't write
Subscription Services	Don't write	Recreational/Pet	Don't write
Social Club/Organization	Don't write	Identity Theft	Don't write
_____ : Other	Don't write	_____ : Other	Don't write
Subtotal	Don't write	**Subtotal**	Don't write
Other Fixed Expenses			
_____ : Other	Don't write	_____ : Other	Don't write
_____ : Other	Don't write	_____ : Other	Don't write
Subtotal	Don't write	**Subtotal**	Don't write

Third Manila Folder

The third manila folder is labelled *Household Variable Expenses*. It's used to compile copies of receipts and handwritten notes for all payments made during the tracking period for items that change from month-to-month and are unpredictable. The easiest way to do this is to save receipts from all transactions and to create handwritten notes for purchases where receipts aren't provided (or are lost), and to store them in the folder.

After 30 days, all items should be tallied by variable expense category and the sum entered on the following table.

Variable Expense Category	Monthly Amount	Variable Expense Category	Monthly Amount
Variable Food Expenses		*Variable Personal Care Expenses*	
Dine At Home (Groceries)	Don't write	Adult Clothing/Cleaning	Don't write
Dine Out (Convenience)	Don't write	Beauty Care	Don't write
Dine Out (Entertainment)	Don't write	Hygiene Products	Don't write
On-the-Go Snacks	Don't write	Aids (Glasses/Contacts)	Don't write
_____ : Other	Don't write	_____ : Other	Don't write
Subtotal	Don't write	**Subtotal**	Don't write
Variable Household Expenses		*Variable Kid-Related Expenses*	
Home Furnishings	Don't write	Books/Toys/Games	Don't write
Home Cleaning Supplies	Don't write	Supervision (Babysitting)	Don't write
Lawn/Snow Maintenance	Don't write	Camps/Athletics/Lessons	Don't write
Pest Control	Don't write	Infant (Diapers/Formula)	Don't write
Tools	Don't write	Kid Clothing	Don't write
_____ : Other	Don't write	_____ : Other	Don't write
Subtotal	Don't write	**Subtotal**	Don't write
Variable Utility Expenses		*Variable Transportation Expenses*	
Electricity	Don't write	Fuel	Don't write
Gas/Propane/Kerosene	Don't write	Maintenance & Supplies	Don't write
Home Phone	Don't write	Periodic Tolls/Parking	Don't write
Mobile Phone	Don't write	Mass Transit (Bus/Train)	Don't write
_____ : Other	Don't write	_____ : Other	Don't write
Subtotal	Don't write	**Subtotal**	Don't write
Variable Entertainment Expenses		*Variable Gift Expenses*	
Media, Books, Apps	Don't write	Charitable Cash Donations	Don't write
Games, Hobbies Fun	Don't write	Family	Don't write
Events (Sports/Theatre)	Don't write	Friends	Don't write
Vacation (Travel/Hotel/Auto)	Don't write	Special (Weddings/Retirement)	Don't write
_____ : Other	Don't write	_____ : Other	Don't write
Subtotal	Don't write	**Subtotal**	Don't write

Variable Education Expenses		Variable Pet Expenses	
School Hot Lunch	Don't write	Supplies (Food/Medicine)	Don't write
Athletic/Extracurricular	Don't write	Veterinarian	Don't write
Books/Supplies	Don't write	Grooming	Don't write
_____ : Other	Don't write	_____ : Other	Don't write
Subtotal	Don't write	**Subtotal**	Don't write
Variable Health Care Expenses		*Variable Bank & Financing Expenses*	
Over-the-Counter Meds	Don't write	Finance Charges	Don't write
Therapy (Massage/Chiropractor)	Don't write	Bank Fees/Checks/ATM Fees	Don't write
Vitamins/Supplements	Don't write	Debt Payments	Don't write
_____ : Other	Don't write	_____ : Other	Don't write
Subtotal	Don't write	**Subtotal**	Don't write
Variable Technology Expenses		*Variable Household Expenses*	
Hardware	Don't write	Repairs/Improvements	Don't write
Software	Don't write	Stationary/Postage	Don't write
_____ : Other	Don't write	_____ : Other	Don't write
Subtotal	Don't write	**Subtotal**	Don't write
Other Variable Expenses			
_____ : Other	Don't write	_____ : Other	Don't write
_____ : Other	Don't write	_____ : Other	Don't write
Subtotal	Don't write	**Subtotal**	Don't write

SAMPLE ADVISOR CANDIDATE QUESTIONS

O nce *DIY financial planners* decide to interview multiple financial advisors and assemble lists of candidates, it's wise for them to ask a wider range of questions and to take copious notes of their responses.

Following are sample questions that they might ask potential debt counselors, insurance intermediaries, investment brokers, lawyers, and tax, retirement and wealth planners.

Candidate's Niche and Focus		
Sample interview questions include:	Important to me?	
	Yes	No
▪ What is your personal area of expertise in the financial services industry?	○	○
▪ Describe your typical client.	○	○
▪ What is your organization's area of expertise in the financial services industry?	○	○
▪ Describe your organization's typical client.	○	○
▪ If you have minimum client requirements, what are they (e.g., minimum account balance, minimum assets)?	○	○
▪ How do I fit into your overall client mix?	○	○
▪ What specific benefits will I receive because of your niche and focus?	○	○

Candidate's Experience, Knowledge, and Ethics		
Sample interview questions include:	Important to me?	
	Yes	No
▪ How long have you personally provided advisory services?	○	○
▪ How long has your organization provided advisory services?	○	○
▪ What is your educational background and what are you doing to further your professional expertise?	○	○
▪ What relevant professional licenses, certifications, and registrations do you currently hold? How long have you held them?	○	○
▪ What professional designations have you earned or are you pursuing that will help me achieve my goals?	○	○
▪ What industry associations or groups do you belong to, and how are you personally involved?	○	○
▪ What qualifies you to help me achieve my goals?	○	○
▪ Do you formally embrace an ethical code of conduct? If so, describe.	○	○
▪ Has unethical conduct by you or your organization ever resulted in an industry association or group terminating your membership or participation?	○	○
▪ What legal action has been taken against you and your firm in the past 5 years?	○	○
▪ What complaints have been registered against you with federal or state regulatory organizations, or watchdog groups, in the past 5 years?	○	○
▪ How many clients have terminated your services in the past three years, and what were their reasons?	○	○
▪ Will you allow me to talk to a few current clients?	○	○
▪ Will you agree in writing to always act in my best interests?	○	○
▪ (For Investment Advisors Only) Will you agree in writing to abide by the "fiduciary standard" of care?	○	○

Candidate's Capacity for Strategy and Planning		
Sample interview questions include:	**Important to me?**	
	Yes	No
▪ What is your philosophy, attitude, or formula, for managing my personal financial needs?	○	○
▪ How will you help me identify and assess my needs and goals?	○	○
▪ How will you help me set realistic goals?	○	○
▪ How will you tailor a plan that meets my personal needs and circumstances?	○	○
▪ How will you notify me of changes that might affect my goals, strategies, or plans?	○	○
▪ What criteria will you use to determine which products are most suitable for me and my needs?	○	○
▪ What other advisors will you consult or engage in the development of my personal financial plan?	○	○
▪ How often will you review my plan to ensure I remain on track to meet my goals, and how often will you report to me?	○	○
▪ What tools will you use to assess the risks and measure the success of my plan?	○	○
▪ What do you expect from me in the relationship?	○	○
▪ How will you protect my personal and confidential information?	○	○
▪ With whom will you share my personal and confidential information?	○	○
▪ Will you notify me in writing before sharing my personal and confidential information?	○	○
▪ What is your philosophy, attitude, or formula, for managing my personal financial needs?	○	○

Candidate's Services and Resources		
Sample interview questions include:	**Important to me?**	
	Yes	**No**
▪ What services are you able to provide me?	○	○
▪ What specific services are you proposing to provide me?	○	○
▪ What tools will you provide, and how will they help me?	○	○
▪ What education will you routinely provide to me, and what topics will you cover?	○	○
▪ Who is involved in the daily and periodic servicing of my account(s), and – if others are involved – how are they managed and held accountable?	○	○
▪ What is the name, title, and professional background of the individual who will be my day-to-day service contact (if not the advisor), and when can we meet?	○	○
▪ What are the names, titles, and professional backgrounds of in-house experts you might engage to help me achieve my goals?	○	○
▪ What standards does your organization establish for timely replies to email, phone, and in-person inquiries?	○	○
▪ What individual or organization oversees or audits your organization?	○	○
▪ Under what circumstances will you transfer me to another advisor?	○	○
▪ How will you partner with external experts to help me achieve my goals?	○	○
▪ Under what circumstances will you or your organization NOT work with other advisors?	○	○
▪ How will you disclose any conflicts of interest that you might have?	○	○

Candidate's Measurement and Reporting Capabilities		
Sample interview questions include:	**Important to me?**	
	Yes	**No**
▪ How will you assess my current needs and circumstances relative to others that are similar to me?	○	○
▪ Ongoing, how will you measure and report progress toward my goals?	○	○
▪ Ongoing, how will you present data necessary to make periodic decisions and evaluations?	○	○
▪ What tools will you use to help me select the best tools for my needs?	○	○
▪ Who provides you with data, information, and analysis that you will use to make recommendations and provide advice?	○	○
▪ (*For Investment Advisors Only*) Will you report investment performance net of compensation, fees, and expenses?	○	○
▪ (*For Investment Advisors Only*) Will you illustrate the impact of taxation on portfolio performance?	○	○

Candidate's Compensation and Fees		
Sample interview questions include:	**Important to me?**	
	Yes	**No**
▪ How are you compensated for providing your services?	○	○
▪ How will you charge me for rendered services?	○	○
▪ Will you provide written confirmation that you will fully disclose all compensation derived from products and services I purchase from you and your organization?	○	○
▪ How will you disclose and explain compensation you and your organization receive by providing me with products or services?	○	○
▪ What, if any, additional fees or expenses will I insure related to the products and services your organization provides?	○	○
▪ Am I required to sign a contract with you or your organization? If so, provide a sample agreement.	○	○
▪ What penalties or fees will I incur if I sever our relationship or seek to terminate a product before the end of formal agreements?	○	○

Compare Candidate Responses

To improve the search, *DIY financial planners* should compare the candidates' responses to the highest priority questions. In the following example, 11 questions are identified as extremely important and a simple grading scale is used to assess the responses provided by each candidate (e.g., "3" is "Excellent", "2" is "Average", "1" is "Poor").

Sample Candidate Comparison Worksheet "Extremely Important Questions"	Candidate		
	Pam	Lou	Jan
• What is your personal area of expertise in the financial services industry?	3	3	1
• Describe your typical client.	3	2	1
• What qualifies you to help me achieve my goals?	3	2	1
• How can you assure me that I will be more successful with you advising me than if I work with someone else?	2	1	1
• How will you notify me of changes that might affect my financial strategy?	3	2	1
• How will you help me set realistic goals?	2	2	1
• Will you agree in writing to always act in my best interests?	3	2	1
• Ongoing, how will you measure and report progress toward my goals?	2	3	1
• Who provides the tools you will use to recommend strategies, products, and actions?	3	1	1
• Who provides you with data, information, and analysis that you will use to make recommendations and provide advice?	3	1	1
• How will you disclose and explain compensation you and your organization receive by providing me with products or services?	2	2	1
Total Score	29	21	11

ACKNOWLEDGEMENTS

In Our Reach is in your hands because loving and supportive individuals sustained me, directly and indirectly, throughout this endeavor.

Foremost, thank you to *Michelle Verheyen, AuD*, my sounding board, unrelenting champion, best friend, and soulmate, and our extraordinary kids. This couldn't have happened without your patience, sacrifice, and help. I'm eternally grateful to the four of them.

Similarly, thank you to reviewers that endured early manuscripts: *Bruce McNeil, Esq.* and *Heather Cambray*, people that I admire and the first to suffer thru my work; *George Verheyen*, my dad and 45-year financial services advisor, who shared his knowledge and obligingly bit his tongue; *Claremarie Verheyen*, my godmother and Professor at Univ. of Houston, who lovingly dispensed candid, line-by-line feedback; *Jeff Kinghorn*, gifted novelist, poet, and playwright, who picked me up and shared vital insights when they were most needed; and *Nick Verheyen, JD*, my brother and stellar sales rep, for helping me see via his minor proof edits that it was time to engage external reviewers.

Thank you to extraordinary subject matter experts that reviewed the full and final manuscript: *Brandon Diersch*, Treasury Group Manager at Microsoft Corp.; and *Anna Rappaport, FSA*, retired pension actuary and President of Anna Rappaport Consulting. These two individuals exceeded any reasonable expectations. And thank you to those that reviewed key segments of the final copy: *Stacey Emerton*, Dir. of HR at Harvard Law School; *Ken Raskin, Esq.*, past Chair for the Plan Sponsor Council of America; *Carol Bogosian, ASA*, retired pension actuary and President of CAB Consulting; and *Dave Murray*, President of David R. Murray & Associates.

Thank you to creative people that gave life to the cover: *Brenna Verheyen* for her appropriate cover design and sketch; *Jodi Lukach* for her exceptional photography; and *Scott Lynch* for his superb touch with the back cover.

Thank you to business leaders that gave me opportunities over the years to combine my passions for total rewards and workplace financial wellness:

Jeff Tolsma, Head of Business Services, and *Lynn Schloesser*, HR Mgr. at Gelita USA; *Kevin Moug*, CFO, and *Karen Sundahl*, Dir. of Benefits, at Otter Tail Corp.; *Pete Wasberg*, Dir. of HR, *Teri Viger*, Comp & Benefits Analyst, and *Marie Hartos* and *Shari Reidl*, Benefit Mgrs., at Otter Tail Power Co.; *Michelle Parkinson*, Dir. of HR, at DMS Health; *Myrna Hoekstra*, Dir. of HR, at BTD Mfg.; *Rebecca Wincell*, Dir. of HR, at Bell Ambulance; *Heather Cambray*, Dir. of HR, at Greatland Corp.; *Kerstin Esser*, Dir. of HR, at PPC Partners; and *Randy Schauman*, Dir. of HR, at Muza Metal Products. Thank you also to *Annette Grabow*, *CEBS*, *CPSP*, Retirement Plan Mgr. at M. A. Mortenson Company.

Thank you to people that were unknowingly valuable to this project: *Jeff Verheyen*, my late-uncle and a proud Union Operating Engineer; and *Punam Anand Keller*, Dep. Dean of The Tuck School of Business at Dartmouth Univ. And to those that provided technical insights: *Jennifer Loftus*, Principal at Astron Solutions; *Ashley Courtney*, Director at Businessolver; and *Joan Miller*, Reid Cinema Archives in the College of Film Studies and the Moving Image at Wesleyan University.

Thank you to those at Plan Sponsor Council of America that encouraged me to write: *Bruce McNeil, Esq.*, a prolific author and Editor-In-Chief of *The Journal of Pension Planning & Compliance* and *The Journal of Deferred Compensation*; and *Tim Kohn*, Head of Retirement Distribution at Dimensional Fund Advisors. And to *Ted Moss*, Vice President at Roscoe Moss Co., for his generous and unheralded contributions to an important mission that I'll forever appreciate.

Thank you to teachers that provided valuable mentoring and memorable opportunities to develop my writing style: *Phyllis Newman*, English teacher at Saint Francis Cabrini school; and *Paul Stoelting, PhD.*, Professor Emeritus of Geography at the Univ. of Wisconsin-La Crosse. And a long-overdue thank you to *Rafique Ahmed, PhD.*, Professor Emeritus of Geography at the Univ. of Wisconsin-La Crosse, for his selfless and kind acts, and in whose honor I strive to pay it forward as a teacher, mentor, and advisor. Outside of my immediate family, no one ever gave me as much as these three people did without asking anything in return.

Finally, thank you to *God* for introducing me to so many extraordinary people, *Jesus Christ* for opening the gates to Heaven, *Mother Mary* for her calming presence, and *Saint Joseph* for lending me his carpenter's saw when I was stuck.

BIBLIOGRAPHY

1. American Board of Internal Medicine. "5 Questions to Ask Your Doctor Before You Get Any Test, Treatment, or Procedure." ABIM Foundation, *Choosing Wisely* campaign, 2012.
2. The Associated Press. "Paris Hilton Hacker Gets 11 Months." CBS News, September 14, 2005. www.cbsnews.com/news/paris-hilton-hackter-gets-11-months/.
3. The Associated Press, "Man Held on Identity-Theft Charges." Los Angeles Times, March 21, 2001. www.latimes.com/archives/la-xpm-2001-mar-21-fi-40550-story.html.
4. Backman, Maurie. "Most Americans Don't Trust Their Financial Advisors. Should They?" The Motley Fool, July 11, 2017. www.fool.com/retirement/2017/07/11/most-americans-dont-trust-their-financial-advisors.aspx
5. Benjamin, Jeff. "Bucket strategies provide a pot of 'safe money'." Investment News, March 27, 2011. https://www.investmentnews.com/bucket-strategies-provide-a-pot-of-safe-money-35240
6. Board of Governors of the Federal Reserve System. *Report on the Economic Well-Being of U.S. Households in 2019*. Washington, DC, Federal Reserve Board, 2020.
7. Bureau of Labor Statistics. "BLS Reports: Consumer Expenditures in 2017." Washington, DC, U.S. Department of Labor, April, 2019.
8. Bureau of Labor Statistics. "The Employment Situation – February 2020." Washington, DC, U.S. Department of Labor, 2020.
9. Capra, Frank, dir. *It's A Wonderful Life*. 1947, Los Angeles, CA, Republic Entertainment. DVD.
10. CareerBuilder. "Living Paycheck to Paycheck is a Way of Life for Majority of U.S. Workers." Chicago and Atlanta, CareerBuilder, 2017.

11. Cilluffo, Anthony, Geiger, A.W., and Fry, Richard. "More U.S. households are renting than at any point in 50 years." Washington, DC, Pew Research Center, 2017. www.pewresearch.org.

12. Consumer Financial Protection Bureau. "What is a debt-to-income ratio? Why is the 43% debt-to-income ratio important?" Washington, DC, CFPB, November 15, 2019. www.consumerfinance.gov.

13. Employee Benefits Research Institute. "Savings Needed for Medicare Beneficiaries' Health Expenses Declines." Washington, DC, EBRI, May 28, 2020.

14. Fair Isaac Corporation. "What's in my FICO® Scores?" Fair Isaac Corporation, 2020. www.myfico.com, June 26, 2020.

15. Farber, Madeline. "Nearly Two-Thirds of Americans Can't Pass a Basic Test of Financial Literacy" Fortune, July 12, 2016. www.fortune.com/2016/07/12/financial-literacy/

16. Federal Deposit Insurance Corporation. *Crisis and Response: An FDIC History, 2008-2013*. Washington, DC: FDIC, 2017.

17. Genworth Financial. "Cost of Care Survey" Genworth Financial, 2020. www.genworth.com./aging-and-you/finances/cost-of-care.html.

18. Granata, Charles L. *I Just Wasn't Made for These Times: Brian Wilson and the Making of the Beach Boys' Pet Sounds*. London, Unanimous, 2003.

19. Grant, Kelli. "This job challenge should scare older workers." CNBC, January 5, 2019. www.cnbc.com/2019/01/04/how-to-navigate-a-late-career-job-loss.html.

20. Greenwald & Associates for Society of Actuaries (SOA). *Aging and Retirement: 2019 Risks and Process of Retirement Survey*. Schaumburg, Illinois, SOA, 2020.

21. Harry, Bill. *The Beatles Encyclopedia: Revised and Updated*. London, Virgin, 2000.

22. Identity Theft Resource Center (ITRC) and CyberScout. *2017 Annual Data Breach Year-End Review*. San Diego, ITRC, 2017.

23. Institute for the Future for Dell Technologies. *The Next Era of Human Machine Partnerships: Emerging Technologies' Impact on Society & Work in 2030*. Palo Alto, Dell Technologies, 2017.

24. Insurance Information Institute. "Facts + Statistics: Auto insurance." Insurance Information Institute, 2020. www.iii.org.

25. Insurance Information Institute. "Facts + Statistics: Homeowners and renters insurance." Insurance Information Institute, 2020. www.iii.org.
26. Kaiser Family Foundation. "2019 Employer Health Benefits Survey." KFF, September 25, 2020. www.kff.org/health-costs/report/2019-employer-health-benefits-survey/.
27. Kantrowitz, Mark. "College Scholarships Statistics." Saving For College, October 23, 2019. www.savingforcollege.com.
28. Kilgannon, Corey. "The Truth About Alligators in the Sewers of New York." New York Times, February 26, 2020. www.nytimes.com.
29. Lavezzoli, Peter. *The Dawn of Indian Music in the West: Bhairavi*. New York and London, Continuum, 2006.
30. Mandell, Andrea. "7 Legendary stars who died without wills: Aretha Franklin, Prince, and more." USA Today, August 22, 2018. https://www.usatoday.com/story/life/people/2018/08/22/legendary-stars-who-died-without-wills-aretha-franklin/83550424/.
31. National Association of Insurance Commissioners. "NAIC Releases Report on Homeowners Insurance." Washington, DC, NAIC, November 25, 2019.
32. Nguyen, Vivian. "AARP Public Policy Institute Fact Sheet: Long-Term Support and Services." Washington, DC, AARP Public Policy Institute, 2017.
33. Nitro College. "The Details of Debt: How Debt Impacts Americans' Quality of Life." Nitro College, 2020. www.nitrocollege.com.
34. Noel-Miller, Carol. "Insight on the Issues: Medicare Beneficiaries' Out-of-Pocket Spending for Health Care." Washington, DC, AARP Public Policy Institute, 2020.
35. Office of Federal Student Aid. "Federal Pell Grants are usually awarded only to undergraduate students." Washington, DC, U.S. Department of Education, 2020. www.studentaid.gov/undersand-aid/types/grants/pell.
36. Office of Tax Analysis. "HSA-Tables.pdf." Washington, DC, U.S. Treasury, January 6, 2017. www.treasury.gov/resource-center/tax-policy/tax-analysis/documents/hsa-tables.pdf.
37. Parker, Tim. "Planning on Retiring Later? Think Again." Investopedia, October 31, 2019. www.investopedia.com/articles/personal-finance/101515/planning-retiring-later-think-again.asp.

38. Parker, Tim. "What's the Average 401(k) Balance by Age." Investopedia, October 30, 2020. www.investopedia.com/articles/personal-finance/010616/whats-average-401k-balance-age.asp.

39. P!nk. "Behind the Music." YouTube, August 2012. www.youtube.com/watch?v=6sWTiBg_9qA

40. Ruane, Bill. "26 CFR 601.602: Tax forms and instructions." Washington, DC, Office of Associate Chief Counsel (Income Tax & Accounting), Internal Revenue Service, 2020. www.irs.gov/pub/irs-drop/rp-20-32.pdf.

41. Serjeant, Jill. "Jennifer Aniston named as victim in salon fraud." Reuters, August 18, 2010. www.reuters.com.

42. Seshan, Balasubramanyam. "P!nk welcomes baby Willow Sage Hart into the World." London, International Business Times, 2011.

43. Social Security Administration. "Disability Benefits: How You Qualify." Washington, DC, SSA, 2020. www.ssa.gov/benefits/disability/qualify.html.

44. Social Security Administration. "Fact Sheet: Social Security." Washington, DC, SSA, 2020. www.ssa.gov/news/press/factsheets/basicfact-alt.pdf.

45. U.S. Bureau of Labor Statistics. *Consumer Expenditure Survey, 2019.* Washington, DC, BLS, 2020. www.bls.gov/cex/2019/combined/age.pdf.

46. Unattributed. "Terri Schiavo's Story." www.terrischiavo.org/story/.

47. Verheyen, Tony, pres. "Financial Readiness Basics." Elm Grove, WI, The Richfield Companies, 2006.

48. Verheyen, Tony. "Richfield's Financial Readiness Services Help Client Earn 'Best of Show' From Profit Sharing/401(k) Council of America." October 4, 2007.

49. Verheyen, Tony. "Building A Holistic Financial Education Plan." Chicago, IL, Mid-Sized Pension Conference, University Conference Services, October, 9, 2007.

50. Verheyen, Tony, pres. "$mart Money & Personal Finance." Elm Grove, WI, The Richfield Companies, 2007.

51. Verheyen, Tony, pres. "Advanced Investment Concepts." Elm Grove, WI, The Richfield Companies, 2007.

52. Verheyen, Tony, pres. "Estate Planning Basics." Elm Grove, WI, The Richfield Companies, 2008.

53. Verheyen, Tony, pres. "Insurance in Retirement." Elm Grove, WI, The Richfield Companies, 2009.
54. Verheyen, Tony, pres. "College Planning Basics." Elm Grove, WI, The Richfield Companies, 2009.
55. Verheyen, Tony, pres. "Employee Benefits & Workplace Retirement Programs." Washington, DC, Plan Sponsor Council of America for Save Our Savings Coalition, 2017.
56. Weisbaum, Herb. "More than 1 million children were victims of ID theft last year." NBC News, June 21, 2018. www.nbcnews.com/business/consumer/more-1-million-children-were-victims-id-theft-last-year-n885351.
57. Whelehan, Barbara. "The average 401(k) balance by age." Bankrate, March 13, 2020. www.bankrate.com/retirement/average-401k-balance-by-age/.

HELPFUL ORGANIZATIONS

1. *American Association of Retired Persons* (*AARP*) is a nonprofit member-ship organization for people Age 50 and over. It's dedicated to enhancing quality of life for all as they age by leading positive social change and de-livering value to members through information, advocacy and service.

2. *American Board of Internal Medicine* (*ABIM*) is a non-profit, independent evaluation organization led by doctors who want to achieve higher stand-ards for better care in a rapidly changing world. Its mission is to enhance the quality of health care by certifying internists and subspecialists who demonstrate the knowledge, skills and attitudes essential for excellent patient care.

3. *American College of Trust and Estate Counsel* (*ACTEC*) is a nonprofit asso-ciation of lawyers established in 1949. Its members are elected to the institution by demonstrating the highest level of integrity, commitment to the profession, competence and experience as trust and estate coun-selors. All members make substantial contributions to the field of trusts and estates law through writing, teaching and bar leadership activities.

4. *American Institute of CPAs* (*AICPA*), via 360 Degrees of Financial Literacy, is a national volunteer effort of the nation's Certified Public Accountants to help Americans understand personal finance and develop money man-agement skills. It focuses on financial education as a lifelong pursuit, from children learning about the value of money to adults achieving a secure retirement. It features a website that offers free tools and resources to help people manage their finances through every stage of life.

5. *America's Health Insurance Plans* (*AHIP*) is an association whose mem-bers provide coverage for health care and related services to hundreds of millions of Americans every day. Through these offerings, their members improve and protect the health and financial security of consumers, fam-ilies, businesses, communities, and nation. They're committed to market-based solutions and public-private partnerships that improve affordabil-ity, value, access, and wellbeing for consumers.

6. *American Savings Education Council* (*ASEC*) is a national non-profit coalition of public- and private-sector institutions committed to making saving and retirement planning a priority for all Americans.
7. *Better Business Bureau* (*BBB*) is a non-profit that seeks to create an ethical marketplace where buyers and sellers trust each other. It achieves its' mission by setting standards for marketplace trust, encouraging and supporting best practices, educating consumers and businesses, celebrating marketplace role models, addressing substandard marketplace behavior, and creating a community of trustworthy businesses and charities.
8. *Certified Financial Planner Board of Standards* (*CFP Board*) is a non-profit that serves the public by fostering professional standards in personal financial planning. It sets and enforces the requirements for the Certified Financial Planner™ certification to create competent and ethical financial planners who are committed to putting clients' best interests first.
9. *Chartered Financial Analyst Institute* (*CFAI*) is the global association of investment professionals that sets the standard for professional excellence and credentials. It's a champion of ethical behavior in investment markets and a respected source of financial knowledge in the global community. Its aim is to create an environment where investors' interests come first, markets function at their best, and economies grow.
10. *Consumer Federation of America* (*CFA*), via American Save campaign, is a broad coalition of nonprofit, corporate, and government groups helping individuals and families save and build wealth. Through information, advice, and encouragement, it assists those who wish to pay down their debt, build an emergency fund, or save for a home, education, or retirement.
11. *Consumer Financial Protection Bureau* (*CFPB*) is a federal government agency that helps consumer finance markets work by making rules more effective, by consistently and fairly enforcing those rules, and by empowering consumers to take more control over their economic lives.
12. *Consumer Reports* (*CF*) is a non-profit consumer organization that works side-by-side with consumers for truth, transparency, and fairness in the marketplace. It's committed to unbiased public education, product testing, investigative journalism, consumer-oriented research, and consumer advocacy. It empowers and informs consumers, incentivizes corporations

to act responsibly, and helps policymakers prioritize the rights and interests of consumers to shape a truly consumer-driven marketplace.

13. *Data & Marketing Association* (*DMA*), part of the *Association of National Advertisers* (*ANA*), is dedicated to comprehensively serving virtually every aspect of marketing with distinction and professionalism. The ANA strives to enhance consumer engagement and business value through innovative, data-driven marketing.

14. *Employee Benefits Research Institute* (*EBRI*) is a non-profit that contributes to sound employee benefit programs and public policy through independent, objective, fact-based research and education. Its mission is to produce and communicate original research on health, savings, retirement, and economic security issues, like retirement plan coverage data, post-retirement income adequacy, health coverage and the uninsured, and economic security of the elderly.

15. *Employee Benefits Security Administration* (*EBSA*) is a government agency that protects the integrity of pensions, health plans, and other employee benefits for more than 150 million people. Its offers a variety of consumer information at www.askebsa.dol.gov/savingsfitness/worksheets.

16. *Equifax* is one of the three major national credit reporting agencies. It's for-profit and empowers individual consumers to manage their personal.

17. *Experian* is one of the three major national credit reporting agencies. It's for-profit, and it promotes better financial health and opportunity among consumers by enabling them to understand, manage, and protect their personal credit information.

18. *Federal Citizens Information Center* (*FCIC*), or USAGov, is a department of the U.S. government's General Services Administration. It's focused on answering citizens' questions about the federal government and everyday consumer issues. It watches emerging consumer issues and topics and regularly reviews new information coming from Federal agencies and consumer organizations.

19. *Federal Deposit Insurance Corporation* (*FDIC*), via Money Smart, is a training program that helps adults outside the financial mainstream enhance their money skills and create positive banking relationships.

20. *Federal Emergency Management Agency* (*FEMA*), an agency of the U.S. Department of Homeland Security, supports citizens and emergency personnel to build, sustain, and improve the nation's capability to prepare for, protect against, respond to, recover from, and mitigate all hazards.

21. *Financial Counseling Association of America* (*FCAA*) is a non-profit representing financial counseling companies that provide hundreds of thousands of consumers annually with consumer credit counseling, housing counseling, student loan counseling, bankruptcy counseling, debt management, and various financial education services.

22. *Financial Industry Regulatory Authority* (*FINRA*) is a private corporation that acts as a self-regulatory organization, and oversees member brokerage firms and exchange markets. It's dedicated to protecting investors and safeguarding market integrity in a manner that facilitates vibrant capital markets.

23. *Funeral Consumer Alliance* (*FCA*) is a national consumer organization that monitors the funeral industry. It keeps a close eye on industry trends and advocates for fair practices on behalf of consumers. It's goal is to ensure that consumers are fully prepared and protected when they're planning a funeral, and its network of volunteers work directly with consumers, and alongside those fighting for legal and regulatory reform.

24. *Identity Theft Resource Center* (*ITRC*) is a non-profit established to empower and guide consumers, victims, business and government to minimize risk and mitigate the impact of identity compromise and crime. It conducts training and presentations on best practices and risk reduction for both businesses and consumers.

25. *Insurance Information Institute* (*III*) seeks to improve public understanding of what insurance does and how it works. For over 60 years, it's provided definitive insurance information and is recognized by governments, regulatory organizations, universities, media, and the public as a primary source of information, analysis and referral concerning insurance.

26. *Investopedia* is a leading source of online financial content, ranging from market news to retirement strategies, investing education to advisor insights. It offers financial and investment dictionaries, advice, reviews, ratings, and product comparisons.

27. *Kaiser Family Foundation* (*KFF*) is a non-profit, private operating foundation focusing on the major health care issues facing the U.S., with a

growing role in global health. It's a leader in health policy and communications, and it develops and runs its own research and communications programs (sometimes in partnership with other non-profit research organizations or major media companies).

28. *Morningstar* is a for-profit provider of independent investment research in the United States and in major international markets. Its mission is to create reliable products that help investors reach their financial goals. It's a trusted source for information on stocks, mutual funds, variable annuities, closed-end funds, exchange-traded funds, separate accounts, hedge funds, and 529 college savings plans.

29. *National Association for Home Care & Hospice Care* is a non-profit trade association representing the interests and concerns of home care agencies, hospices, and home care aide organizations.

30. *National Association of Insurance Commissioners* (*NAIC*) is the organization of insurance regulators from the 50 states, the District of Columbia, and the 5 U.S. territories. It provides a forum for the development of uniform policy when uniformity is appropriate.

31. *National Credit Union Share Insurance Fund* (*NCUSIF*) is an insurance fund backed by the government for credit union deposits. It insures deposits up to specified maximums that are held in federally insured credit unions.

32. *National Foundation for Consumer Credit* (*NFCC*) is a national voice for its members, which are nonprofit, mission driven, community-based agencies. It promotes financially responsible behavior and builds capacity for its members to deliver the highest quality financial education and counseling services.

33. *National Funeral Directors Association* (*NFDA*) is a resource and advocate across all facets of funeral service dedicated to high ethical standards and helping members provide meaningful service to families. Its members stand for credibility, ethics, excellence and trust.

34. *National Institute of Certified College Planners* (*NICCP*) serves the public interest by promoting the value of professional, competent, and ethical college financial planning services. It's the governing body for the Certified College Planning Specialist (CCPS) designation.

35. *Social Security Administration* (*SSA*) mission is to advance the economic security of the nation's people through compassionate and vigilant leadership in shaping and managing America's Social Security programs.

36. *Society of Actuaries* (*SOA*) is the world's largest actuarial professional or-
    ganization. Through research and education, its mission is to advance
    actuarial knowledge and to enhance the ability of actuaries to provide
    expert advice and relevant solutions for financial, business and societal
    challenges. Its vision is for actuaries to be the leading professionals in the
    measurement and management of risk.
37. *Transunion* is one of the three major national credit reporting agencies. It
    is for-profit, and works with businesses and consumers to gather, analyze
    and deliver information that critical to build strong economies through-
    out the world.
38. *U.S. Department of Education, Office of Student Financial Aid*, is the U.S.
    Department of Education's site for free information on preparing for and
    funding education beyond high school.
39. *U.S. Federal Trade Commission* (*FTC*) is the only federal agency with both
    consumer protection and competition jurisdiction in broad sectors of the
    economy. It pursues vigorous and effective law enforcement, advances
    consumers' interests, develops policy and research tools, and creates ed-
    ucational programs for consumers and businesses.
40. *U.S. Financial Literacy and Education Commission* is dedicated to teaching
    Americans the basics about personal finance, such as balancing a check-
    book, planning to buy a home, or investing in their workplace retirement
    plans.
41. *Women's Institute For A Secure Retirement* (*WISER*) is a non-profit dedi-
    cated to education and advocacy that'll improve the long-term financial
    quality of life for women. It supports women's opportunities to secure
    adequate retirement income through training workshops, strategic part-
    nerships, research, education materials, media outreach, policy analysis,
    and advocacy.

INDEX

TONY VERHEYEN, MA, CEBS

S ince entering the financial services industry in 1995, Tony's addressed financial wellbeing as an association leader, total rewards consultant, workplace educator, adjunct professor, entrepreneur, sales rep, and employer. Having viewed the topic from so many angles, he feels there's nothing more professionally gratifying than serving others as their trusted financial advisor.

Tony's unique and relevant experiences give him insights that other authors lack. He's helped tens of thousands of people – from shop floors to the halls of Congress – understand the connection between workplace resources and personal finance, and his thoughts have been included in prominent media outlets like *USA Today*, *Pensions & Investments*, *The Street*, *The Journal of Pension Planning & Compliance*, and *PLANSPONSOR Magazine*.

He founded The Richfield Companies, a firm focused on disability income, retirement income, and life insurance solutions for individuals and families. His pioneering work in workplace financial education helped a client receive the 401(k)/Profit Sharing Council of America's highest recognition. Ten years later, the same organization acknowledged his commitment to help employers fight to preserve a free enterprise approach to retirement security with a *Volunteer Service Award*. And his distinguished service as a military instructor led to his receipt of an *Ohio Commendation Medal*.

He earned his Certified Employee Benefits Specialist (CEBS) designation from the International Foundation for Employee Benefit Plans and the Wharton School of the University of Pennsylvania, and an M.A. from The Ohio State University and a B.S. from the University of Wisconsin – La Crosse.

Prior to and early in his career, he served in the U.S. Army Reserves, and in the Wisconsin and Ohio Army National Guard.

Tony and his wife of over 25 years have three kids and a dog. He enjoys family vacations, football, live music, and good coffee.

CPSIA information can be obtained
at www.ICGtesting.com
Printed in the USA
BVHW032226090721
611566BV00012B/923/J